FUNDAMENTALS OF SOFTWARE INTEGRATION

Kay Hammer
Founder and Former CEO, Evolutionary Technologies International

Tina Timmerman
Chief Solution Architect, Evolutionary Technologies International

JONES AND BARTLETT PUBLISHERS
Sudbury, Massachusetts
BOSTON   TORONTO   LONDON   SINGAPORE

World Headquarters

Jones and Bartlett Publishers
40 Tall Pine Drive
Sudbury, MA 01776
978-443-5000
info@jbpub.com
www.jbpub.com

Jones and Bartlett Publishers
Canada
6339 Ormindale Way
Mississauga, Ontario L5V 1J2
Canada

Jones and Bartlett Publishers
International
Barb House, Barb Mews
London W6 7PA
United Kingdom

Jones and Bartlett's books and products are available through most bookstores and online booksellers. To contact Jones and Bartlett Publishers directly, call 800-832-0034, fax 978-443-8000, or visit our website www.jbpub.com.

Substantial discounts on bulk quantities of Jones and Bartlett's publications are available to corporations, professional associations, and other qualified organizations. For details and specific discount information, contact the special sales department at Jones and Bartlett via the above contact information or send an email to specialsales@jbpub.com.

Production Credits
Acquisitions Editor: Timothy Anderson
Production Director: Amy Rose
Production Editor: Diana Coe
Editorial Assistant: Melissa Elmore
Senior Marketing Manager: Andrea DeFronzo
Manufacturing Buyer: Therese Connell
Composition: NK Graphics
Cover Design: Diana Coe
Cover Image: © Sapsiwai/ShutterStock, Inc.
Printing and Binding: Malloy, Inc.
Cover Printing: Malloy, Inc.

Library of Congress Cataloging-in-Publication Data
Hammer, Kay.
   Fundamentals of software integration / Kay Hammer and Tina Timmerman.—1st ed.
      p. cm.
   Includes bibliographical references and index.
   ISBN-13: 978-0-7637-4133-4
   ISBN-10: 0-7637-4133-7
   1. Systems migration. 2. Software maintenance. 3. Software engineering—Management. I. Timmerman, Tina. II. Title.
   QA76.9.S9H355, 2007
   005.1068'4—dc22
                              2007040651
6048
Printed in the United States of America
11 10 09 08 07   10 9 8 7 6 5 4 3 2 1

This book is dedicated to
Admiral Bobby R. Inman, U. S. Navy, (Ret.)
Charter investor in ETI
and
friend to the entrepreneur

ACKNOWLEDGMENTS

We would like to thank our colleagues and customers from Evolutionary Technologies International for the experiences that gave us the background to write this text. But we would particularly like to thank Adam E. Hampton and Chris Crafford for their valuable comments and suggestions on previous drafts. Thanks to Sandeep Purao, Penn State University, and Philip Cannata, University of Texas Austin, for reviewing this manuscript. We are grateful for the support and patience of Tim Anderson and Laura Pagluica from Jones and Bartlett and that of our families—Katherine and Evelyn Hammer and Craig Timmerman. Finally, thanks also to Stan Wakefield for believing in the ideas behind this book and finding the excellent firm of Jones and Bartlett to publish it. Finally, great thanks to Diana Coe, our production editor at Jones and Bartlett, for shepherding us through the final process and designing such a wonderful cover.

CONTENTS

PREFACE

To the Student

People frequently use the term *architecture* to apply to the high-level design of a software system. In many ways, this is an excellent metaphor. Architects design buildings and spaces to serve some purpose for a particular set of people, and the characteristics of the design can be judged as to how well it meets the needs of that group. Spaces that are suitable for a city hall are not suitable for apartments. Materials like marble and granite that are used in luxury homes are not cost-effective for athletic facilities. However, there are many levels of design required to move from the stage of architectural design to a fully functional building—electrical, plumbing, heating, cooling, and so on. The success of the construction depends on many design decisions that few people appreciate unless they are done badly. The inconvenient light switch, the offices on one hall that are freezing while those on another are sweltering, the placement of faucets and shelves in the laundry room that force the door of the front-loading washer to face away from the person trying to load the machine are all examples of shortcomings in design that do not make a building unusable, but do make it less effective for the people it is supposed to serve.

There are analogies to all these attributes in the design of software applications. Different applications have different requirements based on the purpose they are to serve. Efficient, high-resolution graphics are critical to a layout application, a "nice-to-have" in an end-user report writer. Data integrity is critical to banking and less important to marketing. The fact that the algorithm for numbering bulleted items in a word processor is flawed makes it annoying to use. However, it is still preferable to the older line-oriented editors where the user had to manually insert commands that explicitly told the application how many spaces to indent.

There is one aspect of the architecture analogy that has not been properly emphasized in the past that is important to understanding the purpose of this book—the fact that good design cannot take place in a vacuum. Just as an architect must consider a number of external factors (for example the lot, the climate, government regulations), the software architect has a similar number of constraints ranging from cost to the number and geographic locations of the users. In fact, successful software architecture is a lot more like renovation than the design and construction of a new building because even a new application must often exchange information with existing systems when it is installed. Ask any architect or electrical contractor which is harder—building a new structure or renovating an old. They will unanimously agree that renovation is harder because it is impossible to anticipate all the problems they might encounter with the existing infrastructure before they start the job. In fact, they will often argue that it can be cheaper, and the result may be better to tear down a building and start from scratch rather than trying to work with what is in place.

Starting over is not feasible with software. Organizations need the information stored in their legacy systems to run their day-to-day business. They cannot simply shut down their applications while new ones are built and populated with historical information. As a result, when a company does acquire and implement a new application, the new application not only must work in concert with the other applications in use, but also must often work parallel to the application it will replace for some period of time. The customer must verify that the new application behaves appropriately and all users must be trained before the actual switchover takes place. Historically, we have not provided students in computer science and software engineering with the kind of training needed for "remodeling." Just as a plumber who needs to do renovations must understand the benefits and shortcomings of different eras of plumbing materials (for example, the differences among iron, copper, and PVC pipes, and what is possible when mixing them) in order to anticipate what can be used and what must be replaced, a software designer must have a similar historical perspective of software technology to be effective in the design and implementation of new software technology and applications.

There is no aspect of life that has not been affected by the digital revolution. Computers have permeated every aspect of what we do from making phone calls to planning a car trip, yet we are not able to share the critical information that we need to respond effectively to natural emergencies or to detect illegal activity. For advances in software technology to bring the value they promise, they must be easy to integrate and deploy in *existing* information technology (IT) environments. The goal of this book is to give the reader not just the background required to address today's integration challenges, but a set of conceptual tools and a methodology for anticipating when some new technology runs the risk of reintroducing problems that have previously been recognized and solved.

To the Instructor

About the Book

Integration is one of the most critical technical challenges in software today. This is evident by the lack of progress established governments have made in information sharing, and the cost and difficulty that companies are having in documenting regulatory compliance; nor is there any sign that integration will decrease in importance. With the advent of web services and service-oriented architectures (SOA), software development is actually becoming more of an integration and configuration effort than one that involves the more traditional processes of design, implementation, and testing—even with a methodology that supports spiral design. In fact, the Software Engineering Institute at Carnegie Mellon has instituted a program called ISIS—or Integration of Software-Intensive Systems—maintaining that a new methodology is required because classic software engineering depends on a basic understanding of the system being built. In contrast, Fisher and Smith (2004) maintain that, "With modern systems development and the need to develop complex systems of systems, most systems are no longer 'closed'; rather they are 'unbounded' because they involve an unknown number of participants or otherwise require individual participants to act and interact in the absence of needed information."

For SOA to work, it must be possible to "wrap" the interfaces to legacy systems with code that mediates between the native formats of the legacy systems and the Extensible Markup Language (XML) messages expected by the SOA directory of services. If we are to prepare students to address these challenges, they need a solid understanding of:

- How legacy systems have been implemented and what this means for large-scale integration initiatives
- How the evolution of execution and communication protocols has complicated data integrity and auditability
- The importance of the value metadata acquisition brings to efficient change management
- How technology choices in software architecture can affect everything from performance and change management to accuracy and the skill level required of users

Relationship to College Curricula

A Joint Task Force from the ACM is currently in the process of defining a proposal for Computing Curricula 2005 (CC2005) geared at addressing the fact that there are now a number of different types of undergraduate programs that address computing. The course numbers that follow refer to the course descriptions found in that document.

The authors of CC2005 maintain that one of the three areas of work for computer scientists is "designing and implementing software" and that programs in software engineering have been developed because CS programs "have not been successful at reliably producing graduates able to work effectively on complex software systems which require engineering expertise beyond the level of programming fundamentals." In the case of both types of departments, the authors of CC2005 argue that software design is an important knowledge area and systems/large scale programming should be an area of competence for graduates of either discipline. Programming fundamentals and an understanding of operating systems is a good start, but few if any software products today are designed and built "from the ground up." Instead, they are built on top of a hierarchy of software systems for graphics, search, database, communication, and web services. The challenge in developing a curriculum to prepare graduates for this environment is deciding what material to teach. Usually there is a programming language du jour. In some cases, the one advocated by the academy (e.g., Pascal) is never taken up by the industry; in other cases (e.g., Java) there is clearly a consensus. But beyond that, software technology evolves too quickly to invest substantive resources in developing material that may be timely when it is being taught, but will quite likely be passé by graduation.

It is for this reason that the area of integration is an excellent pedagogical tool for teaching the skills of designing large scale software systems. Although software technology may evolve at warp speed, the rate at which software is displaced by newer technology is significantly slower in large organizations. In fact, industry analysts claim that between 70% and 80% of the data in operational systems in large organizations still reside in COBOL-based systems. Moreover, integration problems are both computationally and conceptually complex, requiring that students consider multiple dimensions (e.g., ease of use, security, scalability). Perhaps the most compelling reason to study integration is the insight that can be gained from studying the evolution of software. Armed with this insight, students will be able to anticipate when advances in one technology will cause problems in another, and will be able to recognize a situation in which a method used to solve an earlier problem can be applied to a new one. As the old saw goes, "Those who fail to learn from history are destined to repeat it."

For these reasons, we see this book as suitable for use as a secondary text in the following types of courses:

CS290 Software Development
CS292 Software Development and Professional Practice

CS392 Advanced Software Development
CS392 Software Design
CS396 Component-Based Computing
CS397 Programming Environments

SE211 Software Construction
SE213 Design and Architecture of Large Software Systems
SE311 Software Design and Architecture

These courses typically focus on current best practices using a particular programming language and/or development environment. In contrast, this text provides students with a historical perspective of the evolution of software and its impact on application development in order to provide students with the background they need to address software system design in practice.

Approach

Too often the relationship between science and technology is articulated as linear. On one end is the area of pure science, which focuses on theory and algorithms, and on the other is technology, which focuses on the process of applying artifacts from computer science—that is, particular implementations of software—to solve particular problems. In reality, the relationship is something much closer to the finite state machine depicted in Figure P.1 where difficulties encountered in technology define problems that lead to new areas of scientific research and analysis.

Although individuals may focus their careers on one aspect of the process, it is important for them to keep a watchful eye on what is happening in the other areas. For example, by understanding what makes it difficult for people and organizations to use certain types of software, a computer scientist is better positioned to pursue research that will lead to "new uses of computers."

For this reason, this book provides students with a high-level history of the evolution of software technology and the forces that have affected its development, placing particular emphasis on the technical and organizational challenges that must be faced in the adoption of new technology. In this process, we provide the students with a framework for characterizing a functional space in terms of the distribution and types of users, the data requirements for an envisioned application, and how the distribution and types of technology involved constrain acceptable solutions. Students

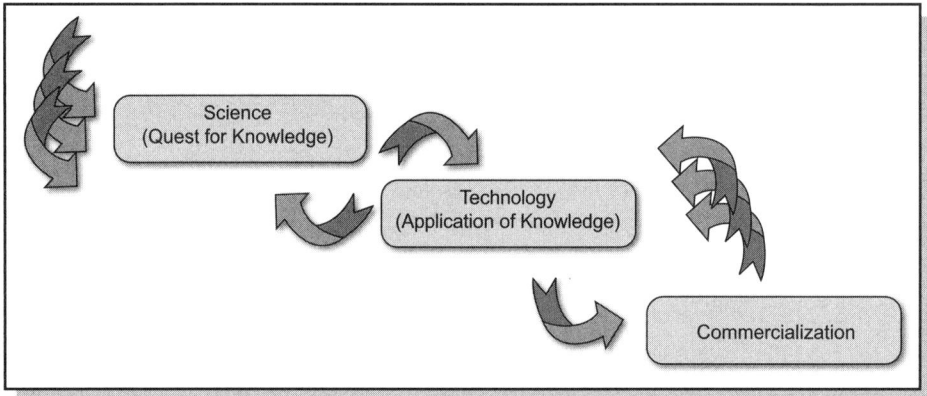

Figure P.1   Issues in Technology Drive Science

will also see how some problems were solved during one period only to be re-introduced at a later time, and how some problems have never been solved but continue to grow (e.g., the representation of meaning, which we will focus on in Chapter 6 and which is key to the ultimate success of XML). At every point we consider the impact on performance, agility (i.e., the ease with which systems can be modified), scalability, and the ability to maintain data integrity. In fact, we pay particular attention to challenges in data integration, because ultimately it is providing users with timely access to accurate information that determines the value of any software application.

The material should enable students to evaluate an application scenario, determine what's non-negotiable in terms of functionality, understand how these requirements affect integration with the data sources, and define the integration technologies and methodologies that will produce acceptable results. There are two types of assignments provided:

- Exercises and problems that require short answers or pseudocode to assess the student's grasp of the factual material
- Assignments that provide the student with an opportunity to apply this knowledge to the types of real-world scenarios that they might find in requests for proposals

In the spirit of WAC (Writing Across the Curriculum), we encourage you to have students prepare their answers to exercises in essay form, and include a brief description of techniques in expository writing in Appendix A.

About the Authors

Together, the authors have 30-plus years of combined commercial experience in system software, with particular emphasis on integration, as well as 12 years of college teaching experience. In 1991, Kay Hammer founded Evolutionary Technologies International (ETI), the first spin-off from MCC (the first U.S. for-profit, industry-backed computer research consortium) to productize the results of a 3-year research initiative to build a development platform for automating data integration. Hammer served as CEO of that company until December 2005 and has been the author of more than 40 articles on this topic during that period. Tina Timmerman assisted Hammer in obtaining the research funding at MCC and now serves as Chief Solution Architect at ETI, where she has had 7-plus years of consulting experience in data integration initiatives with Global 1000–size companies and the Department of Defense.

   Hammer has a PhD in English Linguistics, 10 years of experience teaching at the college level (including freshman composition), and over 20 years of experience in systems software and technical management at Texas Instruments, MCC, and ETI. Timmerman has a BS and MS in Computer Science from Texas State University and 25-plus years of experience in the software industry.

Organization

   Chapter 1, *Integration as a Mission-Critical Initiative,* discusses the range of factors that make integration hard and provides an explanation as to why integration has only recently emerged as a critical area for innovation.

   Chapter 2, *From Calculation to Collaboration,* uses the five Ws from journalism (who, what, when, where, and why) to analyze five major eras in software technology. Even at this gross level of granularity, it is possible to illustrate several principles at work that could be important to system design (e.g., increases in productivity are typically accompanied by the need for individuals with new types of specialized skills).

   Chapter 3, *The Evolution of Database Technology,* provides a technical overview of the evolution of database technology, with particular emphasis on the benefits and drawbacks of different data models in terms of performance, conceptual complexity, and the replication of data. We also include a discussion of common practices that IT shops have used to circumvent the shortcomings of navigational systems.

   Chapter 4, *Communication and Execution Protocols,* explores how advances in networking have changed the paradigm for computing and how the need to support multiple execution protocols has vastly complicated the task of maintaining data integrity.

   Chapter 5, *The Evolution of Application Development,* provides a model for the application and its environment based on the types of effort required to implement and maintain the application. It then explores how development platforms and methodologies have changed to address new uses of computers, with particular attention to how disruptive service-oriented architecture will be to traditional methods for test and data management.

Chapter 6, *The Representation of Meaning,* argues that the inherent differences in the way people and computers process information complicates the successful representation of semantic information and suggests how systems could be designed to bridge this gap.

Chapter 7, *Metadata and Change Management,* discusses how the scope and importance of metadata are expanding. The chapter focuses on challenges in metadata representation and acquisition, as well as factors affecting the success of standards initiatives in this area.

Chapter 8, *An Overview of Integration Technology,* describes the major types of integration technology and the class of integration problems that they were created to address, paying particular attention to the architectural strengths and weaknesses of each technology.

Chapter 9, *Defining an Integration Strategy,* provides a methodology for using the application model to define the most critical architectural and functional requirements for an integration strategy that will not only meet the immediate needs of a critical IT initiative, but also help an organization evolve to an integration architecture that best meets its long-term needs.

Chapter 10, *Topics for Further Study,* summarizes the major findings of the book and provides a description of topics in software integration that would benefit from deeper investigation.

Appendix A, *On the Process of Writing,* discusses how to develop a strategy for organizing different types of documents based on a model of the reader and the intended effect of the document.

Instructor's Online Resources

Instructors using this text in a classroom setting have access to the following support materials at http://www.jbpub.com/catalog/9780763741334/:

- Strategies for your Course
    Ideas for how to adapt the use of the text to meet different curriculum needs
- Lecture Outlines
    PowerPoint lecture slides for use in the classroom
- Answers to the Text's Exercises
    Suggested answers and discussion points to the exercises
- Sample exams
    A mid-term and final exam, including a summary of the key points for answers
- Glossary

CHAPTER

1

Integration as a Mission-Critical Initiative

Computers pervade every aspect of our existence from our telephones to our refrigerators. They have transformed everything from the way we shop to the way we establish communities. As a result, to the average person it seems strange that government agencies cannot exchange the information needed to respond to national emergencies when the navigational system in a rental car can adapt in real-time when a driver takes a wrong turn. Yet it is important to notice that the most dramatic breakthroughs in software in the past 15 years (e.g., Google, GPS) have not taken place in the context of traditional information technology (IT), despite the fact that there are pressing needs like fraud detection and regulatory compliance that would constitute a huge market for solutions in this area. The failure to address these problems is primarily due to the lack of a methodology for managing large-scale systems integration initiatives. In fact, until recently the integration of IT systems has always been seen as a "necessary evil" in implementing some new application rather than an area that deserved disciplined study in its own right.

There are two primary reasons for this state of affairs:

1. The hope that someday the software industry would settle on an interchange format that would make it easier for new systems to be interoperable. If such a standard were developed and adopted, then the belief was that only two translators would be required for the integration of legacy systems—one to write to the intermediate format and one to read from the intermediate format. In short, the problem of integration would be solved.

2. The fact that IT projects already experience such a high level of failure that managers are hesitant to increase risk by attempting to do more than the absolute minimum required to meet the immediate goal.

In this chapter, we will argue that:

- The nature of software limits the value of common intermediate formats.
- Generations of IT projects that have treated integration as a "one-off" problem have created IT environments that constitute such a huge financial burden to organizations that it in many ways offsets the benefits of using computers.
- The recognition of these previously unacknowledged problems is critical to both the advancement of computer science and software engineering.

1.1 Software Is "Sticky" Technology

Software is essentially a collection of digits stored in electronic format that lets people use computers for different purposes. But software is different from other forms of technology in that it is not easily discarded when superior technology emerges. Usually when some technological advance takes place, it gradually supplants the old. Cassettes replaced 8-track tapes and were themselves replaced by CDs. Lasers are being used in surgery instead of scapels. That is not to say that some people still don't play records and cassettes, but the average person wouldn't want to go to a hospital whose operating facilities used equipment that was 40 years old. Yet in most large organizations, mission-critical applications like billing or managing call detail records are based on software systems that are 30 or 40 years old, primarily because it is so difficult to replace them. This "stickiness" results from the fact that software is symbolic and is only useful because a set of people have reached some agreement about how the representation of data on disk and in memory correlates to some set of entities and the relationships among them.

1.2 The Limitations of Data

Most technologies deal with physical phenomena—materials you can touch, see, or feel. They help us move more quickly, lift heavier loads, or keep us dry and warm. But software helps us remember and saves us time by performing mental tasks that are prone to error. In short, software deals with symbolic phenomena—that is, with abstract representations of both 1) things that physically exist in the world, like automobiles or books or ideas; and 2) conventions for how we deal with them as a society. With social conventions, much of what drives the interaction is unspoken or assumed and therefore confusing to someone who is not familiar with the culture in which that convention exists. In large part, then, the reason that software systems are hard to replace is because the information that is stored on disk is only part of the information required to understand the data.

Consider the case where a file definition contains a field named *SALARY* and a record in that file has the value *120,000* for the salary field. What does that mean? Annual salary in U.S. dollars or monthly salary in dinars? Although this is a pretty obvious example, in many production systems the field names used by the software are frequently abstruse, as illustrated by the following portion of a COBOL copybook:

```
01 CLES-RECORD.
      05 RECTYPE      PIC X(3).
      05 TRANS-DATE   PIC 9(8).
      05 CLES-CLMKYE  PIC X(9).
      05 CLES-POLLOE  PIC X(3).
```

Although a knowledge of English gives the reader some confidence that RECTYPE means "record type" and a knowledge of COBOL that the legal value for that field will be a three-character string, you would have to look at all the records in the file to know what the legal values for the field would be. Even then you couldn't be sure that you would understand what they referred to—or in the case of an infrequent value, that the value wasn't wrong. What "CLES-CLMKYE" means is anybody's guess.

The situation is further complicated by the fact that mission-critical applications are extremely complex, particularly those that have been in use for a long period of time. It is not uncommon to find file definitions that contain tens of thousands of field definitions. The schema for a COTS (commercial off-the-shelf) application from a vendor like Oracle or SAP may contain 3000 tables. An XML document may contain a hierarchy of 1500 complex types, each of which is composed of multiple elements. As a result, few technical people in a company or consulting firm understand the entire database layout and, even if they did, they are unlikely to understand the nuances of how the data is represented because they typically are not the people who actually use the database.

In fact, often the resolution of what some data value means—or what it should mean, or whether the value is legal or valid—comes from correlating knowledge from a number of individuals in different organizations. As illustrated in Figure 1.1, in most organizations, the knowledge required to understand data is distributed across three different types of employees:

- *The data owner*—The person, such as a contracts administrator, who interacts with the applications and knows what the data values refer to.
- *The software developer*—The person who maintains one or more of the production applications. In many companies, these positions are filled by contractors or have been farmed out to outsourcers or offshore developers. As a result, the individual currently in charge of this effort may have only a limited view of the application and its data.
- *The business process owner*—The manager or executive who understands at a global level how the information contained in various

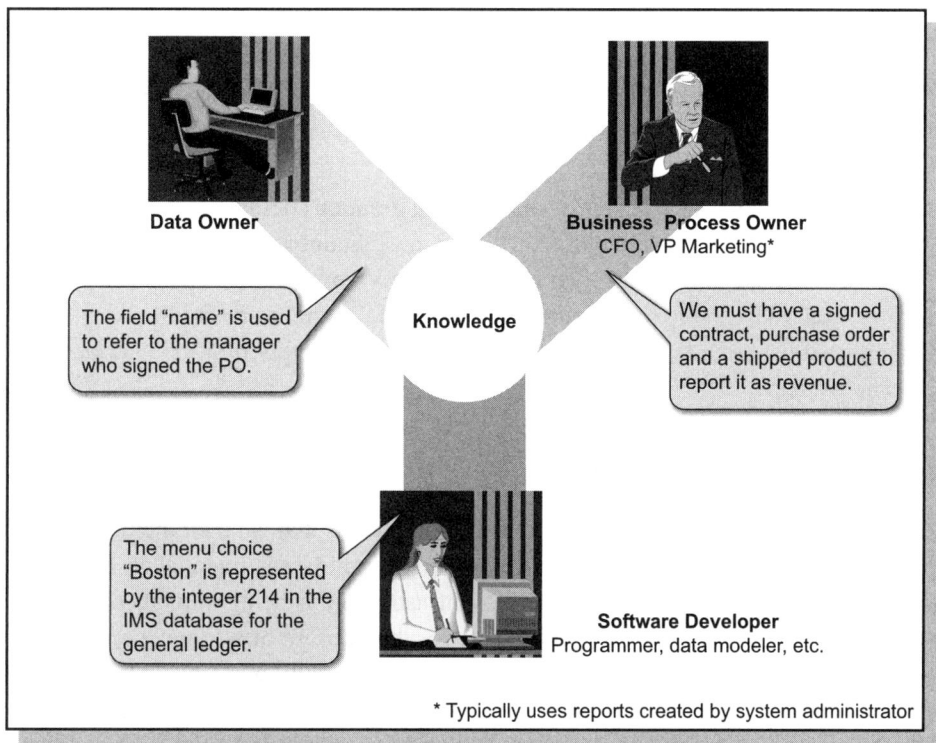

Figure 1.1 The Three Stakeholders

applications is supposed to interrelate and be used in the process of running the business.

Obtaining and correlating the missing information required to understand what data means is not easy for the following reasons:

- Each type of individual has little knowledge about what the other two types of individuals know. In fact, in the case of complex systems, a single data owner may know only one aspect of the data stored in a system.
- The task of explicitly specifying and correlating everything required to understand the meaning of data values is very error-prone. Data owners may reference data fields by the names they see on the screen, whereas developers use the names that appear in the file definition, and business process owners may use accounting terms that

carry additional meaning. For example, when a financial officer of a company uses the term "revenue," it refers to transactions that have met several accounting criteria, whereas a salesman may use the term to refer to transactions that have not yet met those conditions.

As a result, data analysis frequently takes several iterations before an accurate view of the meaning of the data values stored in a system is obtained, and even then it is often hard to understand because it is so complex. Even worse, because each integration initiative has traditionally been treated as a "one-off," there has been little attention to making what has been learned about the data available to other projects interfacing to the same systems.

1.3 The Importance of Data

Probably the most important reason we use computers is that we trust them to give us the "right" answer. Yet too often the task of migrating data is undertaken only after the design is in place and an application or infrastructure is being implemented. Project members may interview different people for the purpose of writing specifications (often called mapping documents), but developers generally don't begin the process of moving and testing the data until at least the first phase of the design is in place. This is usually a mistake, because there is no way to anticipate how long it may take to consolidate all the information required from the various groups in question. In fact, interviews with 400 senior IT managers in 2004 revealed that flawed specifications were the most frequent cause of project failure (IDC, 2004). Data is central to the success of any software project. In fact, one could argue that the functional difference between a calculator and a computer is that computers manipulate persistent data; that is, they can store the results of what they compute.

As a result, often software applications based on older technology cannot be retired because they contain critical data. There is no way to simply abandon existing IT systems without losing the history of what has happened, and losing that history would have devastating results. Would you like your bank balance—and more importantly, what it represents—to just disappear when the bank installs a new application? As a result, we are stuck with the problem of understanding the data that is currently stored in software systems. Unfortunately, until recently most IT initiatives only worried about understanding just enough about the data sources to build the data interfaces, and because the data interfaces were written by hand, there was very little reuse of the information learned across projects. This not only is inefficient, but also has resulted in integration architectures like the one in Figure 1.2.

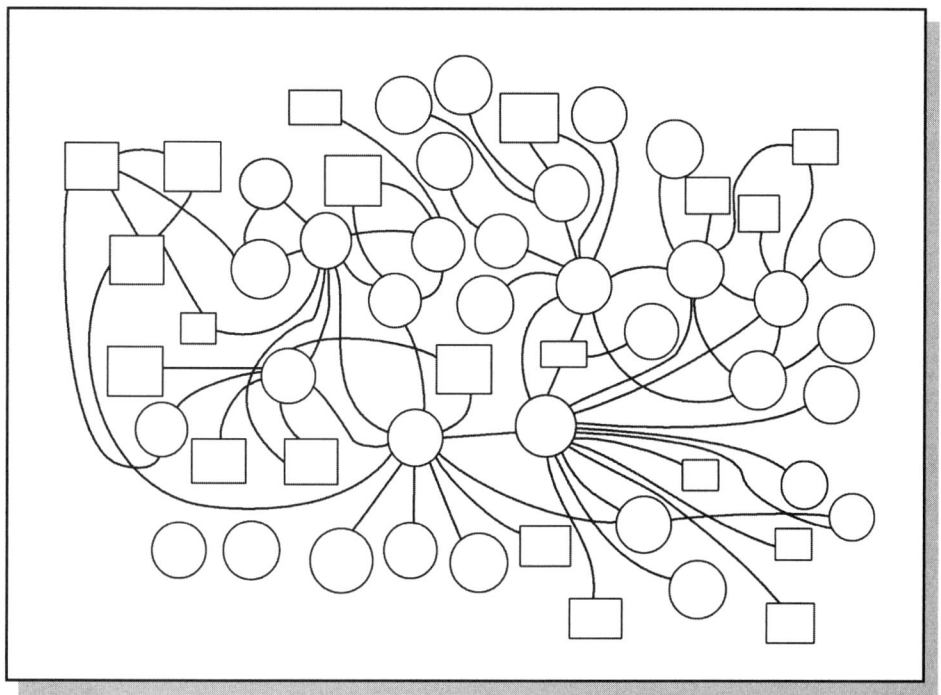

Figure 1.2   A Typical Data Bridge Diagram

The drawing in this figure is a logical representation of the data bridging for a single division of a large energy company. The circles and squares represent the files, databases, and applications used to run the business of that division. The "spaghetti" lines between them represent the data interfaces that have been written on an as-needed basis to keep data consistent and enable automated reporting. This diagram illustrates how the traditional approach to data integration only added to the problem. Whatever was learned about the source and target systems in the process of developing the interfaces was buried in the spaghetti code, including whether anything was done to transform the data values in the process of moving them.

The preceding discussion provides some idea of the difficulties encountered in addressing the integration requirements of any large IT project, but few people realize the impact that these problems have on a company's costs of doing business and its ability to respond to change. Research performed by the Standish Group (2003) reports revealed that:

- Only 34% of IT projects are completed on time and on budget.
- 48% of successfully completed projects were missing some key feature.
- 43% of all successfully completed projects experienced cost overrun.
- 82% of all successfully completed projects experienced schedule overrun.
- 50–80% of a corporation's IT budget is spent on maintenance.

Moreover, not only are organizations extremely inefficient in their implementation and maintenance of software, but as businesses grow and industries change, the cost of meeting IT challenges increases accordingly. To understand why, consider the following.

1.4   How Business Factors Complicate the Problem

Figure 1.2 represented the data bridging for a single division of an international company. Consider the magnitude of the task if a company had 14 divisions with the same kind of integration challenges and then decided to acquire another equally large and complex organization. Add to this a disruptive technology like the Internet that enables a new class of competitors and frequent changes in regulatory policies. Then you have an idea of the challenges that the U.S. telecommunications industry has faced since 1984 when the U.S. Congress determined that AT&T was a monopoly and forced it to break up into seven independent regional companies that were required to make their infrastructure available to any competitor at regulated prices in order to make consistent service available to the customer. Since that time a number of regulations have changed that affected how the telecommunications business was run.

Although the enforced sharing of infrastructure benefited customers by fostering competition, it created a back-office nightmare of cross-billing that became even more complicated with the advent of wireless service. To understand the impact of this regulation on the business, consider the following passage from a policy brief produced by the Brookings Institution:

> In the first six months of 2003, AT&T's 10-Q report shows that it paid $5.4 billion in access and other connection charges out of its $17.8 billion in revenues. **That amounted to 30 percent of costs, and larger than the $4.0 billion that AT&T spent in actually producing its services and products.** *[Boldface type by authors.]* These charges are ludicrously high. The cost of local connections at each end of a call cannot possibly be more than the costs of transporting the call across the nation and then billing for it. These charges distort the decision between toll calls and other means of electronic communication.

In fact, there are over one hundred different configurations of origination and termination charges (depending on whether the calls originate or terminate with a long-distance provider, a local landline incumbent, a competitive entrant in local wire access, or a wireless provider). A key distinction in the charging system is that while some kind of interconnection charges are levied if a call originates or terminates with a wire line provider, there are no such charges on calls routed both ways through wireless carriers. (Litan & Noll, 2004)

The competitive landscape became even more complicated once technology allowed cable companies to offer Voice-over-Internet Protocol (VoIP) service and avoid the charges altogether because that product offering uses none of the infrastructure referenced by the legislation. The situation has become even worse now that AT&T has been allowed to reacquire a number of the "Baby Bells" that the earlier legislation forced it to spin off.

However, there is another layer of complexity for integration in industries like telecom. The applications previously discussed deal with "front office" issues—that is, applications that from a high-level functional point of view are required for almost every business (billing, delivery, customer service, etc.). But most industries use computer technology to actually build and deliver their products and services. As a result, integrating data from these systems is important to the ability to compete. In our telecom example these *backend* systems are their networks and telephone switches. Many of these interfaces are proprietary to the hardware vendors, and the networks and satellites used by most companies span multiple generations.

Given this understanding of the types of pressures faced by industry, let's reconsider the impact of inefficient integration. IT systems that are cobbled together by hand make it costly—if not impossible—for companies to rapidly adapt their systems to support changes in business practices to address new competitors. Finally, when critical data is distributed across multiple computer environments residing in different geographies, it is hard to offer effective customer service. So the next time you are stuck on the phone and have to key in your account number multiple times before you get to the human who asks you for your account number, you have some appreciation as to why.

1.5   Why Study Software Integration?

The focus of science is to acquire knowledge, or what the *New World Webster Dictionary* defines as "systemized knowledge derived from observation, study, and experimentation carried on in order to determine the nature or principles of what is being studied." Scientific theories evolve to achieve greater explanatory power to give them greater predictive capabilities. The scientific method depends upon controlling extraneous variables to enable researchers to see patterns that help them understand the principles of how things work. In clinical trials, subjects are grouped with respect to gender, age, weight, and lifestyle in an effort to ensure that different results in patients' reactions don't result from differences in one of these factors. Computer science relies heavily upon the disciplines of physics and mathematics, both of which are even more rigorous in their formalism than the biological sciences. As a result, it is not surprising that many of the academic courses in the curricula for computer science programs focus on the algorithms and programming techniques that correlate to the theorems and corollaries of these disciplines.

Technology, on the other hand, is the application of science, and as we have seen from the discussion in this chapter, the design and implementation of software systems is far from a rigorous process. In its purest form, computer science is independent of technology. The Turing machine was designed long before the integrated circuit or the discipline of electrical engineering. However, in large part advances in computer science are dependent upon advances in engineering—that is, in our ability to marry what we know from science to what we know about building things to improve the quality of our lives. Technology evolves to improve the way something is achieved, whether that improvement results in buildings that sustain less damage in earthquakes or an internal data representation that supports a more efficient search algorithm for retrieving information from text. In fact, it is frequently the limitations in technology that lead to scientific breakthroughs. For example, one could argue that one of the largest motivations in the creation of computer networking technology was the fact that automating data management had limited value if the data being managed was only accessible from a single computer.

Sometimes scientific breakthroughs result in creating a whole new area for scientific discovery. For example, as we will discuss in Chapter 2, computers were originally used primarily for performing complex mathematical calculations, and it was only after people sought to expand and generalize the application of computers that computer science became a discipline in its own right. In part because computers can be applied to such a broad range of applications, it is becoming hard to design an undergraduate curriculum that covers all the topics in sufficient detail to do the discipline justice.

However, because software is "sticky," most organizations are not utilizing the most advanced software technology. Therefore, for graduates in computer science and software engineering to be effective in many environments, they need an understanding of the evolution of software—that is, the benefits and limitations of different generations of the software technology that are currently in use. Moreover, as we will see, the study of this evolution will provide more than background about the differences in the software technology of different eras. We will also see that the same types of problems crop up across generations of software, and that an awareness of these problems is important to the future of computer science because with this awareness you will design or demand software solutions that can not only be implemented more efficiently, but also maintained more easily.

1.6   The Importance of Proceeding Carefully

Earlier in this chapter, we spent a fair amount of time considering the challenges faced by telecommunications companies because we wanted to point out that the use of information technology in any particular industry is shaped by the nature of its business. Different industries have different requirements, some of which are critical and some of which are "nice to haves." Too often software technology is developed and deployed without a full understanding of what's important to the people affected by it. As we will see in Chapter 3, the failure of the providers of early database management systems to understand the need to enable IT personnel to implement changes quickly—sometimes within a less than 24-hour period—led to many organizations not utilizing some of the product capabilities that ensured data quality. Migration from these systems is extremely difficult because the data is often inconsistent or ill-formed. As a result, rather than replacing applications, companies have resorted to the "spaghetti interfaces" described earlier. Whereas some shortcomings in software products make them difficult to use or the resulting applications difficult to maintain, some had devastating consequences, particularly where the Internet was involved. It is hard to know how much money has been lost due to identity theft, viruses, and practices like "phishing," not to mention heightened risks of terrorism. Many of these problems could have been avoided by anticipating them and designing to take them into account. An understanding of how previous generations of software have fallen short can help designers and computer scientists anticipate problems in new environments—much like envisioning boundary conditions when testing code—to minimize or eliminate these limitations and risks.

In 2000 in an article called "Why the Future Doesn't Need Us," Bill Joy, one of the founders of Sun Microsystems, had the following to say:

> We are being propelled into this new century with no plan, no control, no brakes. Have we already gone too far down the path to alter course? I don't

believe so, but we aren't trying yet, and the last chance to assert control—the fail-safe point—is rapidly approaching....The new Pandora's boxes of genetics, nanotechnology, and robotics are almost open, yet we seem hardly to have noticed. Ideas can't be put back in a box; unlike uranium or plutonium, they don't need to be mined and refined, and they can be freely copied. Once they are out, they are out. Churchill remarked, in a famous left-handed compliment, that the American people and their leaders "invariably do the right thing, after they have examined every other alternative." In this case, however, we must act more presciently, as to do the right thing only at last may be to lose the chance to do it at all.

1.7 The Need for a Conceptual Framework

It is imperative that as students of computer science and software engineering you acquire the skills required to be responsible participants in the creation and deployment of information technology. The first step is acquiring a solid understanding of the current state of software technology as it exists in our industries and governments, in addition to the principles of design that make software easy to modify, integrate, or replace. Armed with this understanding, you will be better able to anticipate the risks associated with new software protocols and technology, and thereby be able to ensure that you create or utilize information technology to its best advantage.

Key to this understanding is the ability to recognize functional similarities across systems that have significant differences in everything from user skill level to communication and execution protocols. It is not reasonable to expect the software industry—nor the consultants and analysts whose job it is to help us understand software—to provide these insights, because they are not financially motivated to make us aware of these similarities. Whether consciously or not, every product is presented as being significantly different from what has come before, with the result that jargon proliferates and creates even more confusion. In the next chapter, we will present a simple, jargon-free framework for characterizing software technology and apply it to the definition of five major periods in the evolution of software.

By using this framework in evaluating a new software technology or product offering in conjunction with what you know about the strengths and weaknesses of the types of software that have preceded it, you should be able to determine the following:

- The nature of the system integration problems you are likely to encounter in different environments and application scenarios

- Whether there is some functional "hole" in an offering that will require either hand-coding or the use of some other product or products
- Whether these shortcomings have been addressed by the new technology if these problems caused some similar technology to fail

Exercises for Chapter 1

1. One of the ways a company can leverage its growth is through mergers and acquisitions. There are two common goals of any M&A transaction. In addition to higher revenue, companies also expect to be able to reduce expenses by eliminating redundant facilities, systems, and staff. Often one of the largest deterrents to achieving these efficiencies comes from difficulties encountered in the integration of their IT systems. Consider the following two scenarios and enumerate the types of challenges you would expect to encounter in integrating the software systems.

   a. A hardware manufacturer acquires its largest competitors
   b. An international bank acquires a bank in a new country

2. As indicated in our discussion of the telecommunications industry, there are many external factors that can complicate an industry's software integration challenges, for example:

   - Increased regulation or changes in regulation
   - Reduced margins due to the availability and/or cost of raw materials
   - New types of competitors
   - Disruptive technology

   It is important to be able to extrapolate how these factors can affect their information systems and anticipate the functionality required to address these problems from what you read in the general press. Use the Internet and business publications to research two of the following industries and write a short report on each that describes 1) at least three external factors that will affect their IT systems within the next 5 years, and 2) the types of additional information and functionality that they will need to acquire.

   Industries: Healthcare providers, software vendors, automobile manufacturers, book publishers

CHAPTER

2

From Calculation to Collaboration

In this chapter, we will examine five major eras of software technology that spanned approximately 50 years and were characterized by significant advances in capabilities in terms of what people could do with computers. Often these advances were possible only because of new hardware or communication technology, but we will focus on the software that most directly affects a person's ability to be more accurate, more efficient, or capable of new types of activities. However, before beginning this discussion, we will establish a framework that we will use to characterize the changes across periods to help crystallize similarities and differences.

2.1   A Framework: The Five Basic Questions

In journalism, students are taught to answer the five Ws in writing an article—who, what, when, where, and why. As it turns out, these five questions are similarly useful when talking about software:

Who: Characterize the skill and knowledge level required of each of the following types of users:

- The developer who implements the software
- The person who uses the software
- The person who maintains the environment in which the software runs

Too frequently people do not give enough attention to the requirements of the developers or technical staff who must maintain applications once they have been implemented and deployed. As we will see in the next chapter, the failure of software vendors to understand the requirements of these users is what has sometimes led to software development platforms being used in a very different fashion from the way they were designed to be used.

What: Characterize what the software does. This includes considering:

- The type of data that can be stored, accessed, and processed with that technology (e.g., numeric, symbolic, structured, unstructured, etc.)
- The type of functionality the technology provides to one or more types of users
- Any tools and system software required to support the technology

When: Characterize the technology with respect to:

- Its scalability or performance across factors like the volume of data or the number of concurrent users and/or transactions
- The support for different execution/communication protocols—that is, how applications are invoked (i.e., scheduled, manually invoked, queue-driven, event-driven, broadcast, service-oriented). (We will discuss each of these in detail in Chapter 4.)

Where: Characterize the "spatial" aspects of the software architecture:

- The geographical distribution of the various classes of users (e.g., in the earliest days of computers, developers had to be in the same physical location as their computer/applications)

- The computational environment, which includes the location and types of hosts involved with respect to geography, processor, operating system, and so on
- The organizational relationship between the user and the owner of the software (e.g., Is the software installed on a host owned and maintained by the company for which the users work, or is it "rented" by the user?)

Why: Characterize the motivation for creating the new software in terms of whether it does one or more of the following:

- Provides significantly improved functionality over previous technology
- Enables a whole new class of user to benefit from the use of computers
- Makes software developers or end users more productive
- Solves a limitation with previous software capabilities

Topic of Interest: Structured vs. Unstructured Data

The term *structured data* is used to refer to datasets with a fixed format—that is, where every instance of a record or every instance of a field has the same offset and data type from the last instance. Most applications for business use are based on structured data stored in files or database management systems. Unstructured data is governed by rules that guide an application in how to interpret it, but each data instance is treated as unique in the sense that a program cannot predict that it will find a particular type of data at a particular location within the instance. Text and graphic files are examples of unstructured data. Unstructured data is constituting a larger and larger portion of the persistent information being stored in computers.

2.2   Five Major Eras of Software Technology

It would be impossible to fully characterize the past 50 years of innovations in software technology in a single book. As a result, the following section is a gross oversimplification, but we have chosen to focus on the four major technical innovations that have affected either 1) expanding the benefits of computers to a new class of users, or 2) the ease or difficulty of maintaining data integrity. Even some of the claims provided in this section are not entirely accurate because technical advances happen incrementally and typically take several years before they are adopted by the mainstream. The purpose of the following discussion therefore is to focus on the technologies whose advent has had the biggest effect on challenges in integration and to illustrate the benefits of answering the five Ws.

The five major eras of software technology we've chosen are:

- The age of the standalone application
- The age of the database
- The age of the network
- The age of the desktop
- The age of the internet

Topic of Interest: Patterns in Technology Acquisition

In 1991, Geoffrey Moore wrote an influential book about the adoption of technology called *Crossing the Chasm.* Moore's background was in marketing, and he noticed that when offering products based on new technology, there was often relatively quick adoption by a small number of companies (companies that he called "the early adopters"), after which sales would stall causing many technology companies to fail. The real growth came for those few companies who successfully "crossed the chasm" between the early adopters and the mainstream. Moore characterized the early adopters as risk takers, willing to try anything with promise even if there was risk of failing. In contrast, the mainstream buyer was risk-averse and only ready to commit to a technology once it had been tried and proven. The challenge, then, for technology companies was to choose a growth strategy that would enable them to move from the buyer who wasn't afraid of making a mistake to those who were and consequently tended to follow a herd mentality.

2.3 The Age of the Standalone Application

This age was characterized by applications that enabled complex calculations and repetitive tasks to be completed more quickly and accurately than could be done by hand. As illustrated in Figure 2.1, during this period an application might use the

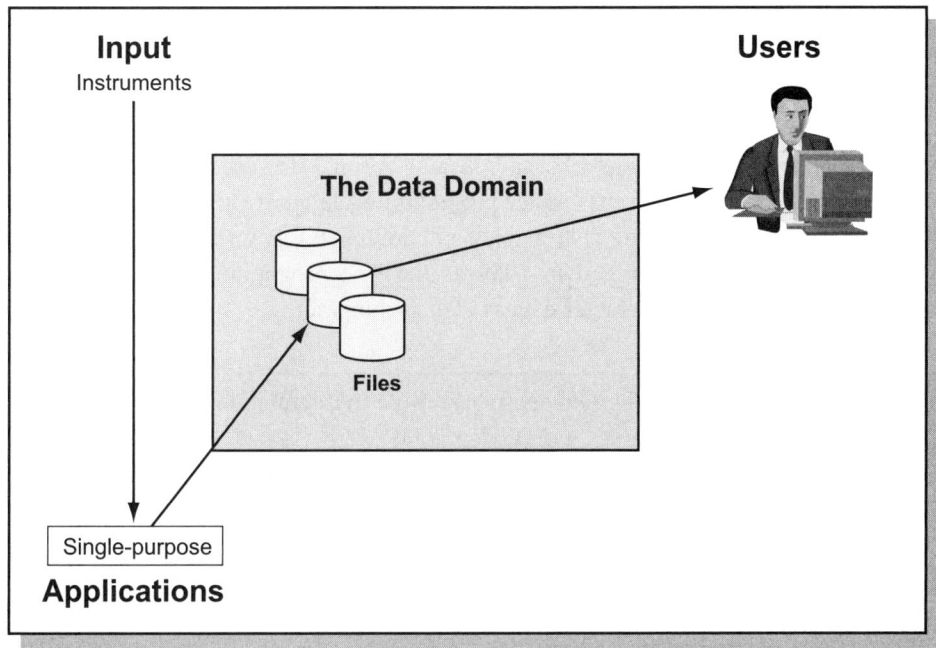

Figure 2.1   The Age of the Standalone Application

same data as input as another application, but it was written as if it was the only application to use that data.

Initially computers were used to compute complex equations that would be either too time-consuming or too error-prone for humans to perform. In fact, some of the earliest uses in the 1950s were in space programs where computers were used to interpret telemetry. Originally the programming took place at the digital level where the "programmers" were technicians who actually flipped switches to 1 or 0 to encode the algorithm. Later computers supported programming in a language called assembler that provided a small set of commands like "move" or "add" that referenced the hardware components that "held" the data that was being processed (e.g., registers and arithmetic units like adders). As a result, programming was a very tedious process and justifiable only when the pay-off was clearly important—for example, some application of huge significance like tracking a spaceship or interpreting seismic data to predict earthquakes.

However, as hardware became more powerful and general purpose, the potential for other types of scientific (i.e., mathematical) computations led to the creation of FORTRAN, the first high-level language that allowed programmers to specify the desired behavior in higher-level terms like "WRITE" and "FORMAT" without referencing hardware components like registers. During this time it became clear that computers could offer similar benefits in speed and accuracy to highly repetitive business applications like payroll and billing. However, to enable this, it was necessary to have an even simpler programming language that could represent and manipulate character data (like names and addresses) as well as it manipulated numbers. COBOL was designed in 1959 as the first programming language with facilities for dealing with character data as well as numeric.

> **Topic of Interest: The Government's Role in Technical Evolution**
> The specifications for the COBOL language were created in 1959 by a committee of government and industry personnel established by the U.S. Department of Defense. Its charter was to recommend a short-range approach to a common business language. The specifications were to a great extent inspired by two languages, one developed by Rear Admiral Grace Hopper called FLOW-MATIC and one called COMTRAN invented by an IBM employee named Bob Bemer. The specifications were published in 1960, COBOL was developed within a 6-month period, and the language is still in widespread use in the 21st century, half a decade later.

One of the greatest benefits FORTRAN and COBOL provided to programmers was that they greatly simplified input and output. Before these "second generation" languages, programmers had to specify exact disk locations in terms of track and sector when they wanted to read from or write to a file. COBOL supported a file definition language that allowed the programmer to associate logical names with different offsets in a sequence of bits or bytes. For example, a programmer could use this language to define a "copybook" that associated a logical name ADDRESS with the characters in positions 11–46 in an EMPLOYEE record.

The Five Ws

Table 2.1 summarizes the answers to the five Ws for standalone applications. Note the second row in the WHY table that is labeled "Unintended outcome." It is a very rare technical advance that doesn't carry with it some problem or limitation. In fact, one of the strongest justifications for investing in the development of new technology is the

Table 2.1   The Age of the Standalone Application

Who	IT Staff	• Scientists, computer technicians; later—application programmers
	User	• Scientists; later—accountants, data entry clerks
What	Applications	• Scientific computation; later—predominantly accounting/financial applications
	Types of Data	• Initially binary or numeric; later—includes character data
When		• Invoked manually or runs all the time initially, later—invoked by schedulers
Where		• Mainframe or special equipment on site with users
Why	The vision	• Enable complex calculations and repetitive tasks to be completed more quickly and accurately than by hand
	Unintended outcome	• Over time, replicated data existing in different files became "out of sync"

claim that it will address the shortcomings of the technology already in place. As a result, we will begin each of the following sections with an assessment of the limitations of the software technology environments that were in widespread use at the time of the innovation.

2.4   The Age of the Database

As illustrated in Figure 2.2, during this period there was an emphasis on the use of software systems that enabled applications to share data for improved data integrity and ease in access.

For the 20 years after COBOL's inception, COBOL-based applications proliferated throughout organizations, although most of the data manipulated by these applications was still being entered by hand. (In fact, at one point in time "data entry

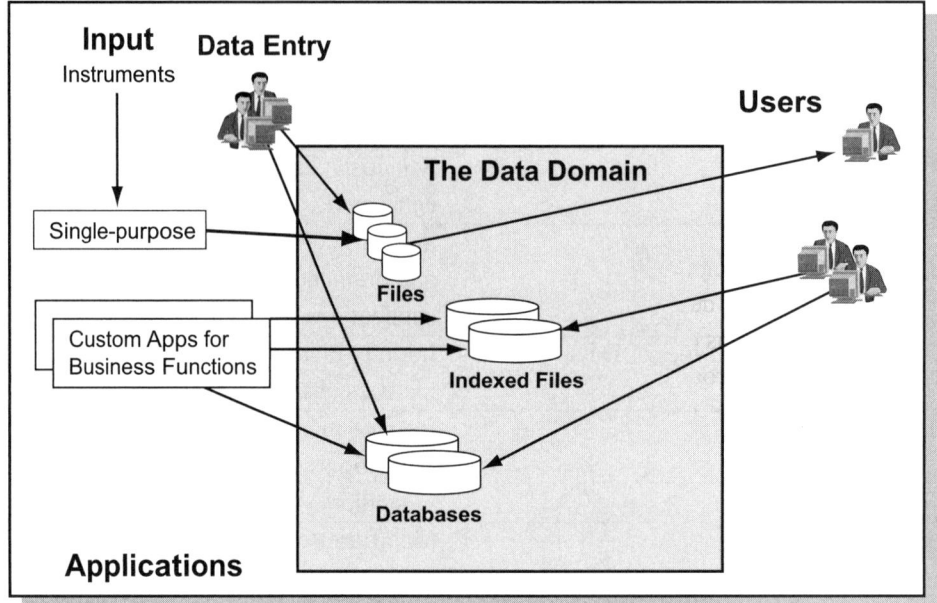

Figure 2.2 The Age of the Database

clerk" was actually a job description.) The output of computers was paper reports that were routed to interested parties and used by other data entry clerks. Because this process depended on human interaction and was therefore error-prone, there were often errors in consistency across files that contained related information. If a retired employee died, the data entry clerk might record the change in status in the personnel file, while the data entry clerk in the accounting department might accidentally skip an entry in entering employee updates to the payroll file. As a result, the company would continue to send benefit checks to the deceased person. In short, there was no way to ensure the *integrity* of common data across files because there was nothing to link them automatically unless the applications were installed on the same computer, in which case companies could hand-code batch update programs to extract updated records from one application and another program to read this information and update the related application. Each of the programs had to be crafted to what often were proprietary file formats used by the various applications; this constituted the earliest of the "spaghetti" interfaces we discussed in Chapter 1.

New Requirements for the Space Program

In the meantime, by the late 1960s the Apollo space program required the representation of extremely complex designs that exceeded the I/O capabilities of COBOL. Although the original impetus was a richer data model, as the concept of a "data manager" became more robust, one of the goals became the elimination of *redundant* or *replicated* data by having all the data needed by an organization stored under the control of a software component called a database management system (DBMS) that would not only handle the details of reading and writing the data, but also ensure that the data being stored was of the correct type. Over the next 20 years, database technology evolved to offer a broad range of capabilities that we will study in some detail in the next chapter. For the purposes of our current discussion there were three important results from the age of the database: Management had more timely access to a wider range of better quality reports, errors in the representation and consistency of data were reduced, and programmers were more productive. However, two new types of specially trained staff were required—the data modeler and the database administrator (DBA).

The *data modeler* was responsible for designing the database—the record definitions (that is, the fields that made up the record) and the way objects represented by the records were related in terms of cardinality (one-to-one, one-to-many, many-to-many). For example, in a database used to represent registration in a college, one department record would be associated with multiple course records, each of which would be associated with one or more section records. As part of their job, data modelers interviewed different users of a proposed database to understand the types of reports they would need to fulfill their jobs. The *database administrator (DBA)* was responsible for adapting the database design to the data model used by the database management system product to ensure that the performance would be adequate to the different database users' needs, using the sample reports as guidance. The DBA was also responsible for configuring the DBMS for security and back-up. In short, although the age of the database provided significantly improved levels of data integrity and made programmers more productive, it required at least two types of technical staff with specialized expertise, as well as creating a whole new class of semi-technical staff (i.e., data entry clerks).

The Five Ws

Table 2.2 summarizes how the age of the database differs from the age of standalone applications.

Table 2.2 The Age of the Database

Who	IT Staff	• Scientists, computer technicians, application programmers • *Data modelers* • *Database administrators*
	User	• Scientists, accountants, data entry clerks • *Diverse employees using reports generated by applications for specific business processes (e.g., marketing, manufacturing)*
What	Applications	• Scientific computation; accounting/financial applications • *A broader range of applications like materials resource planning (MRP) for manufacturing, human resources for payroll, benefits, etc.* • *Database management systems; later, end-user query products* • Binary, numeric, character data
	Types of data	• *Use of binary data reduced; later systems support BLOBs (binary large objects) for graphics, etc.*
When		• Invoked manually, runs all the time, or scheduled • *Triggered*
Where		• Mainframe or special equipment on site with users • *Mainframes and later mini-computers accessible by remote users*
Why	The vision	• Enable complex calculations and repetitive tasks to be completed more quickly and accurately than by hand

| | | • **Improve programmer productivity and data integrity** |
| | Unintended outcome | • **Data integrity depended upon all data being stored under the same installation of the DBMS (i.e., applications were "stovepiped").** |

2.5   The Age of the Network

As illustrated in Figure 2.3, this period was characterized by the first electronic "bridges" that could move data across what had previously been "islands." This was made possible by technology that allowed disparate hardware and operating systems to communicate.

Throughout the 1960s, most large production databases were mainframe-based, but thanks to transistors and core memory, by the 1970s a new class of computers

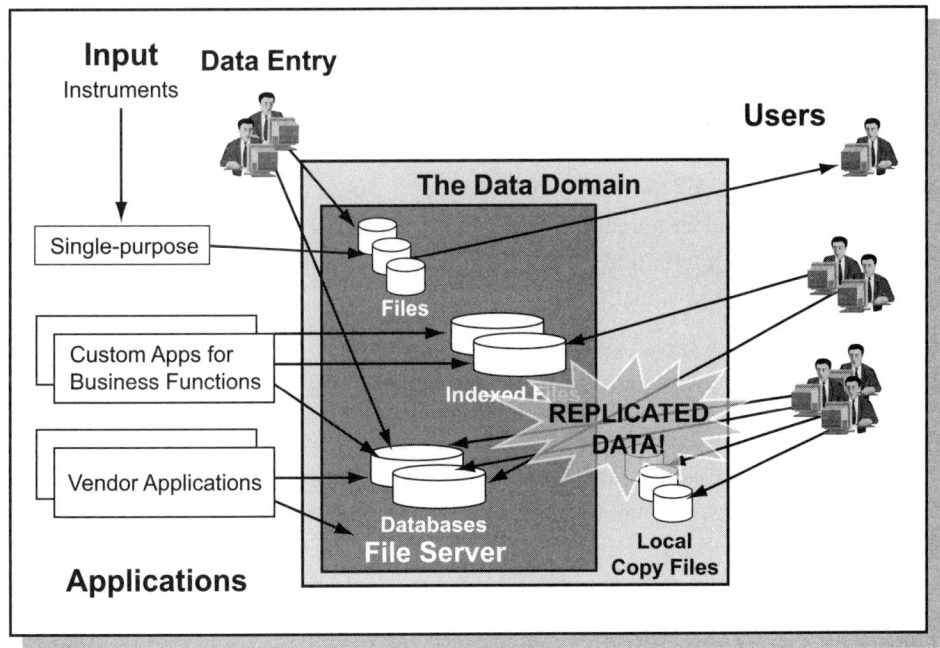

Figure 2.3   The Age of the Network

became widely available—the mini-computer. Systems like the AS400, the VAX, and the TI-990 provided a lower cost solution for companies that could not afford a mainframe and did not want to *timeshare* (that is, buy time on a mainframe available through a third party). However, at that time most applications were owned by a particular department (accounting, human resources, etc.). If the applications weren't installed on the same host, the exchange of information between systems typically required manual data entry, which resulted in delays and frustration.

To understand how time-consuming and error-prone this process was, consider the experience of the authors of this book. At different times in the 1980s, both of us were project managers in software development for a computer manufacturer that sold hardware and a series of software products for that hardware. In order to help the finance department determine whether the company was "on track" with its financial estimates, we had to provide input for monthly financial forecasts. Because all actual expenditures were captured by a mainframe application, the process was as follows: We would schedule a time to use a terminal (typically called a "green screen" because of the color of the display) located in Austin, Texas, that was connected to the mainframe in Plano, Texas, to download and print our actual expenditures for the last month. We would then return to our desks to use a terminal connected to a spreadsheet application on a mini-computer (later a PC using a spreadsheet) to update our budget application with the actual expenditures. We would then make any necessary changes to our planned expenditures for the next month (e.g., additional people, travel, etc.), print out the results, and then take our turn back at the "green screen" terminal to enter our forecasted expenditures. Because there was no error-checking until we submitted the entire report to the mainframe, it would often take multiple submissions to be successful in uploading the data. It would not be unusual for this task to take 2 to 4 hours each month, depending upon the size of the project, where only 20% of the time was spent in actually working with the budget figures.

Advent of a New Application Architecture

As computer chips became more powerful and inexpensive and as networking technology evolved to provide greater throughput and reliability, a whole new architecture for computing emerged—client-server architecture. Rather than having all the computation take place on a remote computer—or having to re-enter information across applications that ran on different computers—one could have local workstations with their own processor and storage (the client) interact directly with applications based on centralized data servers (the server). One of the most appealing aspects of this architecture was that companies could "grow as they go." Because of their large amount of processing power, mainframe access was so expensive that different departments were actually charged a fee for their use of the system. Workstations and servers were significantly less expensive, originally costing in the $10,000–$50,000 range. The vision was that companies could abandon the mainframe and buy only the number of servers and workstations they needed, adding additional servers and workstations as necessary.

New Technical Staff

In addition to new hardware, client-server architecture required two new types of technical expertise: knowledge about the network and knowledge about the operating system. Although many hardware vendors developed proprietary operating systems to support client-server architectures, the industry standard became UNIX, an operating system initially designed at AT&T Bell Labs. UNIX became the standard in large part because several nonprofit organizations made the source code available as freeware in the hope that it would foster a foundation for interoperability between the workstations and file servers from different hardware vendors. This resulted in most universities running UNIX and subsequently a supply of trained system administrators available to IT organizations.

New Types of Applications

Client-server architecture provided local processing power, but because IT organizations were at that time still very concerned about data integrity, they wanted to restrict how the local processing power was used. Most system architects advocated a tiered software architecture that consisted of three logical layers:

- The data layer that provided all the protection and capabilities (locking, etc.) of database technology.
- The business logic layer, where the actual business specific calculations occurred.
- The user interface layer. Originally, these interfaces were pretty basic command-line-driven type-in windows; however, after the introduction of Lisa (Apple's precursor to the personal computer) in the early 1980s, graphical user interfaces like those that we use today became the norm. This local processing capability also enabled the creation of specialized workstations for applications like CAD (computer-aided design) and CAM (computer-aided manufacturing).

Why Client-Server Architecture Never Replaced the Mainframe

In the abstract, client-server architecture seemed like the best of both worlds—efficient for the end user but providing centralized control over data to ensure its security and integrity. However, applications based on client-server architecture have never fully displaced mainframe applications because many of the older database management systems were not available in the client-server environment, and companies had trouble justifying the time and money it would require to port their mainframe applications. (In fact, some large enterprise application vendors like SAP only released their client-server versions in the 1990s, well after the introduction of the personal computer and the desktop.) Because there was no easy way to simply change out the hardware and operating systems, most large companies have a combination of mainframe and client-server applications. As a result, these companies pay for not only the maintenance and upkeep of two types of hardware, but also two sets of system administrators with very different technical skills.

During this period, senior management began to become cynical about software technology despite the fact that computers were now critical to the way they did business. In the early days of client-server architecture, there was a lot of talk about "open standards" and "open systems." There were predictions that the mainframe would be replaced with scalable networks of workstations and servers, all of which could exchange data through a common query language (SQL) and common communication protocols. But it didn't happen, predominantly because the economic realities of the software vendors were diametrically opposed to those of the large corporation. Although most vendors will publicly advocate standards, only small vendors benefit from them when those standards facilitate migration and/or interoperability, unless those standards (e.g., web services) require organizations to make a significant investment in new hardware and/or software. Large, entrenched vendors—those that already "own" the customer—don't want to make it easy for customers to use other companies' products. They assign a considerable number of staff to standards committees that help produce the volumes of documents required, but as the standards they are working on become more detailed, the continual evolution of the standard means that the envisioned benefits almost always fall short. The one exception is for standards that support low-level interoperability between platforms where there is a very limited amount of semantics involved—for example, the representation of characters in files or communication protocols.

The Move Away from Internally Developed Applications

Although applications were available from software vendors as early as the 1960s, many companies chose to stay with the proprietary applications they had developed in house, in large part because of the difficulties involved with migration. During the age of the network, however, upper management decided to stop developing their applications in favor of buying modern commercial off-the-shelf (COTS) products from a vendor, in part due to concerns over the Year 2000 (after which computations on date fields that used two digits to represent year would no longer be correct) and the risk associated with trying to upgrade existing proprietary applications, which had backlogs of functionality requests to be added. This decision had two benefits, the first of which was that when a company was driven to migrate off an old system, they could have a fully functional application in less time. (Since an unlimited use license for a suite of enterprise resource planning applications can cost millions of dollars, it is not clear whether it was actually cheaper.) However, a second—and probably more important—benefit was that by buying a COTS application, the customer had access to a broader range of technical talent, because a larger number of programmers would be familiar with how the products worked than is the case when a small internal team built proprietary applications. During this period more and more large companies started to staff their IT organizations with contractors, individuals that they might pay at a higher rate than their internal staff but to whom they had limited financial obligation. This strategy enabled them to significantly reduce their IT budget in difficult financial times without incurring the termination costs for laying off employees. The downside of this strategy was that, as their computing environments became more heterogeneous and complex, companies had fewer people on staff who understood the technical aspects of how their applications had been configured to meet the company's particular business goals, thereby adding another layer of indirection to integration initiatives.

Topic of Interest: The Rise of COTS Applications

Originally, applications were restricted to a single domain (e.g., general ledger, manufacturing resource planning, human resource benefits, etc.). These standalone applications "knew" nothing about the other types of applications used by the company. Therefore, even though the communication

(continued)

technology was available to support near real-time updates, most updates required the creation of batch programs for extracting changed data from one application and feeding it to another. In the late 1980s and early 1990s, application vendors began to offer suites of applications for what was called *enterprise resource planning (ERP)* that were integrated so that, for example, an update to shipping would trigger the appropriate update to inventory and billing. The problem, of course, was that to benefit from the superior functionality of these integrated application suites, a company had to first migrate all its data from its existing applications to the ERP environment. Industry analysts claim that it can cost anywhere from 4 to 10 times the purchase price of an application to actually implement an ERP application, so many companies never fully completed the job and still have a combination of COTS and proprietary applications.

The Five Ws

In providing the answers to the five Ws, Table 2.3 illustrates how much more complex the IT environment became during the age of the network.

Table 2.3 The Age of the Network

| *Who* | IT Staff | • Scientists, computer technicians, application programmers
• ***Fewer application programmers as more companies began to buy "COTS" applications***
• Data modelers
• Database administrators
• *Network administrators* |
| | User | • Scientists, accountants, data entry clerks |

		• Diverse employees using reports generated by applications for specific business processes (e.g., marketing, manufacturing) • *Addition of more specialized professionals (e.g., engineers, designers)*
What	Applications	• Scientific computation; accounting/financial applications • A broader range of applications like materials resource planning (MRP) for manufacturing, human resources for payroll, benefits, etc. • Database management systems; later, end-user query products
	Types of Data	• Binary, numeric, character data • Use of binary data reduced; later systems support BLOBs (binary large objects) for graphics, etc. • *New standards emerged for handling scientific data (e.g., POSC for the petroleum industry, VHDL for large-scale chip design, EDI for retail, etc.)*
When		• Invoked manually, runs all the time, or scheduled • Triggered • *Event-driven*
Where		• Mainframe or special equipment on site with users • Mainframe and later mini-computers accessible by remote users • *Workstations* • *File servers* • *Sites connected via proprietary telecommunication lines*

(continued)

Table 2.3 The Age of the Network (continued)

Why	The vision	• Enable complex calculations and repetitive tasks to be completed more quickly and accurately than by hand • Improve programmer productivity and data integrity • ***Enable electronic "bridges" across what had previously been "islands" of computing as well as communication across disparate hardware and operating systems***
	Unintended outcome	• ***Replicated data and files***

2.6   The Age of the Desktop

As illustrated in Figure 2.4, this period brought computing to the individual user, resulting in an explosion of data and new problems with data integrity and data sharing.

The next disruptive technology that changed the landscape of software—the birth of the personal computer (PC)—took place outside the confines of the large organization. Many individuals use personal computers in conjunction with the Internet as one of their most basic tools in work or professional development, and therefore may consider themselves expert on the last two major eras of software. However, it is important to realize that even disruptive technology evolves in a stepwise fashion and that the age of the network was in its infancy in most large organizations when the first personal computers were introduced. As we have seen in examining the evolution of software at earlier periods, software is "sticky." Once established in production environments, software and the means of using it are hard to dislodge. As a result, we ask readers to suspend their knowledge of the capabilities that they currently take for granted to consider a time when the concept of the personal computer was first being introduced.

Topic of Interest: The Home Computer vs. the Personal Computer

In the late 1970s, several vendors began to develop relatively low-cost computers for home use—for example, the Commodore 64, the Apple IIe, and the TI 99 4/A. The software for these early systems was limited in capabilities and more suitable for programmers or would-be programmers than for the end user. It wasn't until the release of the Macintosh in 1984 that the first graphical interface and mouse were introduced at a cost that enabled adoption, and with that the PC revolution was launched. But it was IBM's marketing acumen that made Microsoft-based PCs surpass Apple's technical leadership to become market leader.

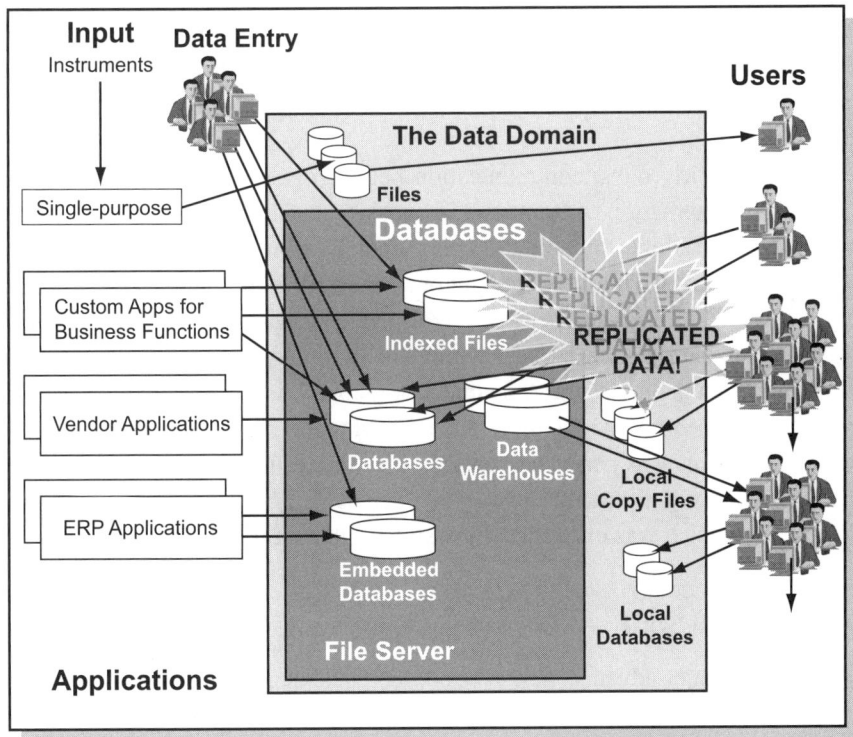

Figure 2.4   The Age of the Desktop

Several factors made the PC possible: the continued decreases in the cost of hardware, increased graphics capabilities, and the recognition of how individuals and small companies could benefit from similar gains in productivity afforded the professional worker by the workstation. In the early days of PCs in the workplace, floppy disks were used to exchange information between workers using PCs, but before long it was possible to connect PCs to the local and wide area networks in use in large organizations. The result was a huge increase in the number of files being shared across an organization—and a new risk of information leaks as large amounts of confidential information could be carried out of a secure environment on floppy disks.

In part because network technology was still in its infancy, even the most sophisticated software applications for the PC were largely designed for the single user by developers with little or no experience in the way large organizations used computers. The situation was exacerbated by the business model adopted by the early PC vendors who actively encouraged third parties to develop software by publishing and distributing their products. In fact, Microsoft historically has fueled much of its growth through third-party "partners" that develop applications and deliver solutions based on their platform. Many of these applications are intended for small and medium businesses, but some have found their way onto desktops in corporations. The result has been to create another type of data integrity problem for large organizations.

In the early days, communication between PCs and other computers in the office was a combination of floppies and sneaker net (that is, an operator moving the tape from one machine to another). Unfortunately, in many organizations PCs were installed on networks with little thought or support for using their applications as anything but personal productivity tools. As a result, data security issues reappeared as people began sharing files while keeping local copies; often it became difficult to know which document was the "document of record." As laptops enabled even greater flexibility for when and where individuals could work, more and more of the creative work in companies was performed on PCs with the result being that highly confidential information was frequently distributed across disparate applications on different PCs, much of which was only partially visible to the organization.

New Technical Staff

As with every major advance, new types of technical expertise were required to install and maintain PC software. Originally the level of difficulty was minimal and managed by other system administrators; however, maintaining PCs in corporate environments has become significantly more complex as the number of PCs and applications has proliferated. The situation is exacerbated by the fact that PC users are often nontechnical and require extra support—or worse, somewhat technical and actually create problems for the PC administrators when they attempt to do their own system administration. In the age of the Internet the situation has become even more complex as PC administrators must cope with such things as computer viruses and firewalls.

The Five Ws

In reviewing Table 2.4, see if you can list four general trends in the impact of introducing new software technology into large organizations.

Table 2.4   The Age of the Desktop

Who	IT Staff	<ul><li>Scientists, computer technicians, application programmers</li><li>Fewer application programmers as more companies began to buy "COTS" applications</li><li>Data modelers</li><li>Database administrators</li><li>Network administrators</li><li>***Application "experts"***</li><li>***PC administrators***</li></ul>
	User	<ul><li>Scientists, accountants, data entry clerks</li><li>Diverse employees using reports generated by applications for specific business processes (e.g., marketing, manufacturing)</li><li>Addition of more specialized professionals (e.g., engineers, designers)</li><li>***An even broader range of users, including small business owners, individual contractors, and publishers***</li></ul>

(continued)

Table 2.4 The Age of the Desktop (continued)

What	Applications	• Scientific computation; accounting/financial applications • A broader range of applications like materials resource planning (MRP) for manufacturing, human resources for payroll, benefits, etc. • Database management systems; later, end-user query products • ***PC applications such as spreadsheets, PowerPoint, desktop publishing, etc.***
	Types of Data	• Binary, numeric, character data • Use of binary data reduced; later systems support BLOBs (binary large objects) for graphics, etc. • New standards emerged for handling scientific data (e.g., POSC for the petroleum industry, VHDL for large-scale chip design, EDI for retail, etc.) • ***Large increase in conventions for representing graphics***
When		• Invoked manually, runs all the time, or scheduled • Triggered • Event-driven
Where		• Mainframe or special equipment on site with users • Mainframes and later mini-computers accessible by remote users • Workstations • File servers • Sites connected via proprietary telecommunication lines • ***PCs***

Why	The vision	• Enable complex calculations and repetitive tasks to be completed more quickly and accurately than by hand
		• Improve programmer productivity and data integrity

2.7 The Age of the Internet

As illustrated in Figure 2.5, this period has been characterized by the ability of individuals and applications to communicate in near real-time regardless of geographic location.

Most of the readers of this book were raised in the Age of the Internet (not to mention the age of wireless technology), so there is no need to discuss the benefits or

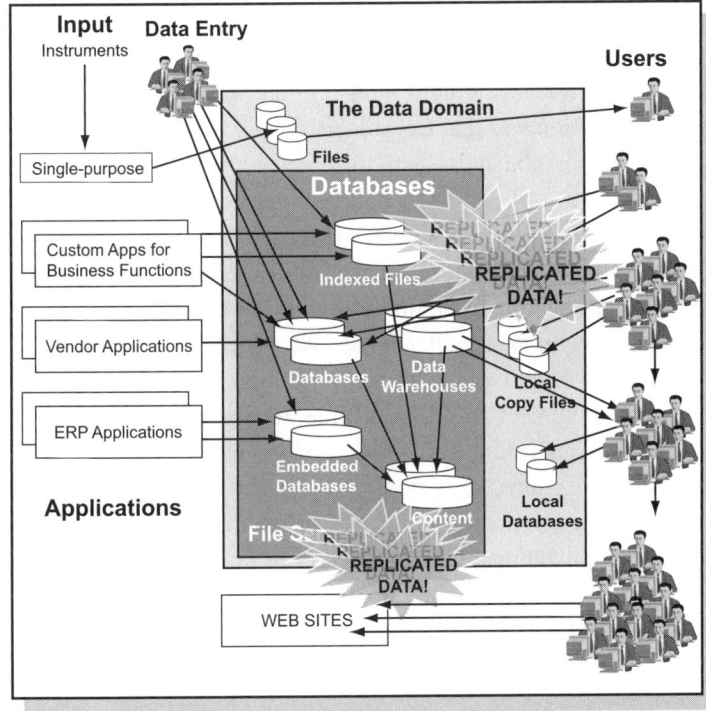

Figure 2.5　The Age of the Internet

risks of having access to the Internet as an individual. The way we communicate with friends and family, collaborate with co-workers, make vacation plans, conduct research, buy and sell products—all of these have been affected by the ubiquity and convenience provided by the Internet. However, few people understand the additional cost that this disruptive technology brought to large corporations, whether they were early adopters or technologically more conservative.

The Fate of Many Early Adopters

During the 1990s, many gurus held forth on how the Internet would transform the way business was performed. The ability to enable B2C (business-to-consumers) communication would allow online retailers to compete effectively with much larger vendors because they wouldn't have to incur the cost of stores and distribution centers. B2B (business-to-business) initiatives would enable manufacturers to conduct real-time negotiations with suppliers so they could minimize the inventory they had to keep in stock, thereby improving their bottom line. Companies like garden.com went public to raise growth capital based on their rapid growth and only the promise of profits. In the year 2000 Jacques Nasser, the CEO of Ford, embraced the vision so thoroughly that Ford founded an ebusiness subsidiary called ConsumerConnect that he claimed would "reinvent the auto industry" and provide Ford with $9 billion in annual savings. The vision was that ConsumerConnect would manage Ford's e-supplier relationships, consumer ebusiness activities, telematics, and customer relationship centers. Two years later—after Nasser had been replaced—Ford closed the company and wrote off almost $200 million in losses (Morgan & Geralds, 2002).

A good part of what made ebusiness difficult was the fact that it was data-driven. Real-time interaction is of little value if a vendor cannot provide accurate information about inventory. Frequently the data needed to respond accurately was spread across different applications based on multiple technologies in different locations—often across countries in different time zones. Second, many of the applications containing the necessary information were not written to communicate in real-time but used programs to periodically extract the pertinent information into files. Finally, the ebusiness paradigm often required the integration of data from multiple independent organizations, making the task of integration even harder.

The Effect on More Conservative Organizations

Early adopters were not the only organizations to experience the downside of electronic business. Even technologically conservative companies were adversely affected by the initial costs of having to support a web presence. Yet they had little choice because once one company in an industry offered an Internet presence, every company in the industry felt the pressure to do so. Although many companies are now benefiting from the ability to interface to their customers via their website—for instance, by saving postage by providing online statements and online payment processing—there are additional overhead and integration demands on production systems.

Changing the Model for Delivering Software

Just as the age of the network and the age of the desktop transformed the landscape of corporate IT, the Internet has transformed the world. The past five years have produced enormous advances in web services that are transforming the software industry. Thanks to standards like SOAP (Simple Object Access Protocol) and WSDL (Web Services Description Language), software companies can provide access to their products via the Internet so that customers no longer have to purchase, install, and maintain applications but can simply use them. (The industry term for this type of business model is *software as a service.*) In fact, many software gurus are predicting that service-oriented architecture (SOA) may provide the means of solving the decades-old integration problem and enable companies to treat their legacy applications as assets and not liabilities.

SOA is based on a directory of services that programmers can consult for software components much like one would look up a type of business in the Yellow Pages. The vision is that programmers will put "wrappers" around the entry points to legacy applications (that is, the transactions they support like "add customer" or "ship product") that would translate between the native application and a representation suitable for communicating with an external application. The Internet provides the near real-time communication across platforms, and the result is that heterogeneous applications that serve the business needs of the enterprise can be developed in a fraction of the time otherwise required. It is an elegant architecture but, as we will see in the following chapters, it is far from easy to implement unless supported by both the appropriate methodology and development tools.

The Five Ws

Table 2.5 provides the answers to the five Ws for the age of the Internet. In the next section, we will draw on the information from the five tables to formulate some trends and tradeoffs that we will use as a starting point to develop a methodology for evaluating integration architectures throughout the rest of the book.

Table 2.5 The Age of the Internet

Who	IT Staff	<ul><li>Scientists, computer technicians, application programmers</li><li>Fewer application programmers as more companies began to buy "COTS" applications</li><li>Data modelers</li><li>Database administrators</li><li>Network administrators</li><li>Application "experts"</li><li>PC administrators</li><li>*XML, JAVA, and/or .NET programmers*</li></ul>
	User	<ul><li>Scientists, accountants, data entry clerks</li><li>Diverse employees using reports generated by applications for specific business processes (e.g., marketing, manufacturing)</li><li>Addition of more specialized professionals (e.g., engineers, designers)</li><li>An even broader range of users, including small business owners, individual contractors, and publishers</li><li>*Users outside the organization in addition to internal users*</li></ul>
What	Applications	<ul><li>Scientific computation; accounting/financial applications</li><li>A broader range of applications like materials resource planning (MRP) for manufacturing, human resources for payroll, benefits, etc.</li><li>Database management systems; later, end-user query products</li></ul>

What		• PC applications such as spreadsheets, PowerPoint, desktop publishing, etc. • *Portals*
	Types of Data	• Binary, numeric, character data • Use of binary data reduced; later systems support BLOBs (binary large objects) for graphics, etc. • New standards emerged for handling scientific data (e.g., POSC for the petroleum industry, VHDL for large-scale chip design, EDI for retail, etc.) • Large increase in conventions for representing graphics • *Addition of video and audio*
When		• Invoked manually, runs all the time, or scheduled • Triggered • Event-driven
Where		• Mainframe or special equipment on site with users • Mainframes and later mini-computers accessible by remote users • Workstations • File servers • Sites connected via proprietary telecommunication lines • PCs • *Global communication via the Internet*
Why		• Improve programmer productivity and data integrity
		(continued)

Table 2.5 The Age of the Internet (continued)

		• Enable electronic "bridges" across what had previously been "islands" of computing as well as communication across disparate hardware and operating systems • Provide benefits of computer use to broader range of individuals, companies • *Increase the speed at which computers can do business*
	Unintended outcome	• *Greater proliferation of data, increased security risks from malware, identity theft, etc.*

2.8 Trends

Software applications have evolved from performing specific tasks that are repetitive and/or error-prone for humans to providing environments that help us improve upon our native abilities to perform complex analysis and design, either individually or in groups. The increased capabilities have been made possible by creating tools that allow both programmers and users to operate at higher and higher levels of abstraction with little or no attention to details of hardware or operating systems. Although programmers initially had to worry about disk sectors and word size, Java allows them to program in a language that will compile to run on any number of hardware platforms under multiple operating systems. Similarly, end users are provided with such powerful graphical interfaces that many never open a manual.

The general principle driving the evolution of software technology could be summarized as favoring the development of products that provide *greater productivity for more users with less training,* where:

- *Greater productivity* applies to:

    - The range of tasks that can be performed, ranging from computation to collaboration

- The speed at which these tasks can be performed, ranging from hours and days to near real-time
- The number of users that can be supported at any one time, ranging from single-user systems to systems that can support hundreds of thousands of users concurrently
- Access independent of geography and time zone

- *More users* applies to:

  - Technical staff responsible for developing and maintaining applications
  - Business users, both within the enterprise and across organizational boundaries
  - Specialized users like designers and/or architects who use computer applications to perform complex specialized tasks, either individually or in groups
  - Customers, citizens, or partners who interface to an organization via Internet-based applications

- *Less training* applies to the skills required for:

  - Application programmers and system administrators
  - Various classes of end users

- *Less programming* applies to:

  - Maximizing reuse
  - Providing GUI-based development and test environments

2.9 Tradeoffs

Nothing is free. There are always tradeoffs. Advances in meeting these goals is not linear, but offset by at least two tradeoffs, namely:

- *Greater productivity for the many requires highly specialized skills of a few.* Much like healthcare, these specialists can be significantly more effective than a general practitioner, but what it means for the company is much like what it means for the individual. Instead of having one regular physician, today a person may have three or four physicians (e.g., an internist, a gynecologist, a dermatologist, and an allergist). Although this specialization provides the patient with individuals who can give expert advice in their domain, it becomes the responsibility of the individual to manage communication among these specialists or to understand how one treatment can impact another in order to ensure overall health. When companies are forced to balance the input from consultants, internal IT employees, contractors, and offshore developers, the ultimate health of the company's IT strategy depends on the skills and commitment of its management.

- *Because software is "sticky," when introduced into an established computing environment, the benefits of increased productivity are offset by:*

  - *Increased complexity*—This problem is probably the most obvious from the tables earlier in the chapter. One of the goals of this book is to explore the scope and nature of the types of complexity that currently limit the value of information technology.

  - *Increased costs*—Whenever new software applications or technology is introduced into a large IT organization, the company will experience either a short-term or long-term increase in overhead above and beyond the cost of the new software, depending upon whether the organization decides to migrate the old applications to the new environment (short-term) or whether the new technology will co-exist with the existing technology (long-term).

  - *Problems in correlating replicated data*—Even when some new technology is dealing with a totally different domain (for example, geographical information systems), any new source of data requires additional integration if information from that data source is going to be used in conjunction with data from other sources. As we will see in subsequent chapters, it is rare for both the format and semantics of data to be identical across independently developed application environments.

  - *Problems in understanding the impact of change*—As our discussion of the telecommunications industry in the last chapter indicated, as external business conditions and regulations change, companies must adapt their IT applications. Unless an organization has put in place some automated means of determining the impact of change, the larger the number of systems involved, the greater will be the effort to implement a change.

  - *Increased risk*—The greater the number of disparate data sources, the greater will be the opportunity for fraud and/or malfeasance.

Exercises for Chapter 2

1. Name five problems that would have affected people in their daily lives (as opposed to computer workers) that might have occurred at 12:01 am on January 1, 2000.

2. What is the problem for companies when they require a number of specialized skills to maintain their IT environment?

3. The *Trade-offs* section in this chapter described the types of problems that have offset the benefits of the deployment of new technology. Use this information to formulate a set of guidelines or principles that an organization should use in evaluating alternative technology solutions.

4. One of the major motivations for the creation of database technology was the elimination of replicated data. Why has that not happened? And what technical innovations have made the situation significantly worse? What are the risks associated with replicated data?

CHAPTER

3

The Evolution of Database Technology

Data is our history, an electronic record of information about a series of events that is sufficiently important to some ongoing activity that we want to maintain it for some period of time. Our ability to build effective software depends on our ability to acquire and maintain accurate data and store it in such a way that it can be easily accessed and correlated with other data. In this chapter, we will consider the evolution of database technology from two perspectives. First, we will examine the major capabilities of a database management system to develop a model that we can use when analyzing other software subsystems. Second, we will consider how database systems evolved over time. Our focus will be external to the systems themselves in that we will not discuss the details of specific algorithms and internal data structures, because that is the material covered in a database course. Nor will we discuss details about how to design databases for the different kinds of systems or how to program against them. Instead, we will approach each type of system by focusing initially on the basic concepts for defining how data will be stored in the system, as well as how those concepts (called the meta-model) correspond to the way the data is actually represented in memory and on disk. In the process, we will consider the strengths and weaknesses of each type of system from the perspective of the challenges that it poses with respect to data integration projects, and how these challenges motivated the next generation of innovation.

It is important for you to have at least a high-level understanding of how legacy systems work because many of them are still in use. By the end of this chapter, you should understand the four major meta-models that have been used in various commercial database management systems and the strengths and weaknesses of these systems with respect to:

- The types of technical staff required
- Their ease of use
- The level of data integrity provided
- How easy they are to maintain

3.1 COBOL Files

The earliest types of databases were simply files of structured data. In 1959 the Conference on Data Systems Languages (CODASYL), a consortium of individuals from industry and government, was established to guide the design and development of a standard programming language. The efforts of this group culminated in the development of COBOL, which is still being used half a century later. In fact, it is estimated that up to 70% of the data in production applications in large organizations is still stored in COBOL-based systems. As discussed in Chapter 2, programmers working in assembler initially had to code directly against the hardware they were using, breaking down every logical step into a sequence of assembler statements where each statement corresponded with an action that took place in the machine. When reading data from or writing data to disk, they had to worry about disk tracks and sectors. As a result, third-generation languages like COBOL and FORTRAN afforded great improvements in productivity because once a programmer defined the physical layout of a record in a COBOL COPYBOOK, he or she could ignore all details of storage and use logical field names to obtain offsets in any record.

However, there were initially two major limitations with COBOL:

1. Every record in a COBOL file had to be the same size (unless additional information was added to the record; see the Topic of Interest on variable length records later in this chapter).

2. COBOL is not strongly typed; that is, the COBOL compiler did no error checking to ensure that the data being stored in a particular location in a record was the type of data declared in the COPYBOOK.

The Problem with Fixed Length Records

The ability to represent differences in cardinality—one-to-many and many-to-many—is critical in representing information about the world. People have more than one child; products contain more than one part. COBOL supported representing one-to-many relationships within a record through an OCCURS clause in the COPYBOOK that allowed the programmer to indicate that there would be some number of instances of a field repeated. For example, the OCCURS clause in the following example defines a "repeating group" of six fields with the name DEP-NAME, each of which contains 40 characters:

```
1 EMPLOYEE-RECORD.
    05 NAME            PIC X(40).
    05 CITY            PIC X(15).
    05 COUNTRY         PIC X(5).
    05 DEPENDENTS   OCCURS 6.
        10 DEP-NAME    PIC X(40).
```

Because each record needed to be the same size, the programmer defining the file had to specify the maximum number of instances that could be found in a single record. If the programmer defining the design chose an upper limit that was higher than the majority of records would contain (for example, 10 dependents), then given that most families have fewer than four children, there would be a lot of wasted disk space. With a lower figure, the question became what to do about the employees who had more than the upper limit, as with the Brady Bunch in Table 3.1. (Often some flag was set so that the overflow information was stored in a subsequent record.)

Table 3.1

Fred Flintstone	Bedrock	USA	Wilma	Pebbles				
Mike Brady	Los Angeles	USA	Carol	Marcia	Cindy	Jan	Greg	Peter...
Gomez Addams	Greenbriar	USA	Morticia	Wednesday	Pugsley			

However, the real problem with fixed length records came when there was a need to add new information to a record. Here there were two choices—the programmer had to either create a new file definition and copy the data from the old file into the new file or make use of the REDEFINES statement. A REDEFINES statement allowed someone to revise a COPYBOOK definition to indicate that some sequence of bytes in the record could be interpreted in a different way, as in the example shown here:

```
01 EMPLOYEE-RECORD.
    05 NAME              PIC X(40).
    05 CITY              PIC X(15).
    05 COUNTRY           PIC X(5).
    05 EMPLOYEE-TYPE     PIC X.
        05 HOURLY.
            10 HOURLY-RATE-STD    PIC 9(3)V99.
            10 HOURLY-RATE-OVER   PIC 9(3)V99.
        05 SALARIED REDEFINES HOURLY.
            10 MONTHLY SALARY     PIC 9(5)V99.
            10 HOURS              PIC 99.
```

This COPYBOOK identifies each employee by type—salaried or hourly. Depending on the value stored in the EMPLOYEE-TYPE field, the programmer would look at the values under HOURLY or the values under SALARIED for payroll information. Note that REDEFINES statements are possible only because COBOL is not strongly typed. The names used for field definitions in a COPYBOOK are used by the compiler to determine offsets and lengths when reading/writing a record and nothing else.

> **Topic of Interest: Variable Length Records**
>
> Sometimes developers wanted to store more than one record type in the same COBOL file, where the record types had a different length. In this case, they created a COPYBOOK definition for a "header" record that would include an identifier that indicated which type of record would be following. In this way the programmer could include conditional logic that would use the appropriate name of the record type for the READ statement.

ISAM and VSAM

Originally COBOL files had to be read sequentially to find a particular record, which resulted in performance problems as the files got larger. Two subsequent enhancements to the COBOL environment addressed this problem. *ISAM,* or Indexed Sequential Access Method, enabled a set of indices to be kept on key fields to enable direct access to particular records if the programmer provided the key as a parameter in asking for the record. *VSAM,* or Virtual Sequential Access Method, was a later, more sophisticated indexing method that supported both primary and secondary keys. These additions not only enabled more effective access to records for application programs, but also enabled transaction-level applications, where a user could use a terminal and transaction monitor to update a record in place without "locking" the entire file.

> **Topic of Interest: Performance on the Mainframe**
>
> Many applications that use COBOL files for data storage run in batch mode, where a large number of records are accessed or updated in the process of executing the program. Because batch jobs are usually compute-intensive, they can keep other applications from accessing the file for a long period of time. As a result, they are often scheduled to run at off hours—in the middle of the night or on the weekend. To illustrate how compute-intensive these applications can be, consider the case of a parts manufacturer in Texas that had a mainframe application it ran against a set of COBOL files every weekend to determine what parts the factory should manufacture the following week. At one point, they had to hire a consultant to rewrite the application because the input files had become so large that the application wasn't finishing until Monday afternoon, forcing them to lose half a day's production.

The Drawback to REDEFINES

Although REDEFINES were a convenient solution for avoiding the need to rebuild a file when additional information had to be added to a record, over time it became difficult to understand how the REDEFINES correlated with the data in the file and the applications using the file. Programmers often documented what data they were adding to the file and why they were adding it, but they often did not document which application used which version of the record or how existing applications might have been modified to account for the change. For example, in some cases an application would be modified to contain a statement like "If the date field is before October 1999, interpret the next 200 bytes this way; otherwise, interpret them that way." If COPYBOOKs were small and the applications simple, it would be easy enough to determine this information by analyzing the COPYBOOK in conjunction with the application code. But it is not uncommon for COPYBOOKs to be thousands of lines long and for the applications that access them to contain hundreds of thousands of lines of code.

Challenges in Migrating from COBOL Files

There are software products from companies like TSRI or SEEC that analyze and refactor (that is, restructure in some principled way) COBOL applications in conjunction with COPYBOOKs to produce a description of how a series of applications interact, usually as a step in migrating them to newer technology. These products were extremely popular during the years preceding the Year 2000 because they could help programmers quickly identify locations in programs that would need to be modified because they used two digits to represent the year in date fields. They are also extremely helpful when a company is trying to port an application to a newer technology base.

However, many companies are hesitant to replace their legacy COBOL applications because they are "mission-critical." It is hard for individuals who use computer applications in a client-server network to appreciate what this means. Short of a disk crash or virus, the worst thing we experience is when the network has a problem or we lose access to the Internet. Even then we are typically able to continue working in some capacity because our applications are based locally, and we have local storage. However, when a mission-critical system fails in a large organization, some aspect of the business simply stops until that application is operational again. Customers can't withdraw money from their account or use their credit card or make an airline reservation. These events are so catastrophic to the organization that the people who support mission-critical systems have someone available 24 hours a day to intervene when there's a problem, and this individual is frequently given only a 1- to 2-hour window in which to get the system up and running again.

As a result, the prospect of eliminating these applications is daunting for a number of reasons, the most important of which is that in order to do so, an organization will need to spend more money in the short term, because it must not only purchase and configure the new application, but also typically engage people who have expertise in the new application at the same time that they are paying people to maintain the current application. The individuals chartered with implementing the new application may have some knowledge of the industry or application, but they are unlikely to understand either the legacy application or company-specific business rules embedded within the legacy application. For this information, they must interview business users and the technical staff responsible for maintaining the legacy application. The technical staff maintaining the legacy application are often also ambivalent, if not hostile, to the idea of a new application because they will either be responsible for maintaining it when they are uncertain of what it will take to keep the application stable or, more likely, be let go in favor of some of the individuals implementing the new application. Note that all these problems are in addition to discovering and correcting the inconsistencies in data in the legacy COBOL files. Given all these factors, it is not surprising that management often decides that it is more cost-effective—and less risky—to make do with what's in place.

Topic of Interest: The Future of COBOL

In April 2004, Microsoft, EDS, and MicroFocus (a leading provider of COBOL development tools) announced the formation of the Mainframe Migration Alliance to provide customers with support in migrating their applications from the mainframe to the lower-cost Microsoft Windows platform. Within 2 years, the alliance had over 50 software vendors and consulting companies as members. Many customers in that timeframe chose to simply "lift and shift" their COBOL applications to the Windows platform; that is, rather than modifying the application to use a more modern database management system, they effectively kept the same files in place. As a result, it is reasonable to assume that COBOL files will remain part of the IT landscape for the foreseeable future.

3.2   The Origins of Database Technology

As the U.S. government sought to expand the use of computers for complex tasks like the design of vehicles for space exploration and the military, there was a need to better coordinate the use of multiple files by multiple people and—in the process—to address some of the limitations of the COBOL file system. In 1967 CODASYL evolved into the DBTG (the Database Task Group) to develop a model for processing data. In the meantime, IBM, working in conjunction with Rockwell and Caterpillar, designed a hierarchical database management system for the Apollo space program that IBM subsequently commercialized under the name IMS (Information Management System). A number of other vendors developed competing products, but none have the installed base of IMS, which is still in active use in many large organizations and has been enhanced to support Java, JDBC, and XML—language protocols that serve as the underpinnings for web services.

However, before we discuss the concepts underlying hierarchical database management systems, let's consider the requirements that motivated aspects of their design. If a software subsystem was to provide support for multiple programmers to successfully share a set of files for the purpose of their work, the system at the minimum had to provide the following capabilities:

- *Locking*—Some mechanism that enforced how records or files are shared so that two programmers didn't try to update the same data element(s) at the same time.
- *Data integrity*—A mechanism to protect programmers from errors made by each other or themselves. If a field in a record was supposed to contain a decimal number, then it shouldn't be possible for a programmer to store a string in that field.
- *Security*—A means for restricting access because not all programmers or users should have access to everything stored in a database.
- *Recovery*—A means for ensuring that data integrity was maintained even if a system crashed. (Otherwise it would be safer to use paper.)

These four capabilities are at the heart of any database management system, although, as we will see in the following discussion, how they have been implemented depends upon many other factors, including the meta-model that is used as the organizing principle of how data is defined, stored, and accessed.

3.3 The Components of a DBMS

Database management systems were the earliest instance of system software productivity tools. The earliest database management systems consisted of two major components, each of which was driven by a different type of command language:

- The *data definition language (DDL)* provided the programmer with a means of defining the schema or database layout. The exact terminology and syntax of the language was typically proprietary to the database management system.
- The *data manipulation language (DML)* defined the commands that the programmer used to retrieve and store data in the database.

As illustrated Figure 3.1, the DDL was used at the time that a database was being designed. The output of the DBMS component used in design was a set of internal data structures used by a *runtime* component (in Figure 3.1, the DBMS Data Manager/Compiler) that compiled the program containing the DML calls. This basic architecture is the same that is used by all productivity software subsystems today, regardless of whether they are helping a system administrator maintain networks, a programmer create a graphical interface, or a financial planner design a spreadsheet.

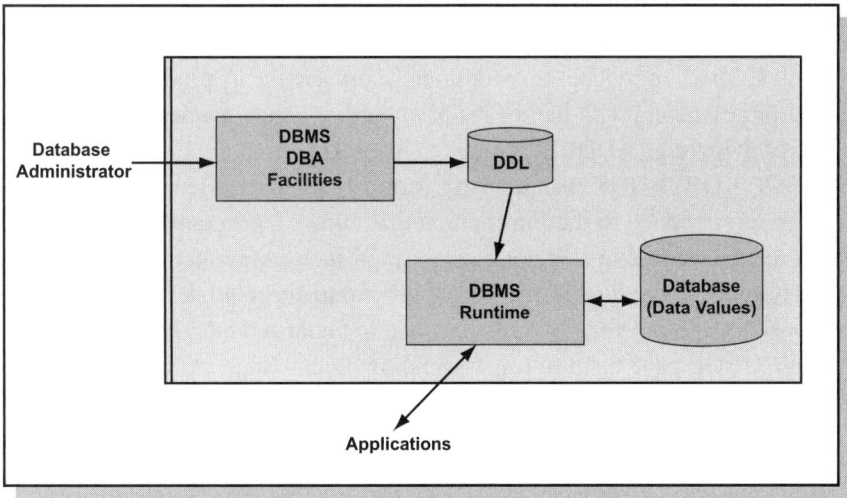

Figure 3.1   Components of a DBMS

The capabilities of a software subsystem are determined by what its design language is capable of expressing. The richer the concepts and set of relationships it supports, the more powerful the runtime component will be. The collection of information that is used to drive the behavior of the runtime component is called *metadata*. As a software designer, your ability to design flexible and powerful software systems will depend upon your ability to analyze and understand the concepts of meta-model, data model, and metadata.

3.4   Metadata: A Common Vocabulary for Man and Machine

The success of any effort to communicate is based on the individuals participating in the communication having a common set of concepts and terminology for discussing those concepts. Communication between humans benefits from the fact that we share similar physical experiences that enable us to communicate without words (e.g., you can point to an object, frown, raise an eyebrow). In contrast, the language that enables humans to communicate with computers must be sufficiently rich to enable the representation of real-world objects and events, but simple and explicit enough to allow a human to specify an unambiguous representation of the desired instructions in a reasonable amount of time.

Internally every data value stored in a computer is represented as a sequence of 1s and 0s. For software to enable programmers to work at a logical level, it must offer some set of conventions for representing objects and actions. As we discussed in Chapter 2, COBOL provided an enormous improvement in productivity simply by providing programmers with the means of assigning logical names and structure to a sequence of bytes (e.g., ADDRESS refers to bytes 31–120 in the EMPLOYEE record). The COBOL COPYBOOK was an early form of metadata. Metadata, or data about data, is the term applied to the information that allows a programmer to describe the nature of the data stored in a file or a database in such a way that a particular type of software system can interpret it. But before programmers could define what a COBOL record looked like in a COPYBOOK, they had to understand the objects and relationships that COBOL gave them to use as building blocks (much as a molecule is made up of atoms).

In representing data to a computer, the term *meta-model* is defined as a model of a model, and refers to the basic types of objects and relationships used to organize the data to be represented in some database. In the relational meta-model, the core concepts include table (or relation), row (or tuple), attribute (or column or field), and join (relationship between tables). A *data model* is the definition of a set of instances of the objects allowed by the meta-model that defines the types of objects and relationships that characterize the contents of a database. For example, a customer data model might contain:

- A table for CUSTOMERS, with columns CUSTOMER-NUMBER and NAME
- A table for ADDRESSES, with columns CUSTOMER-NUMBER, STREET ADDRESS, CITY, STATE, ZIP, and TYPE (Is this a shipping address or a billing address?)
- A relationship between CUSTOMER-NUMBER in CUSTOMERS and CUSTOMER-NUMBER in ADDRESSES

Data models can be quite complex; in fact, some consulting companies actually sell data models for different industries like banking or healthcare to provide customers with a "shortcut" in creating a design for their business intelligence and reporting applications. A *schema* or database design is a description of the data model (or a portion of the data model) in the language used by a DBMS product that tells that product how the information should be physically organized. For example, physically the CITY and STATE might be stored in a separate standard table of zip codes, and only the ZIP stored in the ADDRESS table, both to save space in the database and to make sure the data is consistent.

Figure 3.2 uses the design and construction of a house as an analogy for understanding the difference between the terms. The meta-model provides the database designer with the raw materials to use in constructing the house. Just as different building materials have different properties that can affect the design (e.g., poured concrete differs from brick), the types of objects and relationships between objects supported by a meta-model can affect the types of databases that can be designed. The data model is analogous to the architect's drawing. Although there will be some dimensions on the architect's drawing, a lot of the detailed dimensions and design are left to the contractor. The schema includes all the detailed knowledge required to actually construct the house.

In some ways, what belongs in a meta-model versus a data model seems to be pretty arbitrary. For example, couldn't *table* be an instance of something called "contiguous sequences of bytes representing related information" that occurs in a data model? This is in fact an important point. Often something that starts as a concept requiring a definition later becomes a primitive in a language. Just as humans require less and less explanation of what terms mean when they have come to understand some body of knowledge like astrophysics or scuba diving, over time what was originally a

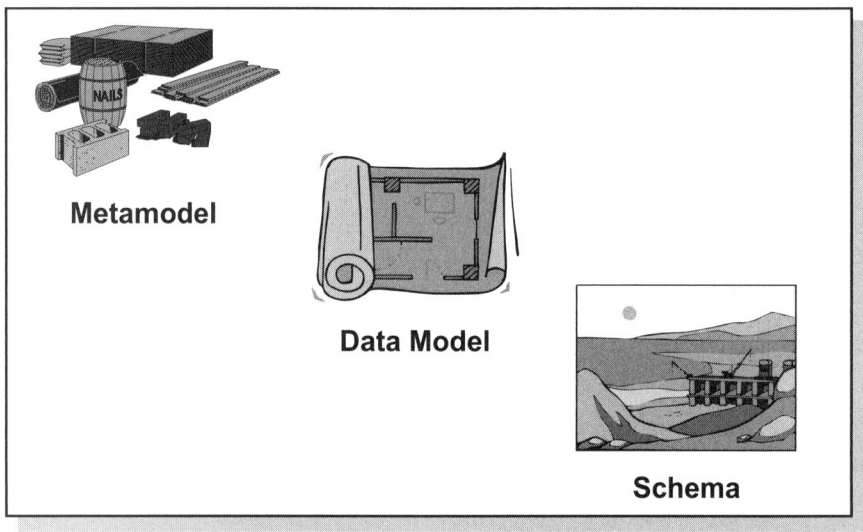

Metamodel

Data Model

Schema

Figure 3.2 Levels of Metadata

construct in software environments (e.g., *date*) has become a primitive data type—something that all modern database management systems understand.

3.5 Hierarchical Database Management Systems

As illustrated in Figure 3.3, in the hierarchical meta-model, a record type can have at most one "parent." The record that serves as the root of the database has no parent and serves as the point of entry for the database. It is not surprising that the earliest DBMS products used a hierarchical meta-model because COBOL records were inherently hierarchical, in the sense that a single record instance could contain multiple levels of repeating groups (that is, where one instance of a repeating group can contain one or more repeating groups). The major advance afforded by the hierarchical DBMS was that it allowed the database designer to represent one-to-many relationships between SEGMENTs, where each SEGMENT was equivalent to a COBOL record. Because the parent-child segments were stored as separate records, there was no need to specify a maximum number of children as would be required if repeating groups were used in a fixed length record.

The earliest database management systems were *navigational* in that they required that the program "walk" the database design to get to the desired information.

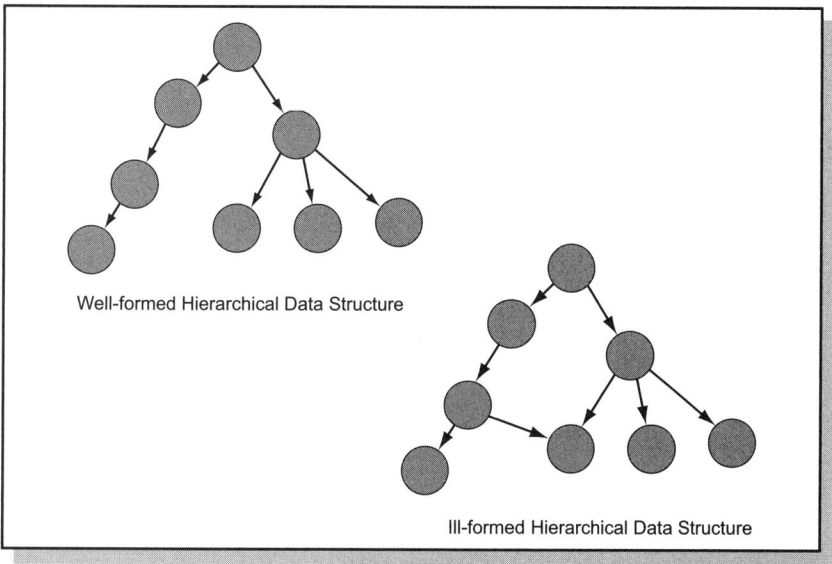

Figure 3.3 Hierarchy: No Record Can Have More Than One Parent

Unless the database designer had declared some type of value in a SEGMENT definition to be a key, the DBMS didn't keep indices that would allow direct access to a particular record instance (analogous to the ISAM and VSAM capabilities in COBOL). In that case, a program would need to contain logic analogous to the following in order to print a report about a course with the number 220 in the German department:

```
MOVE 0 TO END-DEPT.
    PERFORM 3000-PROCESS-DEPARTMENT
        UNTIL END-DEPT > 0.
    ...

3000-PROCESS-DEPARTMENT.
    READ DEPARTMENT-RECORD.
    IF NOT DEPT-END-OF-FILE
        MOVE 1 TO END-DEPT
    ELSE
        IF DEPT-NAME = "GERMAN"
```

```
                              MOVE 0 TO END-COURSE
                              PERFORM 3010-PROCESS-COURSE
               END-IF
          END-IF.

     3010-PROCESS-COURSE.
          READ COURSE-RECORD.
          IF NOT COURSE-END-OF-FILE
               MOVE 1 TO END-COURSE
          ELSE
               IF COURSE-NUMBER = "GERMAN"
                         PERFORM 3020-PROCESS-GERMAN-220
               END-IF
          END-IF.
```

IMS as an Example of a Hierarchical DBMS

IMS's DDL was called DL/1, an abbreviation for Data Language 1. As illustrated in Figure 3.4, a physical IMS record was analogous to a COBOL record, but whereas every COBOL record occupied a contiguous sequence of words in memory/disk, an IMS record could be stored in SEGMENTS of contiguous memory/disk with pointers used to correlate a particular instance of a segment to other segments. In this way, database designers didn't have to commit to either an upper or a lower bound for one-to-many relationships, as they did with COBOL.

Recall that IMS was the result of packaging a set of software capabilities that had been developed over time rather than a system that had been designed "from scratch." As a result, there were a number of options for how the pointers correlating segments could be created and maintained. DL/1 therefore was complex because the database designer had to specify which of the four underlying technologies would be used: HSAM (Hierarchical Sequential Access Method, which was essentially the same as COBOL files), HISAM (Hierarchical Indexed Sequential Access Method, which was analogous to indexed COBOL files), HDAM (Hierarchical Direct Access Method, which used pointers and a hashing scheme), or HIDAM (Hierarchical Indexed Direct Access Method, which used indices to provide direct access to root segments, and pointers to all segments under a root segment). The choice of the underlying technology could have significant consequences on the amount of storage required. For example, as illustrated in Figure 3.4, the choice of HDAM or HIDAM eliminated the need to allocate space that would not be used. DL/1 also had an option

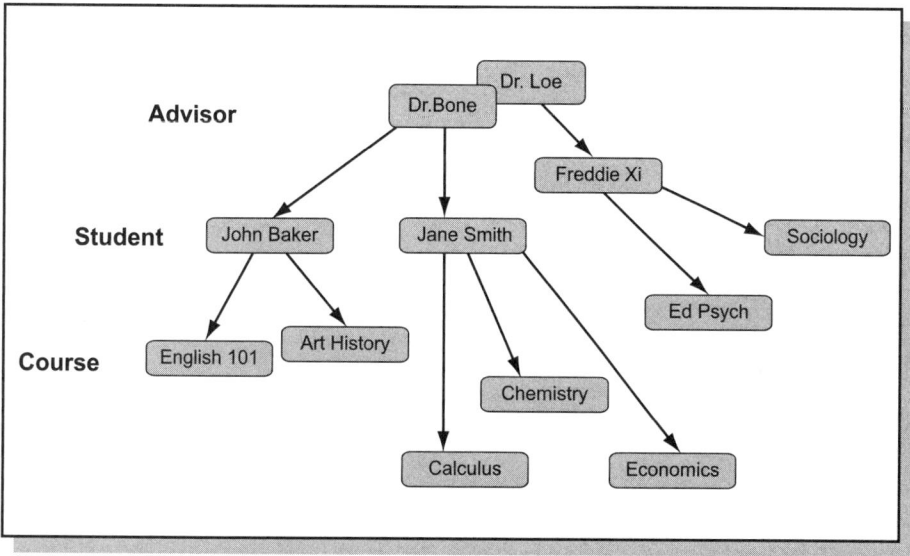

Figure 3.4   HDAM/HIDAM Database

that allowed a database designer to define logical record types in terms of their reference to physical records or subsets of physical records.

Programming Against an IMS Database

If a database designer chose HDAM or HIDAM, there was minimum wasted space in an IMS database because the system would only allocate as much space as needed to store the data. However, IMS application programmers needed not only to know the segment hierarchy to understand how to walk the database, but also to know which DML (data manipulation language) calls to insert in the program because the different storage protocols supported different commands.

But there was even one more complication in programming against IMS. The programmer needed to understand how the program would be executed with respect to other programs that might be running against the same database. Batch programs were invoked by Job Control Language (JCL—the mainframe equivalent of shell or batch scripts), and essentially locked out all other programs from operating against the database until they had completed executing (which is why they were usually scheduled to run late at night or early in the morning). Transaction-driven applications (e.g., ones that supported relatively short-term limited updates) used a "message" protocol, and so on. Some DML commands could only be used in one context rather than another; for example, the SYNC command could only be used in programs that didn't use a "message-driven" protocol. In short, IMS may have eliminated much of the data access code that programmers would have otherwise had to write and provided improved support for representing one-to-many relationships, but it certainly required them to understand what IMS was doing in order to make the appropriate DML calls.

Topic of Interest: The Proliferation of Terminology

If you are getting a headache about this time, it is to be expected. As technology evolves, there is a proliferation of terminology and acronyms. For people who are well-acquainted with a particular domain, it is relatively easy to understand how some new term introduced into the discipline makes an important distinction. For example, if you understand that when it is applied to data access, the term *sequential* means that you have to read the data in the order that it was stored on the disk, then when you're told that the term *direct* means this restriction is lifted, it is an easy concept to grasp. Rather than trying to memorize the specific terms used by a particular system, try to visualize what a program component must do to provide the desired functionality—and what information it needs to maintain to perform that work—because it is this conceptual framework that will help you recognize when two problems are similar in spite of differences in terminology.

How IMS Is Often Utilized

In part because IMS provided a knowledgeable programmer with a variety of features for controlling how the program in question was actually implemented against the hardware, some of the largest and most efficient production databases in the world are still based on IMS. However, as is often the case, many IT organizations did not take advantage of these features because with strong typing (e.g., where the database validates the format of a field as a decimal) there was still no way for them to avoid having to rebuild the database when information needed to be added to a segment. In fact, in many IT shops, the database designers used the IMS DDL only to define the segment hierarchy, defined the storage method as HSAM or HISAM, and used COBOL COPYBOOKs to define the layout of each segment. As a result, these databases suffer from the same use of REDEFINES as COBOL files.

Limitations of the Hierarchical Data Model

The hierarchical data model is appealing because it is simple to understand (the data model itself, not the database system that implemented it!) and code against efficiently. However, hierarchies are of limited value in modeling real world phenomena for two reasons:

- The desired "point of entry" differs depending upon the focus of the application. For example, in a university environment, the accounting office might be interested in organizing its information according to student records, while the registrar might want to organize its records by department and semester. For this reason, organizations that use file-based systems typically maintain (or create from a master file) several different file formats that contain some replicated data. As applications change over time, it is not uncommon for these files to get "out of sync," sometimes with negative results—for example, when the Social Security Office continued to send benefit checks for years after a recipient had died.
- Hierarchies result in redundant data. In the registrar's database, the hierarchical path might be department->semester->course->section-> student. If a student named Freddy Krueger was taking six courses in a particular semester, there would be six instances of a segment representing his name and student ID. Moreover, because a program had no means of knowing how many classes Freddy was taking, it would need to read the whole database before it could be assured that it had obtained Freddy's full schedule.

IMS did provide a means of eliminating redundant records by allowing the database designer to define pointers between physical records. However, the problem of redundant data was one of the motivations for the next major advance in database management technology—database management systems based on a network meta-model.

Challenges in Integrating Hierarchical Databases

As we will discuss in greater detail later in this book, there are two major types of integration initiatives—those that require the extraction and manipulation of large volumes of data and those that interface to the database at the level of the individual transaction. In general, any project that requires integrating large volumes of data from systems based on COBOL files or hierarchical database systems can expect to encounter the following types of problems:

- *Duplicate records*—As discussed earlier, if one is taking data from a lower level segment or repeating group in a hierarchical database, there is the possibility that there will be duplicate data records. For example, if you are reading the database in the example in the previous section to obtain the schedules for multiple students and storing the results in a file, the information for any particular student can be dispersed throughout the resulting output file. If you are merging data from this database with information from another (for example, information where there is only one record per student, as in the database kept by the registrar), you must sort the first file by student before trying to merge, or the merge will be extremely inefficient.

- *Inconsistencies in the data within a single record*—As indicated before, COBOL-based systems are not strongly typed; otherwise it would be impossible to use the REDEFINES construct in a COBOL COPYBOOK definition because the error-checking code generated by the COBOL compiler would signal an error if the wrong kind of data was being read into a particular field. As a result, if an integration project requires moving historical data (as in the case of migrating data from one application to another), it will be important to expect inconsistencies in the data, and if possible, detect them before the data integration project begins by means of a data profiling product. (See Chapter 8.) Note that this also applies to the case of any IMS database that has not fully defined each segment in the DL/1 language.

- *Performance and access*—Depending upon how the hierarchical database is currently being used in a company and the type of data access required for the integration project, access may be restricted to off hours or working against a copy of the COBOL file or a flat file dump of the IMS database. If the project requires that the target database be refreshed on a weekly, daily, or hourly basis, update programs may need to be able to interpret the database log maintained by the hierarchical DBMS to determine which records have been changed since the last time the update program ran.

3.6   Network Database Management Systems

Replicated data was a problem for maintaining the integrity of data stored in hierarchical systems as well as a problem in efficiency and data access. Toward the end of 1969, the DBTG published its first specification for the network database model (often referred to as the CODASYL model), which was designed to address these problems. The network meta-model differs from the hierarchical in the following three ways:

1. A record can have multiple parents, e.g., where records A and B can both "own" or point to a record C.

2. One-to-many relationships can be uni-directional ("simple" networks) or bi-directional ("complex" networks).

3. A network can contain cycles—that is, a record of type X can have a descendant of type X, as long as it is not an immediate descendent—or, to restate as a restriction, a record cannot be a member and an owner of the same set.

Figure 3.5 illustrates three types of structures that can be created with the network meta-model.

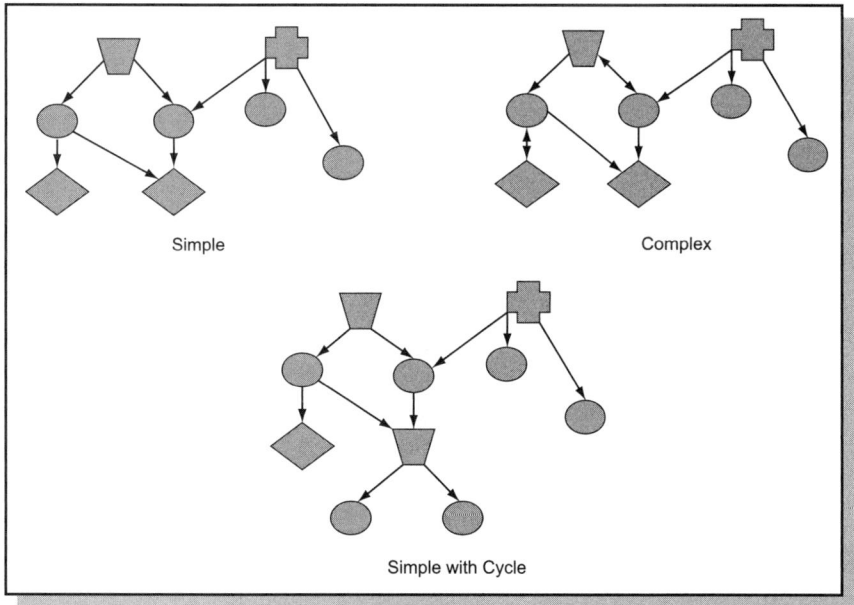

Figure 3.5   Types of Network Structures

The concept of a cycle was important to representing engineering designs, where some object like a *car* would contain (or own) a set of the record type *components,* one of which might be designated as an *engine,* which in turn would contain a set of record type *components,* and so on. This type of data structure was often referred to as a *bill of materials* or *BOM.* As you can see, the network meta-model is a more natural fit for modeling the real-world relationships and minimizing replicated data.

However, this flexibility introduced even more complexity for the application programmer. In a hierarchical DBMS, there was only one path to a type of record; in a network DBMS, there could be many and—depending upon the number of instances of intervening record types—the shortest path (in terms of number of record types traversed) may not be the most efficient, as illustrated in Figure 3.6. Because the database designer was more apt to understand the nature of the data, there were actually two types of DDL for CODASYL databases—a DDL that defined the schema or actual layout of the database and another DDL for defining subschemas that were provided to application programmers. In this way the DBA could create different subschemas for different types of applications to ensure that the programmer was using

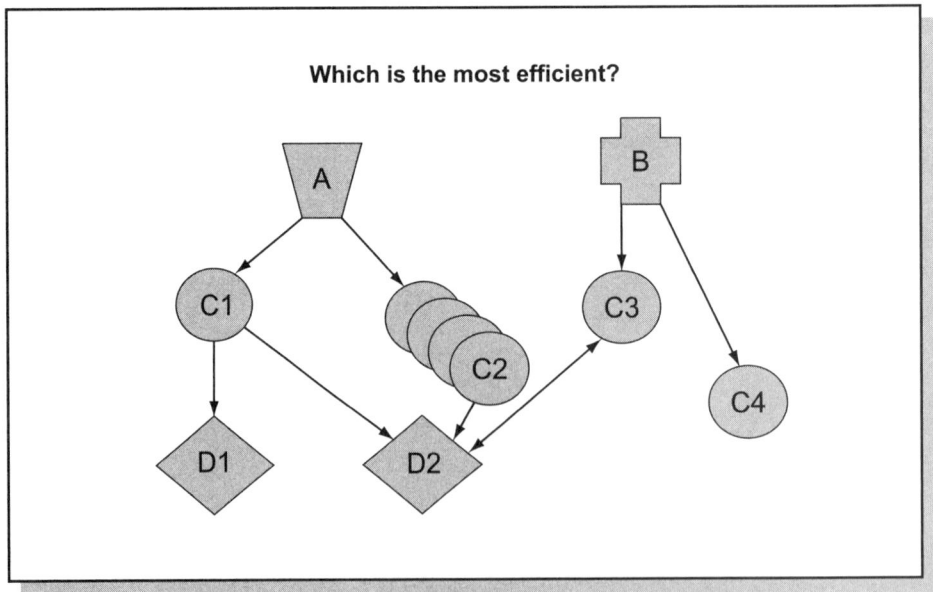

Figure 3.6 Multiple Paths to the Same Record

the path that would provide the optimal performance. (If you're familiar with relational database systems, this would be similar to providing a view over a set of tables.)

IDMS as an Example of a CODASYL DBMS

IDMS (which stands for Integrated Database Management System) was originally developed by the chemical division of B.F. Goodrich and later licensed to John Cullinane for commercialization (first under Cullinane Database Systems, later under the name Cullinet). IDMS is the most widely deployed CODASYL DBMS product with a base of approximately 2500 customers. IDMS augmented its DDL with an Integrated Data Dictionary (IDD) that contained all the database definitions and was itself an IDMS database that could be programmatically searched and augmented to contain additional information. The IDD was a great advance because it allowed designers to write programs to discover information about data relationships, and as such, it was one of the first instances of a metadata repository. (We will discuss metadata repositories in greater detail in Chapter 7.) Whereas today almost all relational DBMS products support an an application programming interface (API) to the metadata defining the databases they manage, IDMS was a technical leader in this respect at the time.

Like IMS, IDMS also gave the DBA control over how the data was stored so that the DBA had to understand how IDMS stored and processed the information to choose between the following storage options: sequential (which was rarely used), CALC (which used a hashing schema to determine on which page a record should be stored), and VIA (which allowed the DBA to indicate which of multiple options would be most often used for traversal).

Advantages and Limitations of Network DBMS

The network meta-model is significantly more expressive than its hierarchical counterpart. A talented DBA could not only minimize replicated data, but also control performance by specifying the appropriate storage options and providing developers with subschemas that forced them to favor the paths that would provide superior performance. However, the result was very complex database designs, and even though the IDD stored these designs in a database, the IDD reports describing a database schema could run hundreds of pages. In addition, if the DBA did not allocate enough pages to an area, the process of rebuilding the database was computationally expensive.

Topic of Interest: Transaction-Level Integrity

As database technology matured, it provided support not only for strong data typing, but also for data integrity. One of the most important of these is *transaction-level integrity.* The term *transaction* is used to refer to an event (for example, shipping an order or transferring funds) where more than one record in a database is affected. Two situations can prevent a transaction from completing successfully: 1) *deadlock,* or 2) a system failure before all the necessary updates are complete.

As indicated in our initial discussion of database functions, locking is used to ensure that only one user/program can update a record at a time. In the situation of a deadlock, user A has record 1 locked and is requesting a lock for record 2, while user B has record 2 locked and is requesting a lock of record 1. An example of a system failure would be in a transfer of funds when the system crashed after funds had been deducted from one account and before they had been added to another. Database management systems provide a pair of commands—BEGIN WORK and COMMIT/END WORK—that allow programmers to bracket all the database updates required for the successful completion of a transaction to ensure that those updates are treated as *atomic:* either all updates take place or none of them take place. They also provide programmers with a ROLLBACK command that will cause the database to undo all updates to the database made since the BEGIN WORK. A programmer might want to use this command if the program encountered some error in the process of executing a transaction; he or she could roll back any associated database modifications to restore the database to the state it was in at the beginning of the transaction.

3.7 Relational Database Management Systems

It is not surprising that database technology was such a strong focus during the initial decades of widespread computer use because persistence in data was a prerequisite if computers were to replace what would otherwise be done with people and paper. During this period of "data processing" we came to understand the functional requirements of what a database management system should do to support multiple users (people and applications) while minimizing replicated data and maintaining data integrity (e.g., support for security, access, locking, logging for recovery, rollback, etc.). However, as organizations sought to design centralized databases that would perform efficiently, the tasks of data modeling and database programming became so complex that the skill and sophistication required on the part of technical staff became a bottleneck, and managers might have to wait months to get a new type of report. A good part of this complexity came from the fact that application programmers had to be intimately familiar with the storage options chosen by the DBA in order to "walk" the schema to retrieve the data they needed. But what was even worse than the complexity of programming against CODASYL databases was the fact that the tight coupling between how the data was stored and how programs requested data meant that any change to the underlying design of a schema could mean that many (if not all) of the programs that accessed that database would also have to be changed.

During the 1960s, Edgar F. ("Ted") Codd, a mathematician who worked as a programmer for IBM, sought to explore a means of building systems that could provide "data independence"—database technology that provided programmers a means of asking for the data they needed without any knowledge of how the data was physically linked in storage. The solution he proposed was to relate data in terms of *values* rather than pointers and use relational algebra to compute the sequence of operations required to obtain the data sets desired by the programmer.

Codd's insights led to database technology that added mathematical rigor to data storage and access while at the same time providing DBAs and programmers with a simple conceptual model. There are four basic concepts in what corresponds to a relational database management system's DML:

- An *entity* or table is a two-dimensional matrix that represents what earlier systems considered a record definition.
- Columns in a table represent *attributes* about the entity and correspond to fields in record-based systems, where attributes are defined as being of a particular data type (e.g., integer, string, date).
- A *tuple* is a row in a table and corresponds to a physical record in a hierarchical or network DBMS or file.
- A *relationship* between entities/tables (also called a *join*) exists when two tuples share the same value for a semantically equivalent attribute, like customer number.

Not only did the relational meta-model significantly reduce the conceptual complexity of defining a data model, but it also significantly simplified the task of programming because the programmer no longer had to explicitly specify how to navigate the schema in order to get to the desired data.

As a result, rather than writing *procedural* code that traverses a network or a hierarchy, programmers could simply *declaratively* ask for what they want:

```
SELECT STUDENT.INFO, DEPT.ID, COURSE.ID, SECTION.ID WHERE
        DEPT.ID = COURSE.DEPT AND COURSE.ID = SECTION.ID
```

Not only did this greatly reduce the task of learning how to use a relational database management system, but it allowed DBAs to optimize the way the tables were actually stored without having to modify any of the existing code operating against the database. The relational meta-model is the prevailing database technology in use today because of all the previous and subsequent meta-models proposed it has provided *greater productivity for more users with less training.*

Topic of Interest: Declarative Programming

SQL is not the first, but is the most pervasive example of what is known as a 4GL, or Fourth Generation Language. Recall that machine language (1s and 0s) is 1GL, assembler languages are 2GL, and procedural languages like COBOL, C, and Pascal are 3GL. SQL differs from procedural languages in that SQL is *declarative*; that is, the commands describe what the programmer wants (e.g., the SELECT) providing a statement of conditions that he or she desires to be true (e.g., the WHERE) and leaves it up to the relational database system to determine how to acquire the desired results. The declarative paradigm is key to interoperability across systems and the basis for most efforts at defining industry standards.

A New Component: The Query Manager

Up until this point in the discussion, a DBMS had two major components—the DDL used to define the database and the DML that allowed programmers to store and access data as a result of compiling that database definition. Because in a relational DBMS (RDBMS) the relationship between records was based on values rather than pointers, it was no longer necessary for programmers to specify the logic required to traverse the underlying data structures. Rather, the query manager parses the SQL query into a set of ordered subqueries against the tables such that, when those subqueries are executed in the defined sequence, a table will be created that corresponds to the information that the programmer has requested. In fact, the relational algebra underlying RDBMS technology is so powerful that it will allow the query manager to compute the answer to arbitrary queries (called *ad hoc queries*) like "Give me a list of all the male employees who have a son with the same name as their father where that son is between the ages of 10 and 12," as long as the individual issuing the query has specified the "join fields" (i.e., the fields that are expected to contain common values). In fact, this capability is valuable because it lets users test hypotheses about relationships between data without visually inspecting it.

Another benefit of relational technology was a closer correlation between internal and external representations of the data. The ability to support ad hoc queries is only valuable if the data returned is in a form that can be understood by the individual issuing the query. As a result, the data values stored in relational databases are user-friendly, as opposed to the data values stored in earlier systems (e.g., a relational database is more likely to contain the data value *Minneapolis* instead of *214*), whereas in navigational databases it is not uncommon to find numeric codes or binary data.

Limitations of Relational Technology: The Need for New Skills

Complexity theory in computer science often discusses trade-offs between the steps required to solve a problem and the space required to store the information used in computation. At a very high level, they are inversely related; that is, reducing the number of steps usually requires storing more information and vice versa. A similar principle applies to relational database technology. Although the constructs in the data definition language are relatively simple, the design of what constitutes a table and the join fields between tables could significantly affect the performance of the relational "engine" that actually manipulates the data to produce the desired results. Relational database technology was developed when the cost of hardware was still relatively high, so there was a high cost associated with poor performance.

As a result, a consulting industry grew up around teaching people the process of relational data modeling. Because data modeling required a different type of domain knowledge from database design, the DBA role was split, with the data modeler in charge of interviewing users within the organization to understand how the data was used by the organization and the DBA focusing on the physical design and administration of the database (e.g., setting up access rights, archiving, performance monitoring, etc.). The data modeler's role was to interview the potential users of the database to understand the types of queries that they were likely to make and to use this information, along with the data required by various applications, to define tables that minimized the amount of redundant data, using keys (that is, columns in different tables that refer to the same information) to relate tables through values. Then, because joining tables on keys can be compute-intensive when large numbers of rows are involved, the data modeler will work with the database administrator to relax the rules regarding redundancy to arrive at a design that will provide an acceptable trade-off between storage and performance, often augmented by keeping additional indices to speed access where necessary.

It is important to note that even in a well-designed relational database, it is possible to create queries that will effectively bring the system to a standstill for other applications, in part because there is nothing to prevent a user from issuing a spurious query like, for example, a listing of all cars in any U.S. state where the license plate number is the same as someone's date of birth in a MMDDYY format. There is nothing ill-formed about such a query, but it could run for quite a while and return an empty set. As a result, in most production environments, nontechnical users are not allowed to issue ad hoc (unplanned) queries. Rather, the DBA or database application programmer will configure an end user query tool that allows the users to define the values for parameters in a set of canned (or preplanned) queries. In these cases, the nontechnical user can specify specific values (e.g., state or part number) to restrict the query results, but is not free to specify which tables are accessed or how they are to be joined.

New Features and New Duties

As database technology evolved, the notion of what constituted a data type also expanded. There is now native support for new data types like DATE, BLOB (binary large object), and even geographic information. There is also a wide range of options that can be declared as part of an attribute definition, such as a defined set of legal values, upper and lower bounds for a number, or a domain like a UPC code. Many relational database management systems also support "triggers" (i.e., the ability to associate a function that should be called whenever a particular field in a table is updated). Triggers are extremely useful in keeping data consistent when data has been replicated for the purposes of performance. Other features include the ability to replicate data across a number of different installations of the database for the purpose of performance or protection against downtime due to planned or unplanned outages.

Changed Data Capture

Up until this point we have been focusing on the way different kinds of database technologies model, store, and provide access to data. However, one of the key benefits of database management systems—as opposed to file systems—is that they all include some means of recovery should the data become corrupted through a hardware or software failure. The recovery mechanism typically involves some type of logging of the activity that takes place against the database, which may involve keeping a "before" image and an "after" image of any record modified. The log can be used in restoring the database to its last consistent state after a system failure (or to reapply changes after a rollback). But these logs are often used for capturing the changes that have been made to a database over a period of time. This ability to capture "changed data" is extremely important when the information from one database is used by another. For example, consider point of sale (POS) computers at a retail chain. These POS computers may maintain a database of products sold at this store. On a periodic basis—perhaps daily—it will be necessary to load changes to the list of products from the company's master database without reloading the entire database on the POS computer. Products that provide changed data capture can be configured to track this information and provide it on a scheduled or event-driven basis. This capability is extremely important when an organization is migrating to a new application, because for some period of time during the migration process both applications will be active and it will be necessary to keep the data in the two systems synchronized until the cutover to the new application can be completed.

RDBMS Products Are Still Evolving

By the late 1970s three relational database management systems were dominant— DB2 from IBM, Oracle from Relational Software Inc. (later renamed Oracle Corporation), and Ingres, available through a source code license from the University of California, Berkeley. Since that time a number of other relational database management systems have appeared on the market ranging from Teradata, a massively parallel RDBMS that runs on proprietary hardware and dominates industries like telecommunications and retail, to scaled down products like Btrieve from Pervasive or OpenEdge from Progress Software that were built to serve as embedded databases in applications. Nor is it clear which vendors will ultimately dominate the large multinational corporations. For example, SQL Server 2005 from Microsoft claims to be able to scale to meet the needs of large mission-critical production systems in Global 1000-sized companies. If this is true, over time its lower price point may help it gain significant market share.

Issues in Integrating Data Stored in an RDBMS

In many ways integration initiatives that require interfacing to data stored under relational DBMS systems are significantly easier than those that require data from their earlier counterparts. RDBMS systems are strongly typed; as a result, one will not find a string value in what has been declared as an integer field. Likewise, because the query manager is capable of performing much of the work required to reorganize the data, there is less need to perform external sorts and merges to structure the data in the way that the target application wants it. However, in addition to performance considerations, there are the problems of recognizing semantic inconsistencies (e.g., salary by month and salary by week) or syntactic inconsistencies (e.g., *J P Gonet* vs. *Joseph P Gonet* vs. *Joseph Peter Gonet*). As we will discuss in Chapter 8, these types of semantic inconsistencies can be among the most difficult to detect.

3.8 Object-Oriented Database Management Systems

Up until the 1980s programming methodologies focused on the design and structure of code; the goal was to maximize the reuse of code by localizing similar operations in the same functions. Programmers used the concepts associated with the meta-model to define their data structures and the data manipulation language to store and retrieve them. In the 1980s, as researchers in artificial intelligence tried to represent even more complex relationships, there was an initiative to represent data objects as actors or agents that reacted to external stimuli or messages. The world was modeled as a hierarchy of classes, where each class not only was defined as a collection of attributes, but also could be declared as a subclass of another class. Each class supported a series of messages or methods that defined how external objects or programs could obtain information about their state, allowing each object to keep the details about its internal state protected.

Figure 3.7 continues an example of a class hierarchy and how it is interpreted when building a specific instance of that hierarchy. An object inherits all the attributes of the classes of which it serves as a subclass, including any default values and all methods. A subclass can override one of the default values or methods. For example, the default for the number of wheels for a class *land vehicle* might be 4, with the definition of the subclass *motorcycle* overriding the number of wheels to be 2. This ability to express exceptions to the norm (e.g., a one-legged man) makes the object-oriented (OO) meta-model efficient for representing complex relationships.

The ability to efficiently model complex relationships through class memberships, inheritance, and exceptions is appealing computationally for the following reasons:

- If modeled correctly, an OO data model will have minimum redundant data and maximum reuse of code. Note: Even though objects are defined through hierarchies, their attributes can contain the object ID (i.e., logical identifier) of one or more other object instances (e.g., an employee object can have a *dependents* attribute that

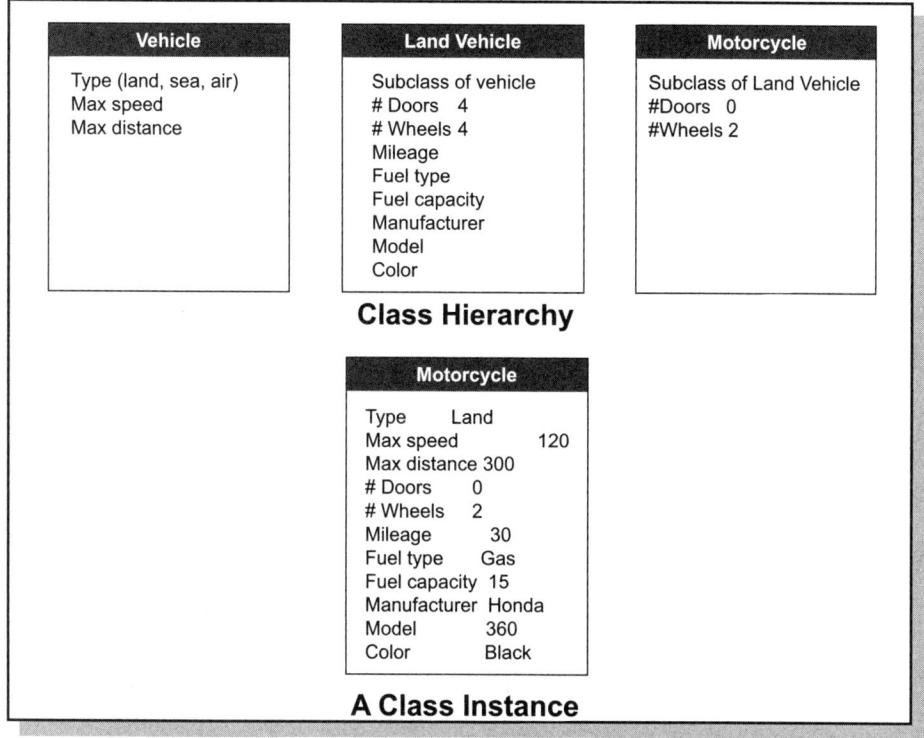

Figure 3.7   Object Oriented Data Model

contains 0–*n* object IDs to an object of type *dependent*). As a result, the meta-model is actually network rather than hierarchical.

- The ability to represent exceptions explicitly both reduces redundancy and makes it much easier to store complex relationships.
- The encapsulation of functional logic as part of the class definition allows the internal structure of the class to evolve without adversely affecting any users of that class because the only thing a programmer needs to know about a class to use it is the set of messages required to interact with the class.

The object-oriented meta-model has transformed the way programmers build systems and—as we will see in the next chapter—has had a profound effect on execution protocols that are at the heart of the new service-oriented architecture.

Object-oriented DBMS have had good success in well-understood technical domains because they provide persistence for applications whose complexity benefits from the object-oriented meta-model. However, they are not in wide use in commercial IT environments for four reasons:

1. Like network database technology, they require sophisticated data modeling and navigational programming.

2. Like RDBMS and network databases, OODBMS products encounter performance problems if the database schema is not tuned to how the data must be accessed.

3. The OO paradigm is more useful in providing programmer productivity in creating a new application than in the manipulation of data, because whenever an instance of an object is retrieved, the OODBMS interprets the class hierarchy and returns a fully instantiated instance of the object that contains a representation of all the attributes.

4. Finally, vendors of relational DBMS have built object layers on top of their relational databases (called object-relational DBMS) that provide enough of the OO functionality without the cost of purchasing and maintaining another database and the attendant costs of training DBAs in the new system. These extensions include the ability to define complex structures in SQL statements that are equivalent to class hierarchies.

3.9   The Emergence of Other Types of Database Technology

At this point we have discussed the major types of systems that manage virtually all of the structured data in operational systems in government and industry today. Most of these systems were developed during the first 25 years after the commercial introduction of computers. However, that is not to say that these systems contain the majority of the electronically stored data. In addition to billions of word processing documents, spreadsheets, and email messages, companies have electronic versions of drawings, source code, graphics, and more. Just as there are database management systems for structured data, there are a large variety of applications that manage these other electronic artifacts—products for document management, source code management, archiving, and so on.

Although most organizations have standardized on a DBMS product to be used for any new development, they have in large part abandoned the hope of consolidating all their applications on a single platform in the foreseeable future. That is not to say that they will not continue to consolidate applications as possible in order to reduce their total cost of IT ownership, but consolidation is not their top priority. There are several reasons for this:

- *Mergers and acquisitions*—Companies frequently acquire other companies as a means of improving their financial performance by availing themselves of economies of scale or removing a competitive product from the marketplace. When this happens, they often acquire duplicate but incompatible applications (e.g., general ledgers, human resources, etc.). Application consolidation is one of the most complex integration initiatives one can undertake and can lead to significant employee turmoil, so many companies postpone it.
- *More complex regulatory requirements*—Companies that operate in different regions of the world must ensure that their applications are in compliance with the laws and regulations of each region or country, and these regulations change. In fact, some governments are now asking for information regarding customer transactions while others require that customer information (for example, healthcare records) be kept private. In fact, in the United States the regulations for certain industries can vary by state.
- *The need to incorporate the Internet and web services into their business practices and the delivery of services and products*—Not only does this require interfacing to production applications in real-time, but it also exposes companies to greater risk of malware (e.g., software like a computer virus that commits fraud or damage).
- *The general increase in the rate of change*—Now that it permeates every aspect of a business, the impact of change often requires changes to multiple systems. As the frequency of change increases, companies wind up spending their resources on maintenance rather than consolidation.

As a result, companies often forego application consolidation in favor of focusing on what it will take to make the systems they have work together by developing an enterprise strategy for integration, where XML will be the language that is used for the exchange of data.

Topic of Interest: Maintenance and the Total Cost of Ownership (TCO)
With most capital purchases like buildings or equipment, the largest cost comes at the time of purchase; periodic expenditures may be required for upkeep or modernization, but typically companies won't make these expenditures if it is cheaper to replace the purchase. With software, the situation is different. For example, as mentioned previously, industry analysts maintain that companies spend 4–10 times the cost of an enterprise software application in implementation—that is, configuring the application to fit the organization's business practices and loading the company's data into the application. But the cost doesn't stop at that point. Software and hardware vendors continually must upgrade their products if they expect them to remain in use. Sometimes the upgrade is required to adapt to changes to the environment in which the product operates (e.g., upgrades to the operating system or communication technology). Other factors include functional enhancements that improve the capabilities of the core product or support for standards like XML and/or to meet new regulatory requirements.

Because companies cannot afford the risk that upgrading to a new release will cause mission-critical applications to fail, IT organizations typically have rigorous regression tests that any new release must pass before it is put into production. Because these tests are labor-intensive, companies often have rules about how often they will introduce upgrades into an organization. As a result, sometimes a large company will have three or four versions of an application (which are sometimes incompatible) in production across different groups.

The preceding activities do not include the overhead incurred when applications are modified for business reasons such as, changes to accommodate new regulations or product offerings. For these reasons, one of the biggest challenges facing organizations is an ever-increasing total cost of software ownership, because every product they introduce into production environments carries a heavy incremental cost.

XML and XML Databases

As we discussed in Chapter 2, for many years there was hope that SQL would emerge as a standard so that data could move freely across relational database management systems. Although it is possible to use a subset of SQL across database environments, most vendors have proprietary syntax for advanced features. Now companies are eager to embrace new standards like HTML, SOAP, and WSDL to avail themselves of the power of the World Wide Web. However, rather than banking on a common meta-model and query language for exchanging data, people are ready to settle for a *lingua franca;* that is, some common language that can be used for the purpose of exchanging data for commerce. XML is that language. But strictly speaking, XML (short for Extensible Markup Language) is not a language but a set of syntactic conventions for using character files to exchange both data and metadata—that is, data that describes what the data in the file will contain as well as the data itself.

The syntactic rules for XML are very simple. Every element in an XML file must be enclosed within a set of tags contained within angle brackets, where the start of the object is signaled by *<tag-name>* and the end by *</tag-name>,* as in the following example:

```
<Employee>
   <Name>Fred Flintstone</Name>
   <HomeAddress>
      <Address>
         <Street>815 Stony Lane</Street>
         <City>Bedrock<City>
      </Address>
   </HomeAddress>
<Salary>1000.00</Salary>
<MaritalStatus>Married</MaritalStatus>
</Employee>
```

Industry groups are working to establish their own XML schemas (collections of tags and structures) for the purpose of data interchange; for example, HL7 for healthcare, CML for chemistry, MNML for music, and so on. However, many organizations are also creating proprietary XML standards that are a superset of the standard for their industry, along with a set of tags to represent distinctions that characterize additional information that is important to their own internal systems. In Chapter 6 we will explore the challenges with the representation of meaning and its importance for whether XML can provide the level of interoperability desired.

Because XML is stored in character files, its inherent structure is hierarchical. Although it is possible to represent network structures in XML, it requires either:

1. A fully qualified path to where the original definition of the element occurred in the file, or

2. A duplicate definition in the schema.

XML is an extremely verbose way of representing data. Its advantage is that it is self-defining; that is, the tags and the nesting of objects allow the application parsing the XML to understand the data relationships. At the current time, there are two types of database support for XML. For structured data, RDBMS vendors like IBM (DB2) and Oracle are XML-enabled in the sense that they can read, store, and produce XML. For XML documents, vendors of content management systems like Documentum and Vignette provide support for document-specific types of attributes like author, revision, and so on. In addition, most application vendors like SAP now provide some level of XML support. However, using XML to exchange data requires that the participants in the exchange have a common understanding of what the tags mean. Many industry groups have defined industry-specific XML schemas, but it is not clear what it will take to correlate independently developed, industry-specific schemas in order to support the kind of information sharing required for recovery from natural or manmade disasters (e.g., where information from transportation agencies, hospitals, and law enforcement will all be required). As we shall see in Chapter 6, this requirement presents a significant technical challenge.

3.10   Integration and Data Integrity

Many of the features provided by database management systems have been geared toward ensuring the accuracy of the data stored in the database by protecting the data from user error or system crash. In today's Internet-based communities this attention to the accuracy of a particular record may seem quaint. Journalists write about the "collective intelligence," the idea being that if someone publishes inaccurate information on a website, others who know better will provide edits or additions that correct the information. These individuals maintain that, given enough time, wikipedia.org, a freeware encyclopedia available on the Web, will rival the *Encyclopedia Britannica.* Yet few of us want to tolerate anything but absolute accuracy if the data in question refers to our bank balance or healthcare. Obviously, the level of inaccuracy tolerated is determined by how the data is to be used and by whom. The goal of a software designer, of course, should be to build systems that minimize errors and inaccuracy and therefore favor integration strategies that foster the rapid discovery and correction of anomalies in the data.

The purpose of software is to manipulate data. As a result, the value of any software application or environment is tied to its ability to provide users with timely data in the form they need it. As we have described in this chapter, there are significant differences in the capabilities and limitations of the various database technologies that store most digital data. However, it's not just a matter of getting and distributing the data some group of users needs, but building an application that preserves the integrity of the data as it is used over time. In the next chapter, we will explore how the evolution of execution protocols has complicated that task.

Exercises for Chapter 3

At this point we have provided a high-level description of the different types of database technology that you are likely to encounter in production systems in large organizations. In any strategic IT initiative it is likely that you will be dealing with one—or more likely several—of these types of systems. Your first challenge in defining an integration strategy will depend upon your enumerating the types of problems that you will be likely to encounter in a particular integration scenario. Note that this is not just a function of the number and types of systems involved, but the amount of data (in terms of duration) that is involved and how the information will be used. The following exercises are geared at helping you apply what you have learned about various types of database technology to this task.

1. Diagram the course schedules in each of the data representations listed. The same instructor name represents the same person.

   Course Schedule:
   Dept: Math
   Class: 101 Basic Math
   Instructor: A. Smith
   Class: 201 Algebra
   Instructor: J. Jones
   Class: 301 Calculus
   Instructor: A. Smith
   Dept: Chemistry
   Class: 101 Basic Chemistry
   Instructor: M. Fields
   Dept: English

Class: 101 Writing
Instructor: R. Milton
Class: 201 Shakespeare
Instructor: M. Fields

Data representations:
- Relational
- Hierarchical
- Network
- Sequential file, single record type, fixed format
- Sequential file, single record type, delimited format
- Sequential file, multiple record type, fixed format
- EDI-style file
- XML file

2. For each of the data representation diagrams you did in Exercise 1, which representation is:

- Most efficient for the amount of storage required?
- Least efficient for the amount of storage required?
- Most efficient for producing a report for each instructor of courses taught?
- Least efficient for producing a report for each instructor of courses taught?
- Most efficient for producing a report of the number of courses taught by each instructor?
- Least efficient for producing a report of the number of courses taught by each instructor?

3. One of the most important tasks in developing an integration strategy is anticipating the types of problems you might encounter in accessing, testing, and modifying the data. These problems will differ depending upon the nature of the project and the nature of the data sources and the data target. List the problems that you would anticipate in the following application scenarios:

a. Migrating a 30-year-old application based on COBOL VSAM files to a COTS package based on Oracle's relational database management system

b. Building an information-sharing application that uses XML to consolidate information from the following agencies: transportation, health and human services, and the department of motor vehicles

c. Consolidating two billing applications after a merger or acquisition

CHAPTER

4

Communication and Execution Protocols

In Chapter 2, we discussed how the advent of networking technology and the reduced cost of hardware enabled software designers to build applications that distributed processing across computers. In this chapter we will examine how this capability evolved as bandwidth increased and the Internet emerged, providing organizations with the potential to improve the efficiency of their business by having their software applications communicate in real-time. Our focus will not be on the details of the communication software and hardware, but on how their evolving capabilities have affected the capabilities of software applications with respect to:

- *Granularity and independence* of application components across users—that is, which application components can be shared and, where they can, what type of additional functionality is required to support multiple users
- *Invocation*—that is, how an application is invoked and how application components interact
- The functionality and information required to maintain a *user's context*

We will then examine the types of problems one encounters when integrating applications that use different execution protocols.

4.1   Early Distributed Applications: Data-centric

Standalone applications had no concept of "user"; rather they were designed to perform some type of computation. When they were invoked with the appropriate parameters or data file, they simply performed the calculation and returned or wrote the result. Persistent data was kept in files, and there was no system support to help organizations keep related data consistent across files. With DBMS technology, a new layer of functionality was inserted between applications and persistent data storage, and with this change in architecture, there came a need to represent users. Sometimes the user was a person, as in the case of a data entry clerk; sometimes the user was an application. Until the advent of networking technology and client-server architectures, the DBMS and applications typically resided on the same host.

When an application ran in *batch mode,* the database it was operating against could not be accessed by any other application. A large batch application like a billing system for a utility company might update millions of records in a single invocation and run more efficiently by locking the entire database rather than requesting locks at the record level. DBMS products also supported applications that run in *transaction mode.* As discussed previously, transactions are database updates that affect only a handful of related records; for example, the transfer of funds from a savings account to a checking account. To support transactions, the underlying design of the DBMS needed to represent users (or sessions) and locking. As products became more sophisticated, these capabilities were enhanced to include access rights (i.e., a mechanism that could restrict an individual or group's ability to view or update only a subset of the data in a database) and transaction-level integrity (i.e., the ability to treat several updates as "atomic" so that either all of a set of database updates completed successfully or none of them would take place).

In either mode of invocation, batch or transaction, very little context had to be maintained about a particular session, and the integrity and security of the data was the responsibility of the DBMS. Likewise, applications were fairly monolithic in the sense that they were typically written to perform a single type of activity (e.g., claims processing, billings). They might share common records or tables in the database, but the application writer could design the application as if the database existed solely for that application alone.

4.2   Client-Server Architecture: The Vision and the Reality

In the 1980s, the sophistication of communication technology and the decreased cost of hardware made it possible for computers to exchange information in near real-time. These capabilities led to a new type of application architecture. In *client-server* architecture, software that needed to be shared across users or applications could be stored on more powerful computers called *servers,* and software that served an individual user or application could reside on a *client* machine, which was typically significantly less expensive. Communication software provided application developers with a simple means of invoking a remote application or procedure with as simple a command as if reading from a file. The initial appeal of client-server architecture was economic. Mainframes were extremely expensive—so expensive that a whole new class of IT vendor appeared that allowed companies to rent access to a mainframe to run their applications when the cost of purchasing and maintaining mainframes was beyond their means. (This process was called time-sharing.) Because workstations and servers were relatively cheap, the vision was that companies could start small with a server and only as many clients as they needed, buying additional hardware when their needs expanded.

In part to facilitate the adoption of client-server technology, a number of key hardware vendors, including Sun Microsystems, adopted the UNIX operating system. UNIX was originally developed at AT&T Bell Labs and was designed to support multiple users and the simultaneous execution of multiple programs in order to eliminate (or minimize) having processors sitting idle. But it was not just the fact that UNIX was highly functional, but the fact that the source code was available as freeware that made it appealing. Because most relational database management systems used SQL (Structured Query Language) as their query language, companies—bolstered by strong support from key vendors—embraced a vision of open systems where they could mix and match hardware and applications with little or no integration effort. These efforts were sponsored by two major industry consortia—X/Open Company, Ltd. and the Open Software Foundation—which merged in 1996 to become The Open Group. The prediction was that with an infrastructure this economical and easy to use, there would be little or no future development on the mainframe. In fact, many industry analysts predicted that the mainframe would die.

Topic of Interest: The True Cost of Client-Server Technology

When determining the cost of a technology solution, it is important to think through all aspects of cost. Client-server architecture certainly offers a lower cost of entry than mainframe time-sharing, and the cost of hardware continues to decrease. However, client-server architecture greatly complicates the tasks of maintenance and security. Now that workstation users have local applications as well as shared applications that run on a separate server, companies have staff not only to maintain and troubleshoot the various PC applications, but also, as more and more employees use computers remotely, to install and maintain systems that serve as "firewalls" to block unauthorized access to the company's servers and/or provide virus protection software to prevent damage to those systems by malware.

In short, as discussed earlier, a software architect must carefully evaluate any claims that one technology is more cost-effective than another, because there are many dimensions to cost above and beyond the expense associated with the initial purchase. In fact, many of the exercises in subsequent chapters require you to perform this type of analysis.

Client-server technology was appealing to software architects because it allowed them to distribute the processing across computers for enhanced user interfaces and better performance. As software architects sought to create designs that would provide the same type of increased productivity provided by database technology, the concept of a three-tiered architecture gained favor, where the code required for user interface, application logic, and database management would all be developed and maintained independently, as shown in Figure 4.1.

In this way, different application developers could share common components in each layer, using remote procedure calls to communicate between layers that resided

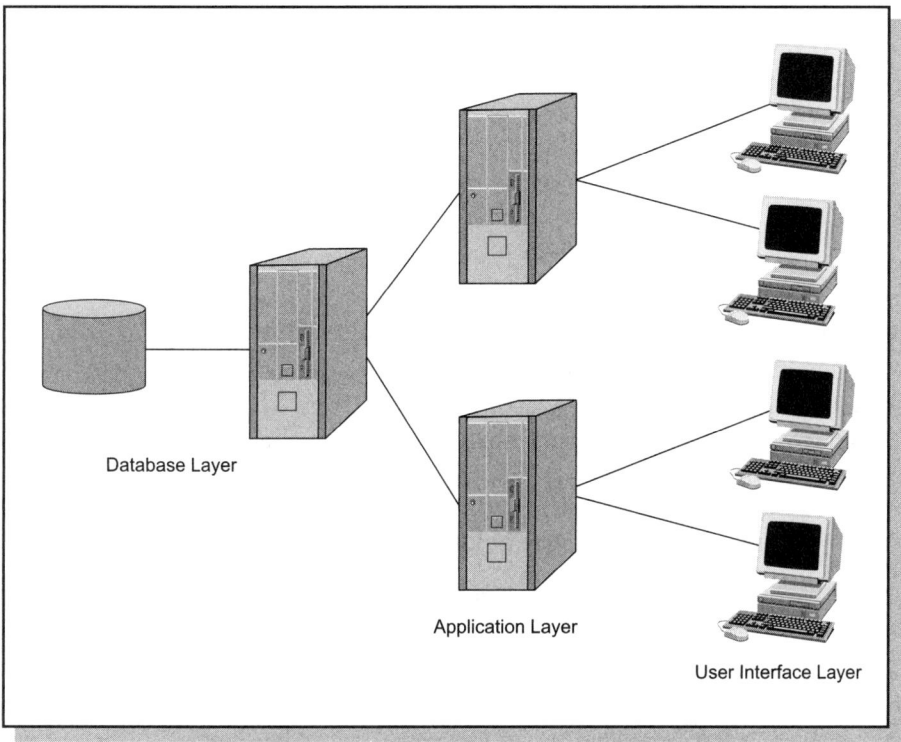

Figure 4.1   Three-Tiered Architecture

on different hosts. As we will see in the next chapter, this influence resulted in significant changes to the way programmers design and implement software.

Factors That Adversely Affected the Client-Server Architecture

Few organizations successfully executed on the vision of replacing the mainframe with internally developed client-server solutions, in large part because of concern about the potential impact of the Year 2000 on legacy applications. Given a hard deadline of December 31, 1999, and the availability of COTS applications, many managers began to question the value of proprietary applications.

The Cost of Developing Proprietary Applications

By the early 1990s, management began to realize that their internal client-server initiatives were long on expense but short on usable deliverables. In an effort to maximize reuse, design teams often spent too much time in analysis and data modeling. In large organizations there may be 40 or 50 representations of customer information. In order to understand how these representations differed, it was necessary to conduct extensive interviews with the individuals who used and maintained those systems, where the majority of these systems resided on mainframes. Because many of these same individuals feared that their job security could be threatened by the organization's migration to newer technology, they were frequently less than helpful, so the attempt to define a common data model for the enterprise often took years of effort with little results. The result was that many internal client-server initiatives were cancelled after the first few years.

The Availability of COTS (or Packaged) Applications

In the meantime, application vendors began to deliver products that ran in the client-server environment. Many of these were *application suites* (sometimes called enterprise resource planning or ERP applications) that consisted of tightly integrated versions of what had previously been standalone applications (e.g., billing, general ledger, materials resource planning). The architecture of these application suites typically allowed individual modules to be purchased and installed as standalone applications, but the tight integration between modules—which eliminated the need for application integration initiatives—offered the dual promise of improved data integrity and reduced maintenance costs because little or no internal development would be required for integration.

As the Year 2000 approached people began to worry that mission-critical applications that represented the year with two digits instead of four might fail. Organizations with these applications had two choices—they could re-engineer their legacy applications or purchase and implement new applications. In most cases, by the mid-1990s it was considered too risky to count on internal development teams to have completed new applications by the hard deadline of December 31, 1999, so internal large-scale initiatives were either halted or curtailed, as companies opted to purchase COTS applications instead.

As a result, many large organizations wound up being more heterogeneous in the decade after the introduction of client-server technology than in the decade before, with a mix of mainframe and client-server–based applications, some that were proprietary and others that were packaged. The result was that systems integration became a major technical requirement for any company that wanted to avail itself of the faster communication capabilities provided by network technology.

Topic of Interest: Why Standards Initiatives Fail

No one can deny the appeal of the concept of standards for software. If only one could define a standard language for representing information, then we could freely mix and match applications. However, all but a limited set of software standards have failed to deliver this type of benefit. There are two major reasons for this, one technical and one resulting from the realities of the marketplace. Technically, the standards that succeed in providing interoperability are those that support limited semantic content. At the lowest level, there are two major standards for representing character data—ASCII (American Standard Code for Information Interchange) and EBCDIC (Extended Binary Coded Decimal Interchange Code). Likewise, standards for supporting basic communication protocols like TCP/IP (Transmission Control Protocol/Internet Protocol) are relatively limited in the range of things that they represent. As a result, it is relatively straightforward for vendors to support them, because they do not require a large ongoing effort.

As the range of functionality—and the semantic scope—increases, standards do not fare as well. Among the most successful is the standard for SQL. Although there is 100% support across vendors for the simpler aspects of the standard, as one moves into the more recent enhancements (for example, support for object-relational constructs), there is much greater variation in terms of what features are supported by different vendors.

But there is a second reason that some standards fail to achieve the envisioned benefits, and that is that they present a risk to large, established software vendors. Small software vendors often base their products on standards because it minimizes the amount of integration required to deploy their product and thereby answers a sales objection. However, enterprise software vendors would be adversely affected if their products could be replaced by less expensive equivalents. As a result, even though large software vendors play key roles in standards initiatives, often their role there does not facilitate the adoption of a standard but actually serves to keep multiple standards in play (e.g., J2EE and .NET, two competing standards used in implementing web services) or otherwise inhibit the standard's timely completion and adoption.

4.3   Heterogeneity and Event-Driven Integration

In developing an integrated application suite based on client-server technology, developers could use remote procedure calls to communicate between applications in near real-time so, for example, a customer order entered into a shipping application could be reflected in near real-time as inventory information in the materials resource planning application. However, this type of integration depends upon each application having knowledge of how it should interact with other related applications. Although the use of remote procedure calls was fairly straightforward for the vendors of integrated application suites, it was of little value to organizations that wanted to integrate a mix of applications, where in many cases they had no access to the source code of one or more applications.

However, even in these cases it was often possible to integrate applications at the level of a transaction through one of three means:

1. Intercepting information sent from a screen

2. Using database "triggers"

3. Using database logs

Intercepting the information involved capturing the data being passed from the user interface to the application. Screen scraper products were designed to capture the format of the "green screen" terminals used for data entry so that developers could acquire the information they needed to create interfaces that simulated user input in order to provide near real-time communication between applications. This capability was so useful that in most implementations of three-tier architecture, application vendors came to publish an API, an application programming interface.

When developers had access to the DBMS used by an application, they could use either database triggers or the database log. If supported by the DBMS technology, a trigger mechanism allows a developer to attach user functions to fields in the database that perform the appropriate remote procedure calls to update related applications. Alternately, databases have logs that are used to restore the state of the database in case of a power or hardware failure. The *database logs* contain a record of every action that was taken against the database since the last time the log was cleared. These logs can be scanned for transactions of interest.

This type of integration is said to use an *event-driven protocol*—that is, where the occurrence of one update causes other updates to happen. In these hand-coded solutions to application integration, the user function looks like just another user to the applications being updated. This type of integration is very efficient in terms of performance but is difficult to implement and maintain for the following reasons:

- It requires a deep knowledge not only of the various applications, but also of how they are supposed to interact. The integration team needs to understand not only the various transactions supported by each application, but also how those transactions should affect each other. Sometimes this might be specific to the way a particular business or industry operates. For example, one company might count a sale as revenue as soon as it ships product, while another might wait until it collects payment. But the knowledge required is even more detailed than understanding how transactions interrelate across applications; the integration team also has to understand the way each application represents equivalent data. For example, a time-management system might track the number of hours worked on a daily basis, whereas a payroll system might require the number of hours worked per month.

- Once the integration was implemented, it was difficult to change, and unfortunately it is quite common for both the data sources and the format of the remote procedure calls (RPCs) to change. Even if the integration team was scrupulous about documenting every piece of code written and how it related to the sequence of "events," this information was usually not stored in a format that could be queried. As a result, changes required careful review of the documentation and having access to developers who understood the appropriate applications and/or technology on which they were based.

4.4 Message-Oriented Middleware

In an effort to provide developers with a less invasive means of real-time integration capabilities, a number of software vendors created a class of software called message-oriented middleware (MOM) as a way for applications to communicate in near real-time without having to modify the application itself. MOM products—like most system software—provide both a set of development tools and a runtime environment (often called an *integration broker*), where the behavior of the runtime is determined by how the product administrator configured the system with the development tool. As illustrated in Figure 4.2, the development platform for MOM products allows the administrator to define each host/application that interfaces to the queue. Developers are then given an API that allows them to define the messages that they want the MOM product to transport, where each message has two parts:

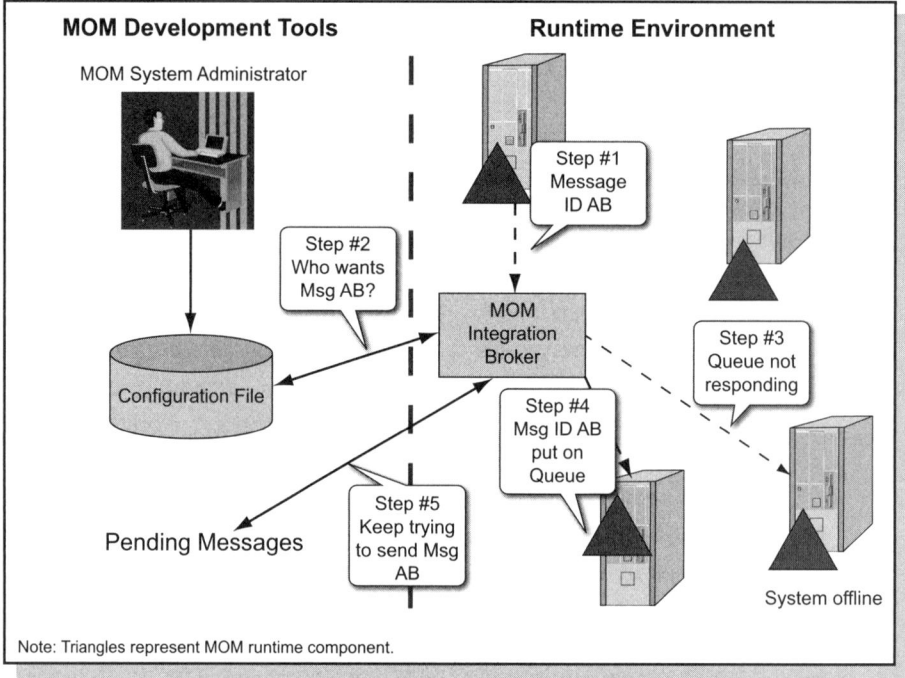

Figure 4.2 Message-Oriented Middleware (MOM)

- A header that contains (among other things) a message identifier and a logical address for one or more target applications
- Content that provides relevant information about the transaction in question

The runtime of a MOM product uses a client-server architecture, where the integration broker resides on the server and runs continuously. When it receives a message, the integration broker consults the destination table to see the type of system(s) that are to receive the message and uses the appropriate format(s) to transfer the message. A relatively small runtime component runs continuously on each computer and is the interface to the message queue that serves as a "mailbox" for messages. This runtime is responsible for either putting messages on the queue or taking messages off and routing them to the appropriate application(s). In addition to routing the messages, the integration broker provides temporary storage for the message if the intended receiver of the message is either down or off the network.

Topic of Interest: The Concept of Runtime

As discussed earlier, many productivity products require a proprietary run-time component to work. In the case of DBMS technology, it is the data manager or query manager; in the case of MOM products, it is both the integration broker and the queue manager than runs on each client that sends or receives messages. Most enterprise software products are licensed by either host and/or number of users, whether those users are named or concurrent. Frequently, software vendors will provide the development tools at little or no cost to make it relatively easy for IT managers to buy their product during the development cycle when relatively few users are involved. Often these managers are more concerned with getting the project delivered on time and on budget rather than the cost of deploying the resulting application across the enterprise. As a result, companies wind up spending far more than originally anticipated as they roll an application out. As you become responsible for weighing the benefits of alternative products, it is important to anticipate these future deployment costs, including the need for additional servers.

The Benefits of MOM

Like RPC calls, MOM products hide the details of differences in operating systems and communication protocols, thereby significantly simplifying application integration. However, the architecture of MOM products offers several advantages over the previous techniques that required either modifying application source code or writing transaction-specific interfaces:

- First and foremost, communication through MOM products is external to the application and therefore more suitable for use with legacy and packaged applications where companies often do not have access to the source code. By intercepting the input to transactions—via a screen scraper or some other technology—the team implementing the integration can create the desired communication between applications without changing their logic and incurring the risk of introducing a problem.
- Communication through MOM products is *asynchronous;* that is, the application that is transmitting the message doesn't have to wait on a

response from the receiving system. In contrast, RPC calls could be *synchronous* causing the application issuing the call to have to wait for a response before proceeding.

- Unlike pipes or file transfer products, MOM products cache the contents of the messages that they send so that information is not lost if there is an error in transmission or the receiving host is offline. As a result, MOM products can guarantee that either the "message" has been received or that they will return an error. Likewise, because the MOM product is responsible for transporting all messages between applications, it can also encrypt messages to ensure that they are secure.

MOM development tools capture sufficient information to be able to create a representation of how information flows between applications. In addition, their runtime logs can capture a history of the message traffic that can be used to audit the communication between applications.

The Drawbacks of MOM

Programming and Maintenance

When using MOM products, an integration team has two major types of tasks:

- Using the MOM development platform to define the messages and participants
- Writing "adapters" that interface between the native format used by the application for each transaction and some representation of the content that can be transmitted as a message and will be understood by the receiving applications

As a result, developers designing the MOM solution still need to have detailed knowledge about each application's representation of data for each transaction (e.g., whether salary is annual, monthly, or weekly). Given this information, the design team has to determine where to put any logic required to transform data values between the source and target applications—either in the source adapter or in the target adapter. In either case, because MOM products usually have no knowledge about the content of messages, they provide no central mechanism for recording information about how the data values are transformed. Even in the case where companies purchase adapter products, developers often have to use handwritten code to perform many of these transformations. As a result, as illustrated in Figure 4.3, MOM-based integration solutions tend to be hard to maintain.

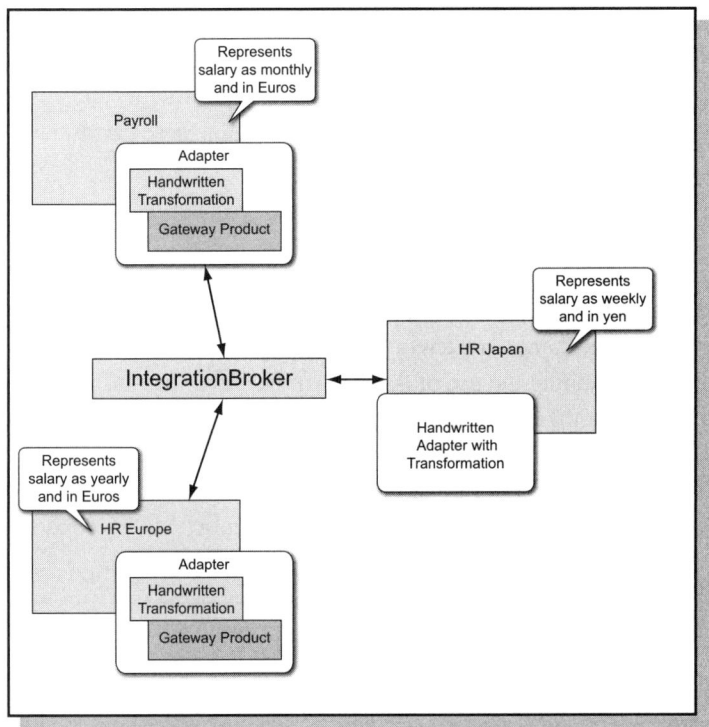

Figure 4.3 Why MOM-Based Applications Are Hard to Maintain

In the scenario in Figure 4.3 the two human resource applications will have to transform the representation of salary in order to inform the payroll system to add a new employee. In short, to integrate applications using a MOM product developers must either have agreed to an intermediate format (for example, an industry standard) for representing common data or understand the details of what data values the other applications expect. In a simple case like the one illustrated in Figure 4.3, this is not particularly difficult, but in large organizations there may be 70 to 100 applications, each of which may have 10 to 15 transactions that must participate. In complex environments like these the creation and maintenance of adapters can be extremely labor-intensive.

Performance

In addition, RPC and MOM technology have potential performance drawbacks. In the case of RPCs, the calling application could either hang when it could not successfully access the target application or it had to contain logic to cache and reissue the calls and/or return an error. On the other hand, the performance of MOM integration brokers can become a bottleneck in the case of heavy messaging traffic. As a result, a number of vendors have added load-balancing functionality to address these performance problems.

Enterprise Service Bus

The term Enterprise Service Bus (ESB) refers to second-generation middleware technology that offers the functionality provided with MOM but without requiring a centralized message server. Like MOM, ESBs can operate across a broad variety of operating systems and hardware environments and provide a means of authorizing, authenticating, and auditing the use of the system. However, as illustrated in Figure 4.4, most ESB products, unlike MOM, do not have a centralized integration broker; rather they act like their name—a bus that "drives" across the network with messages moving freely on and off, depending upon the rules that are used to define the behavior of the ESB runtime on each host. Moreover, whereas most MOM vendors have their

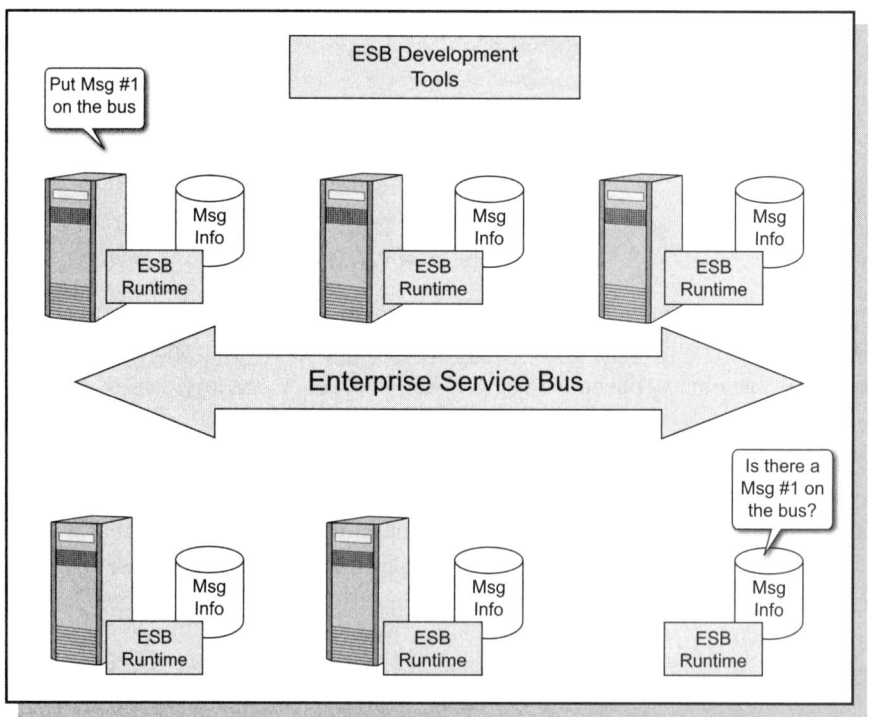

Figure 4.4 The Enterprise Service Bus

own proprietary APIs, most ESB vendors opted to use emerging web service standards and XML for communication. This strategy not only allows them to benefit from the web service support now included as part of many operating systems, but also facilitates integration because most packaged application vendors now support XML as well as their previously proprietary APIs.

The Benefits of an ESB

As you can see from comparing Figures 4.2 and 4.4, the architecture of ESB products has three advantages over that of MOM products:

- They don't rely on an integration broker that can become a performance bottleneck or constitute a point of failure if its server went offline.
- They use XML rather than a proprietary message format, so it is easier to "plug in" new applications and databases because most vendors have XML versions of their APIs. However, custom adapters are often required to accommodate differences in the representation and/or semantics of data.
- ESBs also support a more dynamic integration architecture in that developers for each application can decide which messages to send and which to receive, as opposed to having someone identify all the participating hosts and applications to a central integration broker.

The Drawbacks of an ESB

Although the architecture of ESB products offers an improvement over that of MOM products, they have several limitations:

- Although they provide a robust infrastructure for the near real-time communication between applications that are internal to an organization, the fact that they require a proprietary runtime makes them unsuitable for communicating with applications that are external to an organization, as is required by many e-commerce applications.
- They can be difficult to scale—in both configuration and performance—as the number of applications, hosts, and messages increases.
- It can be difficult to build systems that guarantee reliability and uptime because a single node failure can have significant adverse effects

(for example, when an application is waiting on a message from a host that has gone down).

- They offer limited support for data transformation. Because ESB products use XML, customers can use the Extensible Stylesheet Language Transformations (XSLT) to translate between XML documents. However, this standard is more for the reorganization of XML hierarchies and the utilization of different tags; it does not support complex logic like *if...then...else* or the arithmetic expressions and string manipulation functions often required to correlate data values stored in different applications.

4.5 Enterprise Application Integration (EAI)

The term *enterprise application integration* has been used to refer to the type of event-driven execution paradigm enabled by MOM and ESB products. There are a large number of vendors in this space ranging from large enterprise software providers like IBM (WebSphere MQ) and Oracle to companies like TIBCO and Sonic that focus predominantly on application integration. EAI products enable the *secure and efficient transport* required for integrating applications in near real-time without requiring any modifications to the applications themselves. This *loose coupling* allows the applications to operate as if they are standalone. However, because these products require proprietary runtimes, EAI products are closed systems and not suitable for use in application environments where some applications are external to the organization, as in the case of an electronic trading network.

In the following section we will examine service-oriented architecture (SOA), the next generation of real-time communication architectures that promises to address these limitations by using the Internet for transport, XML for data representation, and a *publish and subscribe* model for communication.

4.6 Service-Oriented Architecture (SOA)

Growing out of work done for DARPA (the U.S. Defense Advanced Research Projects Agency) in the late 1960s, the Internet was based on the concept of an "open network architecture" that passed packets of information by means of a meta-level "internetworking architecture" rather than transferring binary data at the level of circuits (Leiner et al, 2003). Using the original ARPANET (Advanced Research Projects Agency Network), HTTP (Hypertext Transfer Protocol), and HTML (Hypertext

Markup Language) as a base, the Internet grew dramatically because of this open architecture. Because the Internet was in large part originally envisioned as a mechanism for allowing researchers to collaborate, the model for communication was to facilitate communication through logical domain names that were "published" and could be accessed by anyone.

The *publish and subscribe* paradigm has evolved to encompass what is called service-oriented architecture (SOA). As illustrated in Figure 4.5, in the most ambitious vision for this architecture general purpose software components are seen as services (available from "servers," which may or may not be installed on separate hardware) that can publish their services in something comparable to the Yellow Pages of a phone directory. Developers—or applications—are able to look up a particular set of available services under a heading, much like you would look up the available plumbers in an area by looking under the heading "Plumbing." The Java programming language was designed to be hardware-independent so that "applets" could actually be downloaded to a host as part of the process in the case that some runtime was necessary to enable an application to use the service.

Four web service standards are critical for supporting this vision:

- *XML (Extensible Markup Language, discussed in Chapter 3)*—A text-based language for communication of messages

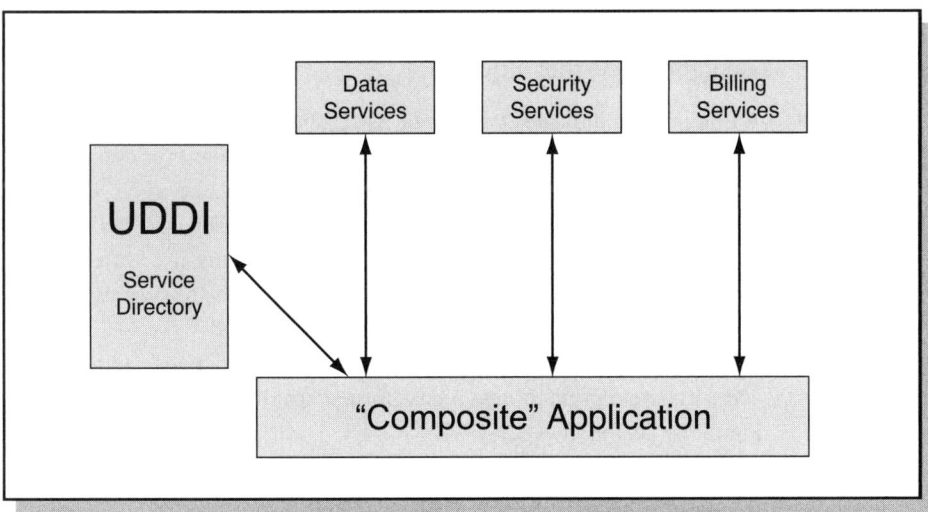

Figure 4.5 Service-Oriented Architecture (SOA)

- *SOAP (Simple Object Access Protocol)*—A protocol for exchanging XML-based messages/documents over a network
- *UDDI (Universal Description, Discovery, and Integration)*—A standard for building an XML-based registry for the purpose of defining services that are available over the Internet
- *WSDL (Web Service Definition Language)*—A standard for describing how to interface to a web service

Ebusiness depends upon interoperability, and because the growth of ebusiness is likely to bring greater revenue to the major vendors of hardware and software, there is considerable support for these standards. Organizations like OASIS (Organization for the Advancement of Structured Information Standards), a not-for-profit global consortium working to establish standards for ebusiness, advocate the establishment of a global registry for businesses worldwide. Whether or not this concept is practical, an XML registry is critical to the success of an SOA.

Each service definition in the registry takes the form of an XML document expressed in a dialect of XML called Web Service Definition Language (WSDL) that contains three types of information:

- A logical definition of the service that consists of the name of the *operation* (e.g., geographic coordinates) and a *message* that describes the data that is being communicated
- Information regarding the class of operations to which this entry belongs called a *port type* (e.g., GIS or geographic information system)
- Binding information that includes:

  - A binding that indicates the *type* of XML document that contains the tags being used. For example, XSD is an XML standard for defining schemas so if the *type* in a WSDL document is declared to be XSD, the calling application can use an internal look-up table for XSDs to understand what the tags mean (much like systems use different tables for character translation in moving between the representation of different languages).
  - A binding that correlates between a logical *port,* a network address, and a concrete protocol and a data format specification for interfacing to the host in question.

As you can see, there is a significant learning curve for developers to become conversant with all the dialects of XML; on the other hand, because XML has been so widely embraced—and because the same standard can be used for both structured and unstructured (e.g., textual) data—the effort of XML-enabling an organization's applications is likely to bring long-term benefit, unlike some other standards initiatives.

Benefits of SOA

A number of things are very appealing about SOA. Like EAI products, SOA provides a noninvasive approach to integration that not only is beneficial when one does not have access to the source code for applications, but also is less likely to adversely affect their performance or stability. However, SOA has four major advantages over EAI products:

- SOA does not require a proprietary runtime on every host, and thus the same infrastructure can be used for both internal services and those provided by external partners in ebusiness scenarios such as electronic exchange.
- The XML registry or directory of services supports a more dynamic architecture because applications—whether internal to the organization or external to it—can query it to determine if new services are available.
- Web service standards are in widespread use and generally operate with efficiency.
- Once they have been given XML wrappers, legacy applications (e.g., those running on mainframes against COBOL files) become assets as valuable and flexible as newer applications that were built on XML.

Of course, XML is still evolving to address issues like the representation of database transactions. Although the level of interest in SOA promises that this standard will emerge quickly—in part because large vendors are likely to sell a lot of hardware and software—there are still some issues about how effectively XML will scale across companies and industries. We will address this problem in some detail in Chapter 6, which deals with semantics and the representation of meaning.

Areas for Discovery with SOA

Although the benefits of SOA that were outlined are appealing, there are a number of areas of concern about whether this architecture can be used to build mission-critical composite applications:

- The granularity of services
- Defining functionality in "unbounded" environments

- Testability
- Security and governance
- Management (e.g., version control, audit)
- The scope and performance of XML

Because the methodology for using SOA architecture to support integration across an enterprise is still immature, the following should be considered as areas for further research. Products and techniques may be developed to address these issues, but they are not yet available. Until they are, it would be advisable to focus these initiatives on targeted, well-understood application areas.

Granularity

As we have discussed previously, one of the major motivations in the development of software technology is providing greater productivity through reuse. Until recently, productivity products have been tied to particular functional domains, each of which supports a fixed set of environments—for example, a graphics package that operates on UNIX and Windows systems. As a result, before a programmer could benefit from the capabilities of a productivity tool, he or she first had to understand its functional domain, internal organization, and APIs. In an SOA environment, all available services are published in a registry in a format that is neutral with respect to the specifics of the location and type of the host on which it is installed, and the semantic definition of what a service does is contained within the XML document. A developer can invoke a service that exists on a totally different kind of platform—including potentially proprietary hardware—and because XML provides a neutral exchange format, use the results as if the service were local. SOA advocates envision developers of the future using SOA to speed the development of applications (called *composite* applications because of their loosely coupled architecture) that are able to utilize services regardless of the technical platform or internal data model. In fact, because the calls in the composite application are essentially logical, a superior service could be used as it became available without having to change the application at all.

What is unclear is how granular a service should be. If a service is so granular that it must be invoked frequently like a remote procedure where the application must wait on the response—as in the case of data transformation or graphics—it is not clear whether an acceptable level of performance is possible. In fact, it is not even clear how one could regulate access to ensure that the capacity of a service would not be overwhelmed without adding a layer of administrative overhead to web services that would significantly compromise the simplicity of the architecture.

Defining Functionality in "Unbounded" Environments

The dynamic nature of an SOA environment leads to an even more subtle problem with designing applications—the fact that a developer must design and implement services with only partial information about how they will be used. Software design typically begins with a description of the desired functionality, so this is in many ways counterintuitive to most software designers. If the domain for a service is highly specialized (e.g., providing geographic coordinates, three-dimensional drawings, or maps, such as with Google's Earth COM API) then it is relatively easy to define the functionality a service can provide because it is fairly limited in terms of semantics. However, if the domain is something that covers a broad range of capabilities (e.g., data transformation) then the situation is much less clear because often the information required to define the desired results may be itself unbounded. (Consider an *if . . . then . . . else* example where multiple table look-ups are involved as well as operations against the data values to perform math or string manipulation.)

Likewise, because services can utilize other services, it is difficult to understand when some change to an underlying service might adversely affect some other service that depends on it. In short, "With modern systems development and the need to develop complex systems of systems, most systems are no longer 'closed'; rather they are 'unbounded' because they involve an unknown number of participants or otherwise require individual participants to act and interact in the absence of needed information" (Fisher & Smith, 2004).

Consider the case where a service is implemented in such a way that it has a side effect on some aspect of the computing environment that is not reflected in its entry in the service registry; for example, it might open a pipe or a cache on behalf of the application that invoked it. If the calling application had some bug that caused it to abort and restart, then over time the service might reach some threshold and no longer be able to accept service requests. Over time a set of best practices will undoubtedly develop that will define what should constitute a service, but until that time, it will be very difficult to debug composite applications.

Some vendors like Computer Associates have recognized these potential problems and are offering web services products that include monitors that allow developers to drill down into the interplay between services in a problem situation, but these capabilities help remedy a problem once it has appeared, as opposed to the way one designs applications in a closed environment, where problems can be anticipated and logic created to prevent them from occurring.

Testability

The non-deterministic nature of an SOA environment also makes it difficult to test applications. Because one cannot guarantee that the same sequence of service invocations will occur every time an application is executed, it is difficult if not impossible to prove that a program or service has not had some unintended and detrimental side effect. In complex event-driven systems where applications are pushing messages on a queue or service bus and the system is closed, it may be computationally impossible to test every path, but with visibility into the feeder-consumer relationships provided by the proprietary runtime of an EAI product, one has a better chance of designing tests that provide a reasonable approximation of the various sequences of messages that could be received by any application participating in the integration environment. Because the service registry can be dynamically modified, testability is even more compromised by an SOA architecture.

It is not possible to anticipate all potential error conditions in an unbounded system, so the best way to alert the system administrator that some service may be amiss would be to add services one at a time and create a set of regression tests that properly processes data. It is then possible to create a utility that automatically runs the tests and compares the results against the validated results every time a new service is added to the registry or an application is added to the environment. If no discrepancies appear, then at least you have some assurance that the new service or application hasn't broken anything that was working before.

Security and Governance

One of the most appealing aspects of SOA is the ability to dynamically modify the services available with minimum impact on existing applications. However, organizations are responsible for the security and behavior of their mission-critical applications. As a result, they have well-defined guidelines for system access and the management of source code, which must be applied to the addition or upgrade of services to the UDDI in an SOA environment. In particular, services that are provided by organizations and/or individuals that are external to the organization must be considered reliable. Because services can themselves be made up of services, it is not clear what type of review process can be used to ensure that policies for security and governance have been followed.

Management (Version Control, Audit)

Almost all system software products maintain some type of log of activity for the purpose of recovery and audit. Vendors often provide access to these logs either by documenting their format and contents or by providing some kind of API, thereby allowing developers or other software vendors to utilize this information to support such things as changed data capture. In environments where an organization has standardized on a particular set of products (e.g., a standard DBMS, operating system, email provider, etc.), it is possible for the system administrator(s) to utilize these logs for back-up and recovery, as well as any documentation required for the purpose of audit. How this type of activity can be maintained in an SOA environment is unclear because there may be less visibility into the behavior of components in composite applications—and even if there was total visibility, the potential complexity of configuring and maintaining these procedures becomes staggering unless the organization significantly restricts the types of services it allows and publishes.

The Scope and Performance of XML

As discussed previously, XML is a file-based language for the description and transmission of both metadata and data. In the early days of computing, data files were complex because developers were trying to conserve disk space; in contrast, XML files are extremely verbose, and are even more so once they are parsed into memory. For example, a 1-megabyte XML file can expand to 8 megabytes when parsed into memory for an XML application. Finally, interoperability with XML depends upon a common understanding of arbitrary tags with little or no support from system software. To appreciate what this means, consider the following. Once you have defined a schema to a relational DBMS, the data/query manager will ensure the integrity of that schema so that no one can, for example, write the wrong type of data value to a particular field. Although there may be XML parsers that can flag certain tags as not part of some standard schema, the validation of the data values provided is left to the application writer. The WDSL describing a service serves as a contract, whereby the service provider must be "trusted" to deliver what he promises. Developers are typically trustworthy people, but they do make mistakes, and XML schemas can be large and complex requiring developers to accurately maintain the semantics for values associated with hundreds if not thousands of tags.

**Topic of Interest: Business Process Management
and Business Activity Monitoring**

The documentation of the data interfaces between applications has always been a problem because most interfaces were at least partially hand-coded and therefore dependent upon programmers' commitment to and accuracy in the process of documentation. Even with the most disciplined staff, the question of where to store the documentation so it could be readily accessed made it difficult to ensure that one had all the information needed to understand the relationships between data elements in different databases. As long as data integration was predominantly batch, however, one didn't need to worry as much about data integrity because batch programs were scheduled to run when both the source and target systems were at a consistent state and IT was responsible for scheduling the jobs. The situation is less clear-cut in event-driven execution protocols that operate at the level of transaction where updates are asynchronous, because one cannot predict in what order and from what source an update may originate.

For example, consider the case where a company has a policy where it does not recognize revenue until it has shipped product, and there are five different applications from which orders can originate: a telephone call center, a mail center, a website, a reseller, and a brick and mortar store. In the batch world, five interfaces might be written to extract orders from each of the five source applications. IT would then be responsible for scheduling each of these jobs, and therefore there would be a single point of contact responsible for ensuring that the orders were sent to the shipping application rather than the general ledger. In the case of using an EAI product, there is nothing to keep a developer from making a mistake and creating a message for the general ledger as well as the shipping application, and because there may be 250 or 300 messages being handled by the EAI product, the error will be hard to detect.

In recognition of this type of problem, two new types of software products have appeared. Business process management (BPM) products provide a graphical interface that allows a company to capture a representation of the workflow that should be followed in integrating data from different systems if the corporate policies are being followed. Business activity monitoring (BAM) products monitor the runtime IT environments and report on business activity and flag discrepancies. At the current time, these products operate in limited environments, but their very presence indicates that the industry recognizes a functional hole in current application integration solutions.

4.7 Trends and Tradeoffs

As communication technology has become more powerful, it has enabled new models for interaction between humans and computers. In the event-driven protocol enabled by EAI products, applications operate like agents with at least one component running continuously. On the other hand, with SOA—as is often the case in the history of software technology—what we see is a cycle, where functional characteristics that were once discarded in favor of a new vision come back into fashion in another environment. For example, the earliest standalone applications operated independently of all other applications using their own proprietary persistent representation of data. In some ways, therefore, a service is analogous to a standalone application because it shares no context with any other application except for its XML interface (i.e., the parameters used to invoke it).

In some ways, there are only three differences between SOA and the hand-coded interfaces illustrated in Figure 4.6, shown also in Chapter 1, page 7:

1. The fact that in SOA the registry serves as a repository that documents what a service (application) does and how to call it.

2. The fact that the programmers use a standard protocol for invoking all services (applications) while the details of transport and access are handled via web services.

3. Services do not share state or persistent data, whereas hand-coded interfaces may.

In both scenarios, hand-coding is still required (i.e., to wrap legacy applications and to perform data value transformations that fall outside the scope of XSLT) although it is significantly reduced in an SOA environment.

Of course, the three differences given here make the two types of integration significantly different. Hand-coded spaghetti interfaces are extremely difficult to maintain; the logical layer for defining services to a common registry should make SOA

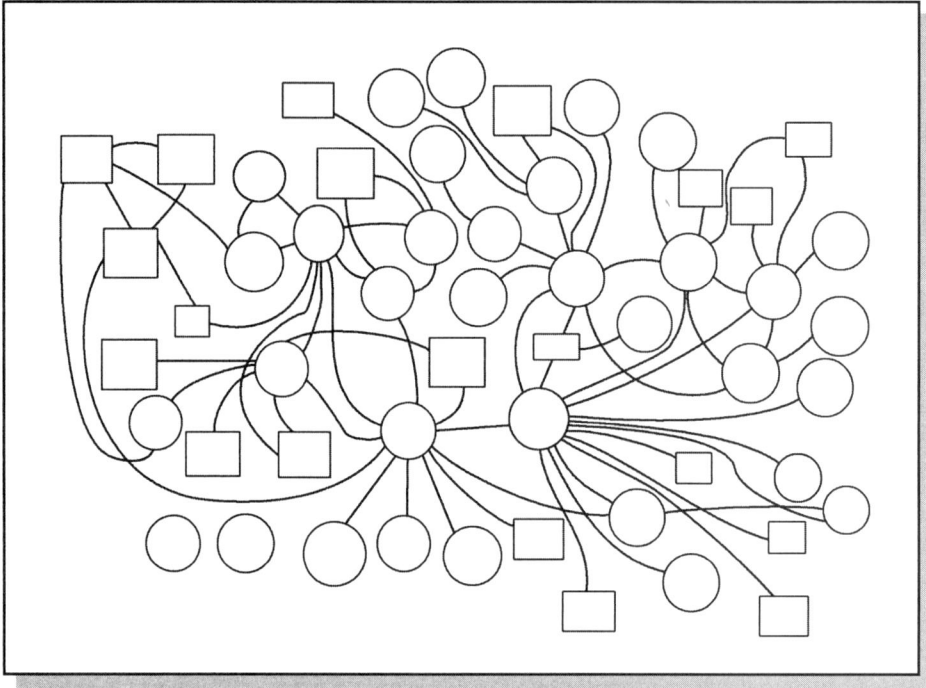

Figure 4.6   A Typical Data Bridge Diagram

architectures easy to maintain and evolve. Nevertheless, this kind of analogy can be extremely valuable because it can provide insights about the problems that some new architecture may encounter. There are at least two similarities that bear serious consideration:

- One of the problems with spaghetti integration is that it provides no visibility into the relationships between data elements. While in an SOA environment the registry externalizes the data elements that a service understands, unless the product producing the XML service calls can correlate those elements with data elements in the underlying data model used by the application to which it serves as an interface, there is a similar lack of visibility.

- Because the registry can be dynamically updated, it is possible that the sequence of specific service calls will differ across different runs of the same composite application.

Both of these limitations suggest that maintaining SOA environments may be significantly more complex than anticipated.

As a software designer, it is important that you learn to anticipate these types of problems before you encounter them, or you are likely to design and implement something that doesn't work. Note that these potential problems don't mean that you should not make use of these newer technologies and execution protocols. Rather, it is important that you recognize the potential shortcomings and devise some means of minimizing their impact. We will come back to some of these topics at later points in the book. In the meantime, the following exercises should help you determine the most promising types of applications for these new technologies.

Exercises for Chapter 4

1. For each of the following application examples, choose and justify the appropriate execution/communication protocol (e.g., batch synchronization between files/databases, a client/server model with a shared database, event-driven, MOM, ESB, SOA). Justify your answer.

   a. Searching for information about some topic of interest
   b. Withdrawing money from an ATM machine
   c. Multiple stores ordering products from the same supplier
   d. Coordinating a sales transaction between departments like Sales and Shipping within the same store
   e. Keeping two different files/databases within the same company in sync within one day of each other
   f. Keeping two different files/databases within the same company in sync within minutes of each other

2. Describe an application where a publish/subscribe model would work well. Explain.

3. Describe an application where a publish/subscribe model would not work well. Explain.

CHAPTER

5

The Evolution of Application Development

In Chapter 4, we discussed how the evolution of network technology affected application architecture and the benefits and drawbacks of the different execution protocols that it enabled. In this chapter, we will consider the evolution of applications from another point of view, including:

- The granularity of the application itself in terms of what it does and how many organizations within an enterprise can use it
- The software productivity products and methodology used to build it
- The skills and personnel required to implement and support it

What we will see is that as the scope and complexity of applications have increased, a greater part of their functionality—for example, display, data storage, and/or communication—has become externalized in that this functionality is achieved through system software products. However, what we will also see is that although this trend may have provided greater productivity to the individual programmer, it has added complexity and cost to the overall process of maintaining application systems. In fact, we will argue that there is really *no way to make the complex simple*—that *simplicity achieved in one area is always accompanied by increased complexity in another.* Relational database management systems made database creation, maintenance, and access significantly simpler at the cost of making both the process of data modeling and database design more complex and database processing more compute-intensive.

In short, particularly in the interactions between humans and computers, there seems to be a principle of *conservation of complexity*—what is complex in digital representation and computation can only be simplified at the expense of what is explicitly represented. Rather than justifying this principle at this point, let's propose an abstract model of what constitutes a computer application and then consider how the changing scope and nature of applications across the five major eras in software have affected that model. Once we see this principle at work, we will develop some guidelines about trends and tradeoffs that you can use in evaluating proposed architectures in your future work.

5.1   A Model for the Application and Its Environment

There are eight major aspects of a computer application—three that pertain to the platform against which the application is implemented, three with the code that is internal to the operation of the application, and two with the environment in which the application operates and must be maintained.

The Platform:

1. *Configuration*—The effort and skills required to define the environment in which the application runs and/or tune the application to behave appropriately in the desired environment. For example, most commercial off-the-shelf (COTS) applications have a rich set of options ranging from currency to report formats that must be specified before deploying the application.

2. *Control*—The execution protocol for the application (i.e., manually invoked, scheduled, event-driven/triggered, publish-and-subscribe). In the case of scheduled applications a developer may need to write a script or JCL (Job Control Language), whereas an event-driven architecture might require that the developer create one or more database triggers to invoke an application at the appropriate time(s).

3. *Communication*—The mechanism(s) by which the application communicates with external entities—for example, a human to a peripheral or other applications or services that may or may not reside on the same host.

The Application Itself:

4. *Context*—The input and data environment(s) required for the application; that is, the data required for it to successfully execute.

5. *Constraints*—The conditions under which some computation should or should not take place.

6. *Computation*—The actual manipulation of data values to produce the desired result.

The Environment:

7. *Confirmation/correctness*—The ability to test and validate that the application will perform correctly without unexpected side effects.

8. *Conversion*—The relative ease with which one can modify and maintain the application.

What we will find as we consider how application architecture has evolved across the five eras of software is a blurring of both the distinction between a function and an application and the distinction between programming and configuration/integration. We will also see how these changes have required significant changes to

Topic of Interest: System Software vs. Application Software

Compilers are productivity tools that allow programmers to use a programming language to describe a logical view of persistent data and a high-level description of sequential operations against data stored in that logical view. Programming languages contain constructs that represent actions (e.g., +, -, READ, WRITE) or control structures (e.g., GOTO, PERFORM...UNTIL...) and have a fixed meaning, but there are no objects inherent to the language. The program is compiled into machine language. Although programmers were able to create external functions—that is, compiled functions that could be reused by multiple programs—the functions were stateless in the sense that they kept no persistent data.

System software, on the other hand, is software that provides greater productivity to programmers by providing them with a set of functions that operate against a set of related (often persistent) data objects in order to eliminate the need for programmers to understand the details of hardware. Database management systems were the first instance of *system software* that occurred above the level of the operating system. The purpose of an operating system is to provide users (or applications, which are a form of user) with a high-level means of interacting with the computer and its peripheral hardware. Operating systems allow programmers to manipulate users, directories, printers, and disks. Database management systems allow programmers to define data objects that represent meaningful artifacts of their work and the relationships between them in such a way that this data can be used by multiple programs/users for multiple purposes. Similar definitions can be given for system software products that manipulate graphics, communication, interaction with the Web, and so on.

Applications can be written without any system software; in fact, the earliest telemetry applications for the space program were coded in binary. The distinguishing characteristic of application software is that it provides an organization with a set of operations and persistent data objects that represent the processes for a functional unit of an organization (e.g., finance, materials resource planning, logistics).

the methodology used to develop software. This evolution is the result of the development of more and more powerful types of system software. However, we will see that although these products can speed the development of an individual application, they have actually complicated the tasks of confirmation (test) and conversion (maintenance).

The Age of the Standalone Application

As we discussed previously, the earliest business applications were developed internally, hard-coded for a particular environment, and performed a relatively limited set of tasks. For example, data entry clerks in shipping might enter orders by means of a simple screen-based interface, and on a monthly basis a billings application might compute and generate bills. When the company received a check, another data entry clerk would enter the payment into an accounting package used to create financial reports for management.

With standalone applications, an individual developer was free to design his or her own file format. At that time the capabilities of hardware were limited and the cost of hardware was high, so there was a considerable effort to be efficient in the use of disk space and computing power. Therefore, it was not unusual to see numeric and/or binary codes for data values like state rather than less efficient string values. The application was in control of both input and output, so confirmation (testing) was relatively easy because programmers only needed to worry about boundary conditions like exceeding a maximum number of tables or files, provided that they included checking the data input through application screens. As illustrated in Figure 5-1,

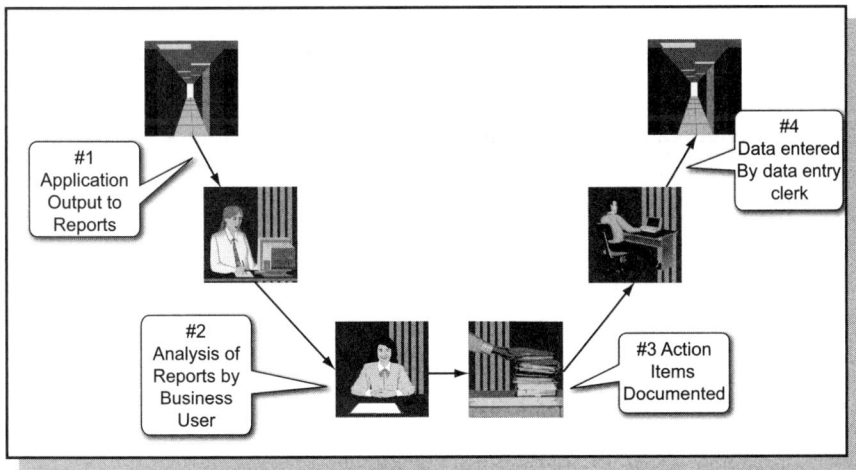

Figure 5.1 Data Integration During the Age of the Standalone Application

when companies wanted to exchange data between applications, they typically wrote a program that extracted the desired data, ran in batch, and initially wrote the data to tape, using "sneaker net" to transfer data between applications. At this point the application development environment was relatively simple, consisting of a compiler (most often COBOL for business applications) and the capabilities afforded by the JCL provided by the computer's operating system that allowed a program to be invoked in batch or transaction mode.

The Origins of Software Engineering

Over time organizations began to formalize their process for application development so that by the beginning of the age of the database, programmers typically used what is called a *waterfall* methodology, a concept first introduced by Winston Royce in 1970. In this methodology the development of an application was seen as a sequential set of processes where each phase had to be completed before the other began. The process included the following phases:

- Analysis of functional requirements to determine what the application needed to do. The deliverable from this phase was a functional specification that described how the application would appear to the user(s).
- Design. Deliverables from this phase included:

  - A design specification that included a definition of the underlying data structures (or later the database design) and a description of each of the functional components of the application and the interfaces for invoking them
  - A development schedule that included the order in which the components would be implemented, integrated, and tested

- Development, where the deliverable was source code and a running application.
- Unit test, where the deliverable was a set of tests and (perhaps) a set of correct results.
- Integration testing, where the deliverable was a set of tests and (perhaps) a set of correct results.
- System test. Deliverables from this phase included:

  - A test plan that described the tests to be performed
  - Test results

In terms of the preceding model, the important point to note is that the bulk of the functionality of the application was the result of the execution of the source code written by the development team—that is, the context (creating and manipulating the data file and input parameters), the constraints (testing for boundary conditions), and the computation (the actual manipulation of the input parameters and persistent data from the file to produce new data). Although over time an IT organization might develop external functions to perform some type of computation that was needed across programs, none of the functionality was provided by third-party system software products.

The Age of the Database

A New Process: Database Design

In the earliest application of database technology, the database management system (DBMS) simplified the task of designing and implementing an application by handling all the details of data storage, validation, and access. However, as we saw in Chapter 3, database management systems required a significant amount of training to understand which options to choose in the process of designing the database to provide the desired functionality and performance. As a result, most companies had at least one individual designated as the database administrator, who was a key part of the design process. In the case of navigational systems, these individuals were typically programmers because they had to understand the implications of different types of pointers in order to design the database, just as programmers had to understand them in order to write programs that "walked" the database.

These skills were not helpful in the design of relational databases, which required a type of analysis called normalization, a process of analysis whose goal is to produce a set of table definitions related by key values that minimizes redundant data values and avoids query results with data anomalies. Normalization was typically performed by data modelers, some of whom were not programmers. The process of normalization requires database modelers to first define all the functional dependencies between data—a time-consuming and error-prone process in the case of complex data environments—and then to apply a number of algorithms to determine what they believe will be an acceptable design. Unfortunately, these algorithms are nondeterministic because they can result in more than one solution, so there is some element of "art" or judgment in deciding on the optimal database design for a particular organization's environment.

However, highly normalized database designs can be extremely inefficient because to answer some queries the DBMS query manager would have to perform a large number of joins between tables. As a result, developing the data model for a relational database also involved understanding the types of queries that different groups were likely to make against the data to do their jobs. Once the data modeler had consolidated this information, the database administrator would relax the rules for normalization to come up with a design that would perform adequately. This process was sufficiently difficult that whole consulting organizations like Yourdon and Database Associates were established to provide training and services in this area. But over time these techniques became so well understood that software tools were developed to help automate the process of migrating a legacy schema to a relational one. Computer-aided software engineering (CASE) products like IEW and ADW from KnowledgeWare or IEF from Texas Instruments were developed. These products imported the schemas used by the legacy network or hierarchical databases and provided a graphical interface to assist the data modeler in designing the schema for the new relational database.

The Effect of Database Technology on Development Methodology

In the early days of the database era, the waterfall methodology still prevailed, so development teams labored under the impression that they shouldn't begin implementing applications until the design of the database schema was complete. The productivity and improved data integrity afforded by DBMS technology required that applications share the same database in order to simplify data consistency. The result of this thought process was that the first phase of most strategic IT initiatives was the task of developing a logical data model. This was a task that could take 10 or 12 people in a large organization because of the need to interview a large number of application users. Some organizations spent years trying to define an *enterprise data model* or *common data model*—a data model that could be used to accurately represent the data required by all applications across the enterprise. It was not unusual for leaders of data modeling teams after some period of time to shake their heads and say things like "Do you know that we have 35 different representations of *customer* in this company?" The result of these multi-year efforts was often only an entity-relationship diagram of the enterprise data model that spanned two or three walls in a room.

There were three problems with making the design of a common data model a precursor to implementation:

- In a large organization it can take years to interview and analyze all the database definitions in use, during which time applications are modified and new applications are introduced that need to be accommodated by the common data model. Even worse, sometimes during that time frame the company would acquire another company, adding a whole new level of analysis to be performed—or there would be some change in regulations that would significantly affect the products or services being offered by the company.

- In the meantime, when reviewing IT budgets, management would become impatient with funding a project that after several years had not contributed any demonstrable benefit to the top or bottom line.

- People were licensing relational database management systems, but they were slow going into production. In the meantime, the applications based on navigational database technology became even more entrenched.

Many license agreements tied maintenance on corporate licenses[1] to the number and type of servers on which the software was installed, so it was in the industry's best interest to address this problem. The solution came in the form of a new methodology and a set of tools to support it. The term *rapid application development (RAD)* was introduced by James Martin, who worked at IBM. This methodology advocated rapid prototyping as a means of incrementally developing applications so that users could both see results and validate the requirements that they specified in a much more timely fashion. RAD emphasized the importance of an efficient change management cycle and recommended the use of CASE tools. These products were possible because the query manager in relational database management systems handled significantly more of the details of data storage and access than the data manager in navigational database systems. As a result, CASE tools not only could help automate the process of the database design, but also could automatically generate certain types of applications from specifications. However, although the RAD methodology and CASE products offered rich functionality, they required an organization to follow a rigorous methodology that required significantly more involvement from nontechnical people within an organization. As a result, RAD had limited success. Moreover, RAD is an incremental bottom-up approach, where a small set of functionality is implemented and tested, and then a new set of incremental functionality is implemented on top of the previous base, and so on. Although this approach is possible for something like a decision support application (for example, an application that

---

1 A corporate license is one where for some large sum, an organization could install as many copies of a product as it wanted.

provides managers with reports about sales), to be efficient and stable, some would say that more complex applications (for example, a financial trading application) need to be driven by a top-down design. In reality, the best applications are designed using a combination of both approaches.

The Effect of Database Technology on Software Applications

The effect of utilizing a DBMS in implementing an application is that the functionality of a significant portion of the application lies outside of the code written by the application developer(s). A good part of the design and development effort—the tasks of designing and implementing the database—is performed by individuals with different skills from the application developer. These efforts serve as part of configuring the application's environment and constitute separate efforts for testing (confirmation) and maintenance (conversion). In fact, because the database design is typically used by multiple applications, it may require a significant amount of performance testing under different types of loads (i.e., numbers of concurrent users and/or applications). In fact, as previously noted, because some queries can have such an adverse affect on the performance of relational DBMS, many database administrators will not let users issue ad hoc queries against the database.

Visualizing the Difference across Eras

One of our goals in comparing the impact of technology across eras is to understand the relative amount of effort that must be spent on each of the eight dimensions of our model of the application. For example, in the age of the standalone application very little effort was spent in configuring software outside the application to enable it to run. The developer merely needed to develop a JCL file that instructed the operating system when the application should be invoked and in what mode—batch or transaction-based. The bulk of the effort required to build the application was spent in writing code that defined the format of the file(s) and accessed the data in that file (context), tested any constraints on the data, and manipulated it to produce the desired result (computation). Testing and modification were relatively easy because the application was a closed system.

As illustrated in Figure 5.2, in the age of the database the amount of time spent writing the application was greatly reduced because the DBMS handled all aspects of the data storage and access, as well as ensuring that the data values met with any constraints specified at the time of database design. However, the need to consider data requirements of multiple applications to arrive at the database design greatly increased the effort spent in configuring the environment in which the application

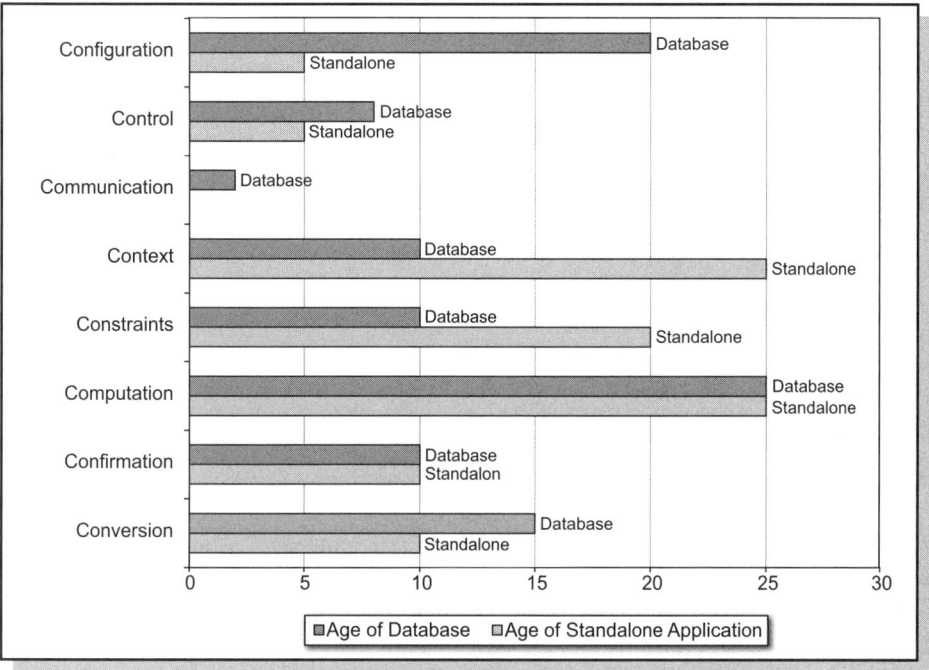

Figure 5.2   Age of the Database

would operate. Likewise, more effort was spent in establishing external controls—access rights, back-up and recovery, and the like—and because changes could potentially affect the database design as well as the application, maintenance (conversion) became somewhat more complex.

Topic of Interest: The Evolution of the Software Marketplace

As early as the late 1960s, vendors started to sell software applications for particular industries like banking and insurance. Originally they sold source code so that companies could modify the applications to meet their particular needs; the result was a support nightmare because customers had to maintain internal support staff or pay consultants to come on site to debug

(continued)

> problems. Likewise, it made it very hard for vendors to sell and implement upgrades. As a result, over time application vendors switched to selling object code. As indicated earlier, database management products originally were targeted predominantly toward companies that were developing applications internally. In the age of the network, the largest source of new sales for relational technology was application vendors who embedded the relational DBMS to manage their persistent storage.

The Age of the Network

New Types of System Software

As we discussed in the previous chapter, the advent of network technology led to the event-driven execution protocol and the concept of a three-tiered architecture for applications, where the code for the user interface, application logic, and database logic were all designed as distinct components and these components might or might not exist on the same host. This architecture led to two other types of system software products—graphical user interface (GUI) toolsets and communications software. GUI toolsets included a set of objects (e.g., window, menu, pointing device, icons, check boxes, etc.) along with a set of messages or APIs for manipulating them (e.g., draw, fill, move, etc.). Sometimes they included a graphical development environment that allowed developers to interactively define a window's layout. Communication packages included a high-level means of defining the hosts on a network, as well as a set of functions that provided programmers with a high-level means of indicating the desired communication between hosts (for example, remote file transfer or remote procedure call). As illustrated in Figure 5.3, like database technology these two types of software packages meet our previous definition of system software in that they provide a high-level language (or API) that allows programmers to ignore details about the hardware and operating systems and are able to store persistent information to enable them to re-create a particular context in an application.

New Skills and New Methodologies

These new productivity platforms allowed the development of complex applications with less code, but they had three consequences. First, because it requires a significant

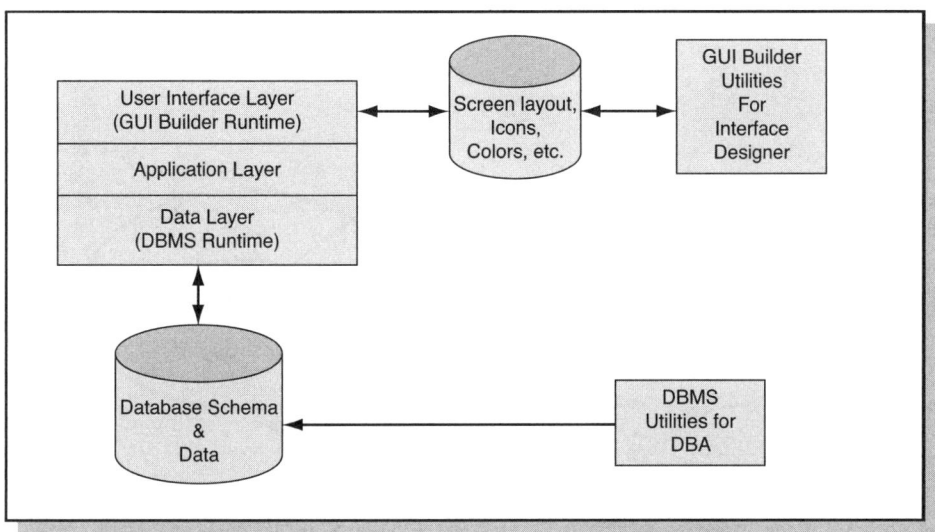

Figure 5.3   System Software and Persistent Data

learning curve to master system software products, their use led to programmers developing specialized skills so that the loss of these skills could significantly affect an organization's ability to meet an implementation deadline. Second, their use required even more thorough design up front (including explicit documentation of the APIs for the different functional subsystems) to enable programmers to work effectively in parallel. Finally, the process of testing also became more complex. With complex applications, it is important that each subsystem be thoroughly tested, since bugs are harder to detect once the subsystems have been integrated because the symptom of the problem may have nothing to do with the actual problem. Likewise, as problems are detected and fixed, it is important to be able to automatically run regression tests at the unit, integration, and system levels to ensure that the fix has not introduced another problem. As a result, a *spiral* methodology became more popular. As illustrated in Figure 5.4, with this methodology the design team has a long-term view of the functionality and a high-level design that encompasses that view. Then a meaningful subset of the core functionality is identified, designed, and implemented. Sometimes this implementation is a prototype, but more often it is something that can be used.

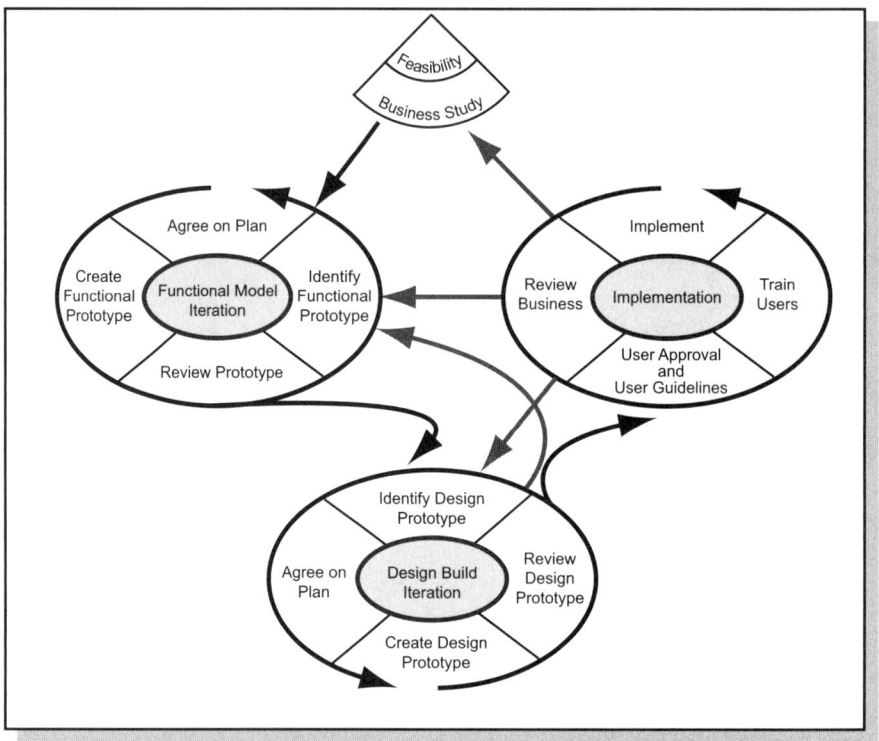

Figure 5.4   Chart Illustrating a Spiral Methodology

Like the waterfall method, a spiral methodology starts with a good understanding of the problem and goals for functionality. However, spiral methodology is inherently iterative. A detailed functional specification and design is required for each phase of the project, although the design may include "stubs" as placeholders for where code for a subsequent cycle would be inserted. The spiral methodology also assumes that earlier stages may need to be reworked when shortcomings are discovered in the design and implementation of a subsequent phase.

The Effect of Network Technology on Software Applications

One benefit of the three-tiered architecture is that the strong functional division between the tiers made it relatively easy to define unit tests. However, when multiple programmers work on a complex application using multiple productivity products (e.g., graphics, communication, database), the process of keeping different versions

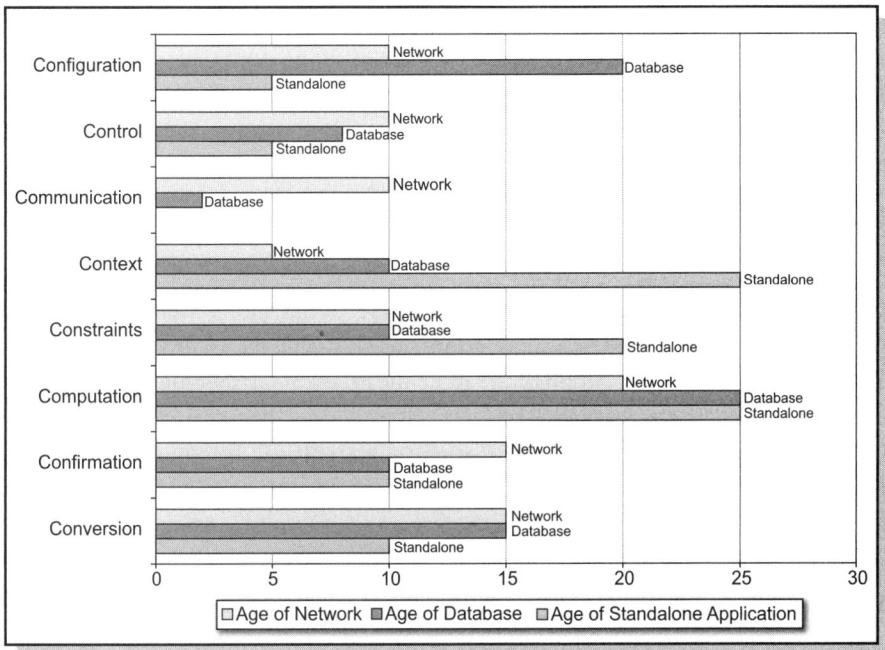

Figure 5.5   Age of the Network

of the source code in sync with the runtimes for the productivity products can be a complex task. In fact, most projects use a source control system to manage the source code and automate the builds of different versions of the application. This process is further complicated when the vendors of the productivity packages issue new releases, where they typically give a date 6–18 months out after which they will no longer provide support for the old release. As shown in Figure 5.5, in the age of the network even more of the functionality of the application falls into the external areas—configuration (database, graphics), communication, and control (as in the case when a database update "triggers" the invocation of another application).

The areas of confirmation (test) and conversion (maintenance) also became more complex with the implementation of applications based on a three-tier architecture. For example, having multiple embedded components often complicates the task of identifying the source of a problem. In fact, it is good for application designers to include debug code in the application that can be triggered by setting a flag and that traps data values that can provide clues as to the location of the bug, because most vendors of embedded runtimes require some proof that the bug is in their code before they will investigate. Likewise, releases are greatly simplified if all the tests used to validate the application before release are captured, along with their results, in a system that automates running them as regression tests that compare the two sets of results and verify that future changes do not negatively impact existing functionality.

The Move Away from Internal Development and the Effect on Integration

Standalone applications and even early database applications were designed and developed to serve the needs of a single organization within the enterprise. With client-server networks came the promise of allowing department-specific applications to share a common database. However, as already discussed, the design of the common data model for these shared databases often took significantly longer than management counted on. At the same time, software vendors were beginning to develop sophisticated applications that provided a rich set of configurable options for business functions for different industries (for example, materials resource planning for manufacturing, logistics for transportation, and claims management for insurance). Because it is costly to create and maintain internally developed applications, over time many organizations opted to stop the internal development of any application for which they could purchase a COTS package. Unlike the commercially available standalone software applications, which tended to focus on a single task (e.g., general ledger, claims processing), these applications are designed to automate the data collection and processing for a full business function like customer relationship management, where the software would be used by staff in call centers, consulting, and sales.

Although these applications provide rich and robust functionality, they are typically based on proprietary data stores because vendors do not want to make it easy for customers to migrate off their products. A number of vendors like SAP offer a full set of integrated modules for enterprise resource planning (ERP), but unless an organization opts to purchase, install, and implement all the modules, it faces a similar problem to the one it had with internally developed standalone applications. The organization will have to integrate the COTS module with its other applications, and although the data stored in these systems may be of better quality, there is no automated way of keeping related and/or equivalent data stored in multiple locations consistent, making confirmation more complex.

Topic of Interest: The Task of Integrating a COTS Application

Earlier we cited leading industry analysts as claiming that it costs four to ten times as much to implement a COTS application as to purchase it. There are several reasons for this, the first being the complexity of the applications themselves. Because a COTS application is designed to anticipate any set of options that a company might want to use, their schemas can be quite complex so that there may be 20,000–30,000 fields that must be populated.

The first task requires that the business users decide how they want the application to behave. The second is to determine how the data in the existing applications correspond to the data needed by the COTS application, including whether data values need to be modified in some way. The third is to generate or write the data interfaces required to move the data and test the results. Once the application is up and tested, any interfaces between the original application and other applications must be rewritten to interface to the COTS applications. Finally—after these interfaces have been verified—the company will need to train the users on the new application before switching over to it. This switchover process can be lengthy. In some cases, an organization may run the old and the new applications in parallel for some period of time as a final form of verification that the new application was functionally equivalent to the old.

The process of data integration in implementing a COTS application can be very error-prone and requires many iterations, but once this effort has been completed, a company spends significantly less in maintenance than with internally developed applications. However, it is important to note that different implementations of the same COTS application are not automatically interoperable just because they are based on the same product. Different choices made during the configuration processes result in differences in the way data values are represented. As a result, if two organizations want to consolidate two implementations of the same COTS package, it can take almost as much effort as if the two applications were on different technology platforms.

The Age of the Desktop

New Applications for the General User

The age of the desktop brought a new class of generic applications to the individual worker. Text editors and word processing software had been available for use on a variety of computer platforms and proprietary hardware for a number of years, but with the personal computer over time they have come to the desktops of practically every white collar worker. To fully utilize these applications takes considerable training, but the key to their success has been the fact that the conventions employed by the graphical user interface (e.g., how to utilize windows, icons [widgets], and radio buttons) are relatively easy to grasp, so the average person can be quite content using a fraction of the application's functionality. In fact, according to the Standish Group (2003), 45% of the features in typical software systems are never actually used by users, and another 19% are only rarely used.

Until now the applications we have discussed—whether proprietary or COTS—were targeted to a particular semantic domain. For example, financial applications contained logic that made them conform to standard accounting practices, insurance applications contained logic regarding claims and accidents, and so on. After the release of the Macintosh, PC software vendors developed a set of functionally rich applications for different types of common activities—word processing, complex calculations, and creating presentations. Specialized applications followed for accounting, desktop publishing, architectural design, and the like that required as much training to use as many enterprise applications, but with these generic applications the average person could learn enough basic commands to obtain some value within a matter of hours.

The Impact of the Desktop on the Organization

PC software applications were originally designed for a single user in a low security environment that allowed any data stored on the hard disk to be copied to a floppy. Even now the support that does exist for the sharing of documents is used at the discretion of the individual creating the document, although new releases of PC operating systems include features that allow PCs to be configured to better support secure, multi-user environments. However, for years many organizations did little to constrain how PCs were used. As a result, organizations now face a whole new range of problems, including:

- Nonsecure copies of confidential and proprietary information, as evidenced by the frequency of news stories describing events like the case where someone broke into the home of an administrator of the Veterans Administration and stole the personal data and Social Security numbers for 26.5 million veterans. (Fox News, 2006)
- Employees using incorrect data when they reference a local copy of a contract or spreadsheet thinking that it contains the most recent information when it doesn't.
- Local spreadsheets and documents created by individuals with PC tools that are used to manage business functions within units and divisions without the review and approval of the legal and financial organizations within the company.
- Local applications built independently by business units using PC databases like FoxPro or dbaseII. These databases can become a huge problem to consolidate because there were no standards for how data should be represented.

To understand how big a problem this can be, consider the case of a large manufacturer of PCs. After rapid growth in the United States, it began to establish distributors internationally with no thought of automating how these distributors would report sales. As a result, each distributor used or developed a distinct PC-based application. When at a later point the manufacturer started to consolidate these applications, it was a hugely expensive task, in part because new distributors were being added at a rate that was more than twice as fast as it took to migrate/consolidate the data from the proprietary database of a single distributor. In short, the use of PC applications greatly complicates the tasks of proving the correctness of financial reporting and the documentation of processes required to comply with regulations like Sarbanes-Oxley or Basel II (a set of standards for evaluating the capital adequacy of banks).

In addition, the proliferation of PCs added an enormous burden to the system administration of large organizations. First, there was the normal problem of ensuring that the use of PC software was in compliance with license agreements, as well as the need to back up disk drives for recovery in case of failure, install upgrades, and so on. Even more disruptive, there was a huge increase in the number of nontechnical users to support, and unlike the nontechnical users of interfaces to production applications, these users were not constrained by application user interfaces that limited what they could do. As a result, they could further complicate problems by trying to "fix it themselves" before calling for support.

Topic of Interest: IT and Regulatory Compliance

At the start of the decade, there were a number of accounting scandals that led to the demise of large public companies, including Enron Corporation, Tyco International, and WorldCom. Enron was probably the most dramatic of these. Before it declared bankruptcy in 2001, Enron employed 21,000 people and had been named "America's Most Innovative Company" for six consecutive years by *Fortune* magazine. The scandal was so serious that it also led to the dissolution of Arthur Andersen, Enron's accounting firm.

In an effort to prevent this kind of fraud from happening again, the U.S. Congress enacted the Sarbanes-Oxley Act of 2002 (Pub. L. No. 107-204, 116 Stat. 745, also known as the Public Company Accounting Reform and Investor Protection Act of 2002 and commonly called SOX or SarbOx). Under this law both the CEO and CFO of a public company have to certify that the company's financials are accurate and were developed in compliance with the company's documented business processes. In fact, they are at risk of criminal liability if the financial statements are incorrect. Moreover, this is not a one-time effort. Annually, the company must review and audit its processes for controls. As part of this, companies have to put in place IT controls that prove that their IT systems are in compliance with their documented business processes. Some of the key responsibilities for IT include documentation of the definition, acquisition, installation, configuration, integration, and maintenance of the IT infrastructure (IT Governance Institute, 2004, p. 23). "When management realizes the cost of compliance with the Sarbanes-Oxley Act, there will be an increasing attention on automated controls. Why document and test a daily manual control for 30 to 50 occurrences, when automated control, supported by adequate security controls and program change controls, may need to be tested only several times?" (p. 25).

The Effect of the Desktop on Software Applications

As indicated earlier, desktop applications either operated independently of production applications (as in the case of desktop publishing) or used data from production applications to serve some useful function for the business unit. Although PC applications had little direct effect on mission-critical applications, they had two major impacts on the challenges faced by IT in the age of the Internet:

1. A realization that the widespread use of computers could significantly improve the productivity of the individual and the perception that one couldn't really do one's job effectively without his or her own desktop (and even perhaps laptop). This change was nowhere more dramatic than in the offices of upper management. In the early 1980s, senior executives did not use keyboards—to do so would be beneath their stature. A decade later all but the established, old-school executives considered a laptop and email critical to their ability to do their job.

2. Although a fairly rigorous methodology was used in developing or implementing production applications, the applications created at the department level using tools like VisiCalc, Lotus 1-2-3, and Excel had no such guidelines. As a result, by the end of this era, large organizations were depending upon hundreds of reports defined with applications created by one or two users, and IT had little or no visibility into how the corporation's proprietary data was being used.

Visualizing the Difference across Eras

Although PC applications are functionally rich, they have an even more limited set of semantics than most system software. Because until recently desktop applications were used in parallel with the applications in IT, they had little effect on what it meant to create a production application; however, as illustrated in Figure 5.6, they significantly increased the complexity of system and network administration—and because the users of these applications drew their data from IT applications, their use has led to additional complications in application maintenance (conversion).

The Age of the Internet

Business users have always been impatient with the output of IT organizations, maintaining that it took too long for them to get the information they needed. With the individual productivity afforded by desktop applications, they became even more impatient. By the time the World Wide Web became available, most computer users had been using the Internet for electronic mail, mailing lists, and bulletin boards and were well aware of its advantages, namely:

- Near real-time communication, where for example on a phone call employee A can say to employee B, "I don't understand what they

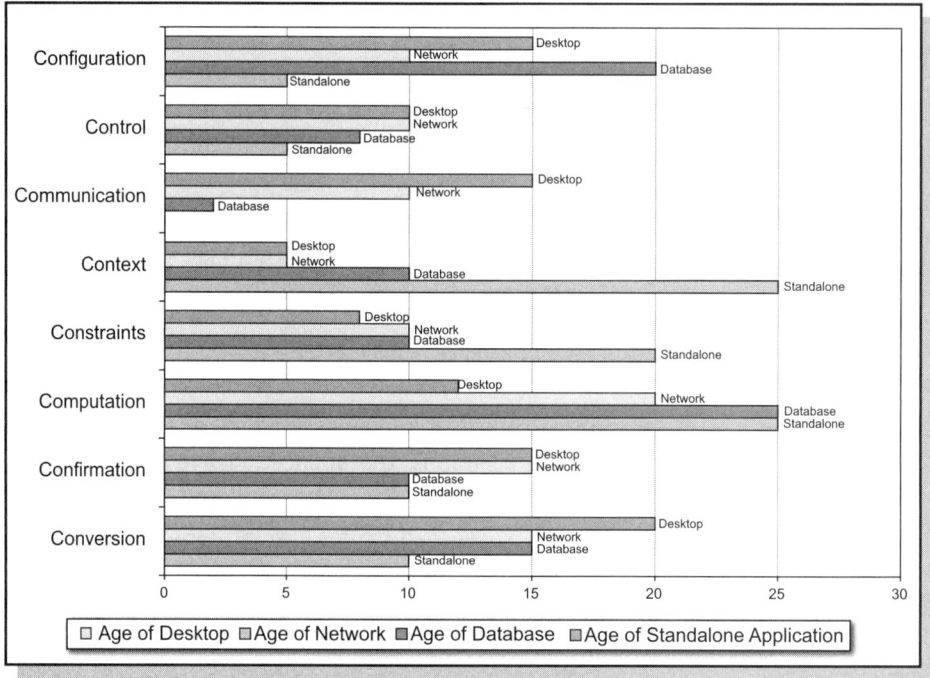

Figure 5.6 Age of the Desktop

mean regarding one of the product requirements. I just sent you the spec. Can you bring it up and look at it and tell me what you think it means?"

- The ability to reliably communicate with an individual by means of a logical (i.e., symbolic) email address.
- The ability to associate a set of email addresses with a group email address to make it easy to broadcast (or *publish*) a message to a large number of individuals. An extension of this concept was the *mailing list* that allowed individuals to add their name (or *subscribe*) to a mailing list devoted to some particular topic(s).

These high-performance/low-cost capabilities were rapidly adopted by individuals who wanted to communicate with each other because they were faster than "snail mail" and asynchronous—that is, unlike a telephone call, they offered the sender (or caller) a simple way to send an arbitrarily complex message to one or more other individuals without requiring them to "pick up the phone."

As a result, when the World Wide Web (WWW or the Web) was introduced as a global read-write information space where resources (e.g., documents, images, video) could be found via short, unique, global identifiers called Uniform Resource Identifiers (URIs), people were quick see its potential for transforming everything from commerce, education, and research to finding a mate. With a ubiquitous, low-cost way of communicating and sharing textual and graphic information came a new vision for doing business, such as virtual storefronts, just-in-time manufacturing, improved communication between healthcare providers, and remote learning.

Heterogeneity as a Fact of Life and the Rise of Middleware

Before the age of the Internet, if you asked the CIOs of most companies to list their top priorities, the goal of consolidating applications and reducing the number of hardware and software platforms would have been one of the top two or three. The motivation was primarily to reduce costs, but reducing their dependence on specialized skills and simplifying the process of implementing changes were also cited as important benefits. However, once organizations addressed their fears about the impact of the Year 2000, this goal began to diminish in priority if not importance for two reasons. First, the rate of change in business was so fast that companies simply didn't have the time to address consolidating applications. Things like the deregulation of industries (e.g., banking, telecommunications) and the advent of disruptive technology (e.g., VoIP, Voice over Internet Protocol) led to an increase in growth by merger and acquisition, which in turn increased the diversity of IT applications found in large companies. To obtain the visibility they needed to run organizations, managers opted to build data warehouses—applications that collected information from diverse operational applications on a periodic basis for the purpose of analysis and management reporting—which in turn added another layer of tools and applications to the IT environment. (We will discuss data warehousing in greater detail in Chapter 8 of this book, along with other integration-intensive application initiatives.)

But the second reason companies tended to forego application consolidation was the fact that ebusiness emerged as a new competitive threat. The Internet promised to enable vendors to enter new geographic markets, manufacturers to develop improved supply chains, and trading partners to communicate more effectively—not to mention that customers came to expect to use the Web as an alternative means of obtaining product information, conducting transactions, and accessing customer support.

The result was that although organizations still see the benefit of consolidating their IT systems in order to reduce operating costs, they have accepted the fact that their IT organizations are likely to contain heterogeneous—and often redundant—applications. As a result, one of the most pressing needs became an efficient means of synchronizing distributed, heterogeneous applications in near real-time to support ebusiness applications. EAI vendors selling message-oriented middleware (MOM) and enterprise service bus (ESB) products emerged to meet this need and were one of the most strategic purchases made by large organizations in the last half of the 1990s.

As discussed in the previous chapter, these products facilitated an event-driven execution protocol where a successfully completed transaction within one application could trigger related updates or transactions in other applications to enable the synchronization of applications in near real-time. A beneficial side effect of this architecture was that EAI tools required an explicit declaration of the interaction between applications, which provided both IT and management with a better understanding of the company's business processes than was provided by integration through batch interfaces. Moreover, MOM and ESB products kept logs of the messages sent and consumed, allowing companies to monitor their business activity and providing an audit trail of the effect of transactions for the purpose of documenting regulatory compliance.

Service-Oriented Architecture: Communicate in Real-Time through the Internet

Integrating applications using MOM and ESB products could be extremely effective within the enterprise, but they were not well-suited to communication across organizational boundaries. Web-based browsers, the earliest web-based applications, provided users with a flexible means of traversing unstructured data (e.g., text and graphics). HTML and links were augmented by search engines culminating in the type of technology provided through companies like Google. Once again, a new set of software programming skills was required—this time in HTML and XML. But creating websites—and keeping them up to date with current information about products and services—was a time-consuming and error-prone task and led to the creation of a whole new class of products for managing and updating material for the Web. Content management products from companies like Vignette or Captiva separate the visual content of a web application from the textual content to help automate the process of updating the material on websites; they include capabilities for helping designers rapidly create the layout of web pages and the links between them, as well the ability to import content from documents and databases.

Websites were initially targeted at creating virtual storefronts or providing another means to service an organization's customers. Now websites exist for everything from technical support and internal communication within an organization to sites maintained by high school students. However, the Web couldn't really deliver on

---

Topic of Interest: The "Dot Bomb"

One of the most common reasons that technical innovations fail is that the vendors and/or implementers have failed to properly assess the technical requirements of deploying the technology for some particular type of application. In most cases, the impact of these failures was limited to a small set of vendors or early adopters. For example, the limited success of object-oriented technology to deliver on its promise adversely affected only a handful of software vendors. However, this was not the case with ebusiness. Thanks to the low cost and efficiency of email, people who never used computers before became believers and could see how the Internet would transform the way business was conducted.

In part because the barrier to entry was so low that many teenagers had their own websites, the number and initial success of the "dot com" businesses founded in the period between 1997 and 2001 made certain industry leaders say that the Internet had changed the rules of business forever. In some regards this claim was true; in others, it was not. Customers still expect prompt delivery of promised goods, and unfortunately this turned out to be harder to do than B2C (business to customer) companies anticipated. Too many "virtual" storefronts couldn't provide accurate inventory or information about delivery because they had underestimated the difficulty of data integration. Some were forced to build warehouses and distribution systems, thereby losing their competitive advantage. As a result, for every amazon.com, there were hundreds of companies like garden.com and toysrus.com that went out of business—and with them many of the software providers of Internet infrastructure and hosting facilities.

---

its promise until operating systems offered robust support that allowed developers to utilize the Web in the way they designed and delivered applications. As illustrated in Figure 5.7, with the advent of the web standards discussed in Chapter 4, a whole new range of application architectures became possible.

With Simple Object Access Protocol (SOAP), communication is efficient and "free," allowing the creation of rich user interfaces with all the features users have come to expect from desktop applications on a "smart client" whose software footprint is not much larger than a traditional browser. Moreover, the application server—

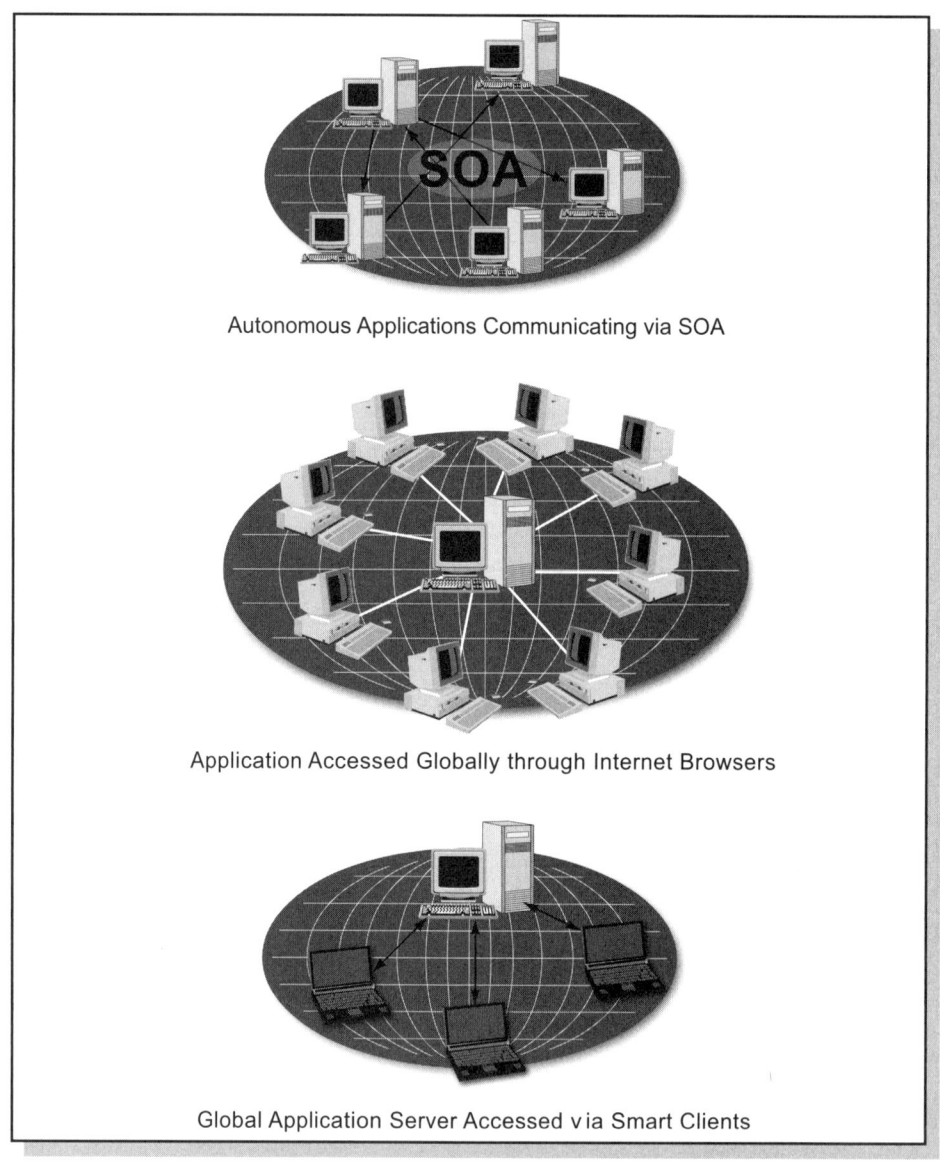

Autonomous Applications Communicating via SOA

Application Accessed Globally through Internet Browsers

Global Application Server Accessed via Smart Clients

Figure 5.7 Application Architectures Enabled by Web Services

or other servers, such as a database server—could be half a world away without adversely affecting the performance of applications. Finally, the wide adoption of Java as a platform-neutral programming language means that if necessary an application can download functional components (called applets) onto a user's desktop.

As a result, software vendors can now sell software on a service basis (a concept called "software as a service," abbreviated SaaS) rather than requiring customers to license, install, and maintain software on their site. Not only is this more cost-effective for the customer, but it has definite advantages for vendors, because by hosting their applications, they reduce their support and training costs. Rather than providing call centers for technical support, they can focus on making their user interfaces for end users more intuitive. Likewise, upgrades require minimal cost to the vendor and no effort for the customer. One of the most successful applications of this architecture is salesforce.com, an application for sales force management that allows salespeople located anywhere in the world to report their activities (e.g., new leads, status of negotiations, details about contracts) into a database that is immediately accessible by management through numerous reporting options.

In short, web services provided the technical infrastructure required to support the original vision for e-commerce by providing a standards-based means of communicating in near real-time that is widely available at extremely low cost and enabled by the Internet and the World Wide Web. The only remaining requirement was a mechanism that allowed organizations to be able to discover who was participating in the web-based interchange and in what capacity. With the UDDI (Universal Description, Discovery, and Integration) standard for building an XML registry, the architecture provides a mechanism through which developers can discover how to interface to other applications for the services they need.

SOA: The vision. In Chapter 4, we discussed the technical reasons that a service-oriented architecture (SOA) is appealing, but from a business perspective, there are also a number of benefits above and beyond enabling e-commerce, namely:

- *Reuse*—Knowledge that workers spend the bulk of their time looking for something that has already been created or—worse still—creating something that is equivalent to something that has already been created (Taylor, 1998). Because SOA has a means of creating a directory of what services are available, it becomes much easier for developers to avail themselves of what the organization already has.
- *Agility*—Because the interfaces between applications are explicitly defined and—because of reuse—there are fewer of them, it is easier to determine the impact of some proposed change (for example, a change in tax code or regulatory reporting) and modify the organization's applications to accommodate it.
- *Greater return on investment (ROI)*—By "wrapping" legacy applications so they can interface to the registry, an organization's past IT

investments can continue to bring value to the organization rather than being seen as something that complicates the organization's ability to obtain consolidated information and deploy new technology.

- *Ability to align IT with business processes*—Because it was relatively difficult to understand and change hard-coded interfaces between applications, it was often difficult to institute or enforce new business processes. The explicitly defined, reusable interfaces of SOA make it easier to make business process changes, sometimes within the SOA interface itself and therefore transparent to the calling application.

As illustrated in Figure 5.8, at the technical level, SOA promises to be the elusive, evolutionary IT infrastructure that can finally solve the problem of integration, thanks to the visibility afforded by the registry and the technology- and implementation-independence afforded by web service standards. In fact, the vision is that in the future some applications—called *composite applications*—may be created predominantly by configuring services in some unique way rather than by writing all new code. Likewise, the cost of maintenance (conversion) can be significantly reduced because the capabilities of applications can be upgraded by providing a new and superior service (for example, some superior method for compression and transmission) with no effort required on the part of the individuals maintaining the application. This ability to evolve the technology being used by an organization by creating new versions of services and adding them as alternatives in the XML registry is made possible by polymorphism (the ability to have multiple services denoted by the same name) and dynamic binding that allows the specific service being invoked to be delayed until deployment.[2]

SOA: The reality. There's a saying in software development that the last 10% of the work takes 90% of the time. SOA is no exception. A number of problems must be addressed for SOA to be successful, and many of these will require that an organization purchase or lease new software components, many of which are still relatively new to the market and may not have all the features required to support mission-critical IT systems. These include the following:

- *Common taxonomies and XML schemas*—The full vision of SOA can only be realized if it is easy for developers to discover what services

---

[2] It would be possible to write applications in an SOA environment so that they dynamically (that is, at runtime) invoked the UDDI to determine which service to invoke, but researchers in the area think that invoking an untested service would be inadvisable.

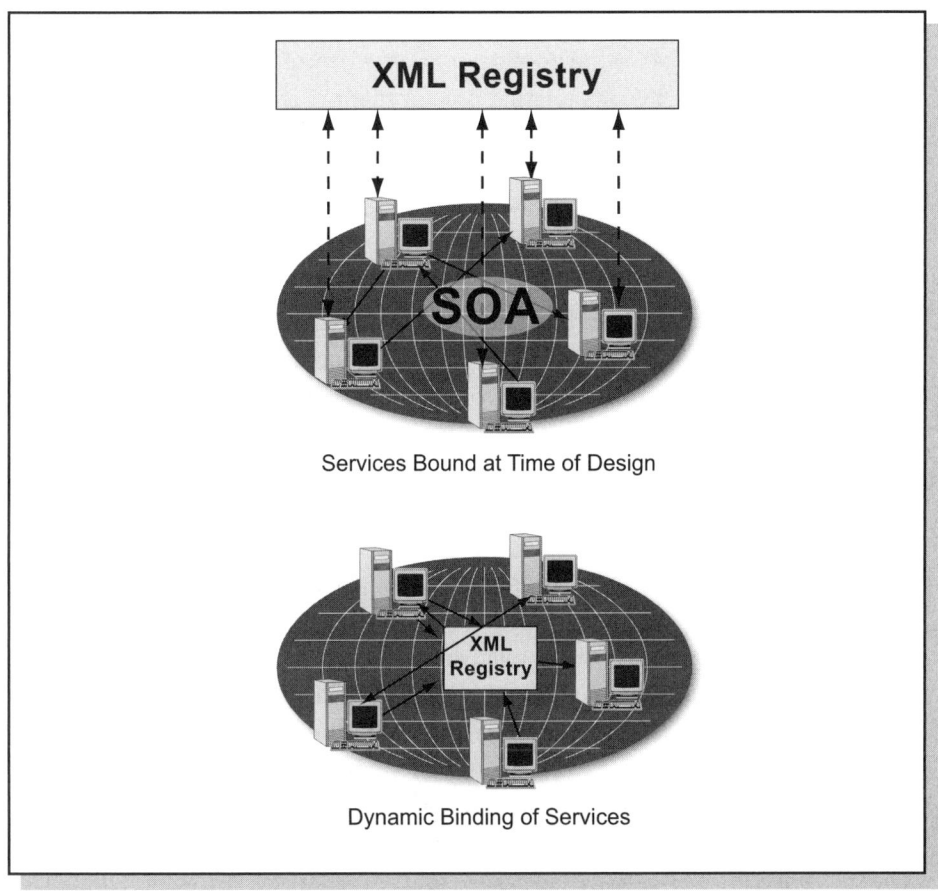

Figure 5.8 The Vision for SOA

are available as well as what they do. There are two aspects to this—
the organization of the registry and the XML schemas that are used
to define the semantic domain of the services. Registry vendors typically provide some taxonomy management functionality that helps
customers easily categorize, label, and organize services based on
business and technical priorities and requirements. These classification systems help developers discover the services that are relevant to
the application they are developing. Similarly, to simplify reuse, services should use a common XML schema to represent data values.

- *A mechanism for testing and validating services*—The vision of SOA can only be realized if the developers in an organization trust the services available to them. As a result, organizations must publish and enforce the processes they use to allow a service to be added to the registry. Most registry products include capabilities for defining and documenting the processes to be followed in the *governance* of services.

- *Security*—Particularly when an SOA environment allows services provided by third parties to participate in the registry, it must include a single sign-on service that provides the requesting service with a security token that allows the user or application access to other services for a period of time. There may also be a need for data encryption.

- *Effective change management*—When a company decides to "wrap" an existing application to create services, it will typically need to create a series of translators to interface between the application's representation of transactions and the XML schema being used as the intermediate format. Often some type of transformation function is required to modify the data values. Although the XML registry provides developers with a relatively simple way to determine which services are affected when something like a tax code or regulatory reporting requirement changes, this information will be of little use in knowing what changes might be required for the translators wrapping legacy applications unless a description of these transformations is captured in an environment that supports a similar type of impact analysis.

- *Auditability*—One of the key benefits of an SOA is its ability to incorporate new services without having to modify the application code. This fact, coupled with the fact that services can run asynchronously, means that one cannot guarantee that exactly the same sequence of events occurs every time an application is invoked. As a result, web service environments need a mechanism for monitoring and logging events as well as a means of alerting the system administrator when some policy has been violated.

As you can see in Figure 5.9 (where the triangles represent translators required to reformat/transform data), the apparent simplicity of the SOA vision becomes significantly more complex as one puts in place the components required to ensure the kind of security and reliability expected of mission-critical applications.

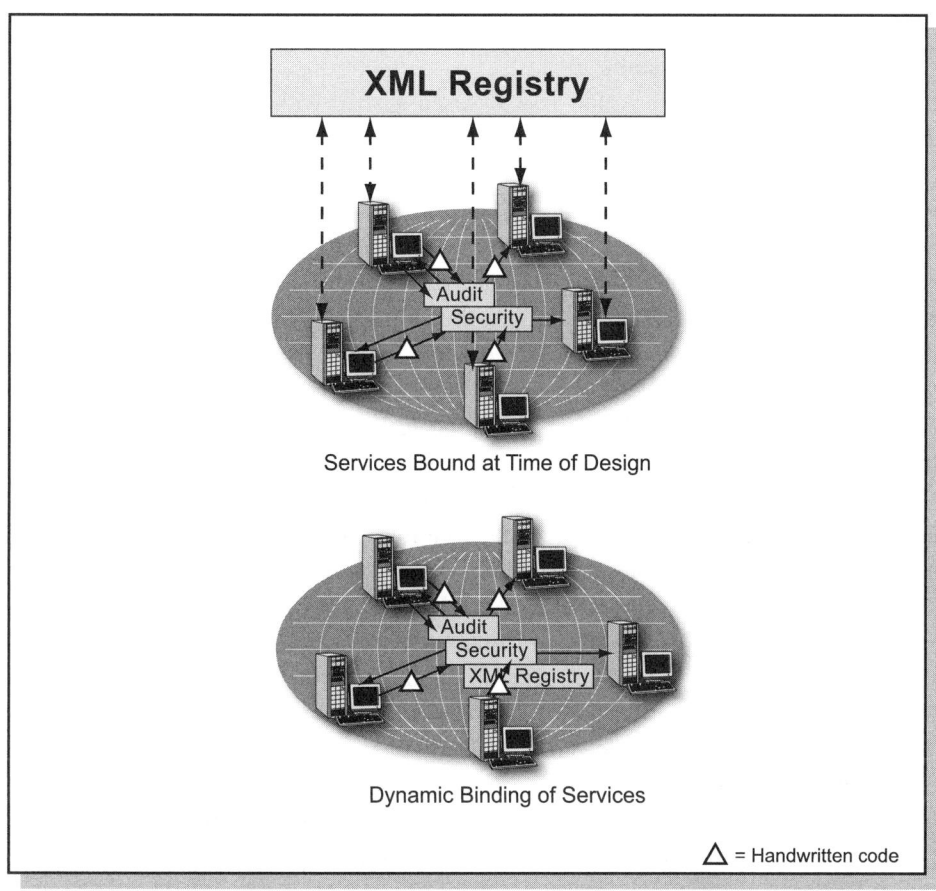

Figure 5.9 The Reality of SOA

Configuration: A New Methodology for Building Applications

As indicated earlier, one of the major benefits of SOA is that it fosters the reuse of code so that in some cases new applications could be created purely by configuring a sequence of calls to services. However, this flexibility comes at a cost of potential instability because the individual creating a new service may make assumptions that could have an adverse effect on some existing application. Recall the quote in the Preface from Fisher and Smith (2004) that says "With modern systems development and the need to develop complex systems of systems, most systems are no longer 'closed'; rather they are 'unbounded' because they involve an unknown number of participants or otherwise require individual participants to act and interact in the absence of needed information." (p.1)

A standalone application was a closed system with an internally consistent set of data structures that exercised control about how new data was entered. As a result, there was an opportunity to constrain and check data values as they were entered. With the advent of applications based on client-server architecture, there was no longer a single thread of control over data because multiple applications could share a database on an event-driven basis. As a result, data integrity was dependent upon the design of the database—not just the definitions of the records or tables, but the specification of constraints and triggers that required some foreknowledge about what the data should look like. System software (e.g., DBMS technology, communication packages) maintains its own internal state based on a finite set of data structures that can only be accessed and updated through proprietary APIs. In short, system software has the same level of control as a standalone application with the ability to maintain the same high level of data integrity because it, like a standalone application, is a closed semantic system.

The UDDI standard is similar to a DBMS product in that it provides a simple set of XML constructs that have very limited semantic content and can be used as "building blocks" in designing a schema where the user has complete control over the configuration and semantics of the objects in that schema. Composite applications will only work correctly *if* the developers creating and consuming services have a common—and correct—understanding of a common schema *and if* all interfaces to existing applications map correctly between the application's APIs and the common schema. But it is not enough for the developers of services and interfaces to the XML registry to understand the syntax and semantics of the common schema; anyone responsible for modifying an application that participates in an SOA environment must also have this understanding or run the risk of corrupting the integrity of the other applications using services based on the application being modified.

In fact, such risks exist whenever an organization seeks to interface autonomous applications. Consider the case a consulting organization actually encountered where a company had a number of applications that interfaced via EAI tools from webMethods and Microsoft. A developer updated one of the applications, and initially everything appeared to work appropriately. A couple of days later the "rumblings" started because the change affected data used by the interfaces to the EAI products and consequently affected the databases in other applications. In this instance the number of interfaces was relatively small, so it was possible after a significant amount of analysis to determine the source of the error. But then there came the task of identifying which updates to various applications had to be backed out or modified.

The situation is even more complex in SOA, where the registry has no knowledge of which services are being used by what applications. Although logging all web service calls would provide the information needed to unravel the problem, this approach only uncovers problems *after the fact,* at which point significant damage may have already been done—not only to the data, but also in terms of the real world transactions that correspond to the transactions represented in applications; that is, the wrong amount of steel may have been shipped to a customer or an incorrect amount of money wired to another bank. Anticipating these problems, the vendors of SOA registry products offer support for companies to define "governance" policies that define the steps that must be followed before a new service is put into production. But following this process is only as good as the testing of that new service and—because of the nondeterministic nature of SOA—one can never guarantee that a new service will not have an adverse effect; one can only guarantee that it has not had an adverse effect on a similar set of events that have been judged as performing correctly. Thus, a rich methodology for the capture and automation of regression tests will be critical to maintaining SOA environments where there is a need for a high degree of accuracy.

Topic of Interest: Determinism vs. Nondeterminism

In computer science, an algorithm is *deterministic* if, given the same input, it will always produce the same result. An algorithm is *nondeterministic* if, given the same input, the algorithm may pass through a different sequence of states and produce different results.

In an ideal world—one where we could guarantee that all services listed under the same category in the UDDI would be functionally equivalent, no server would ever fail, and no service had any adverse side effect—a composite application could be deterministic. Unfortunately, there is no way to guarantee that the three preceding conditions will hold true. There is no way to guarantee that the same sequence of events will occur every time an application is invoked because calls to the services that the application makes could be interleaved with calls from other applications. Moreover, there may not be a software problem at all because sometimes intermittent hardware failures or speed/duplex settings on network hardware can adversely affect the software. For example, in one case, a company spent months trying to find a problem in a web services application where eventually it turned out to be an intermittent short in a network card in one of the machines.

(continued)

As a result, SOA environments must be assumed to be potentially non-deterministic. Therefore, the only way to feel comfortable that a service-based application is likely to deliver the correct results is to perform regular, intensive regression tests, *or* to institute some tight controls that force such testing whenever a new service is introduced.

Impact on the model of the application. Figure 5.10 reveals some unexpected consequences in the balance of different types of effort required to develop applications. Given the discussion in this chapter, one would expect that the amount of effort spent on external configuration and confirmation (testing) would be significantly increased, but not the amount of effort spent in context (data) and constraints (boundary conditions). However, because SOA is a nondeterministic environment, the developers of services are responsible for ensuring that they maintain whatever data they may need

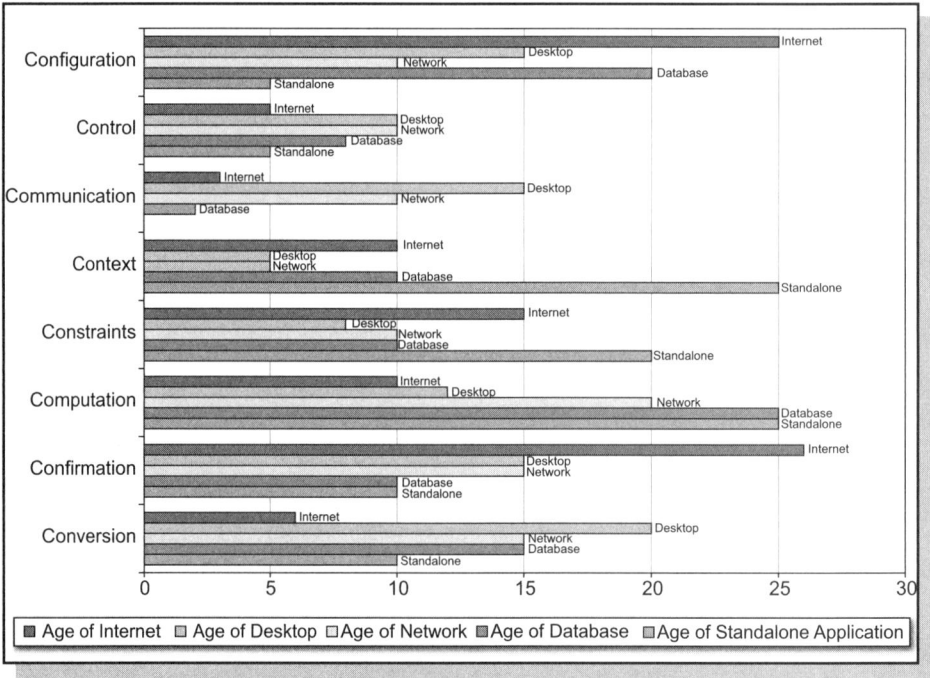

Figure 5.10   Age of the Internet

to ensure the integrity of both their service and any internal database that they maintain. This effort will be fairly limited when the service is achieved by wrapping the APIs to the transactions of a legacy application and may only consist of ensuring that the translation between the XML representation and the API is accurate and that any data values or parameters are of the correct data type, because the internal logic of the application probably contains sufficient error-checking to block an ill-formed transaction. But in creating a new service—even if it is a composite service (that is, made up of a series of calls to other services)—the developer, much like the designer of a system software product, should try to anticipate and block any error that could occur from being called inappropriately. This may require maintaining contextual information regarding historical events in the case that the service expects a series of calls to be made within some period of time (e.g., for an application session).

5.2   Trends

In Chapter 2, we argued that the general principle driving the evolution of software technology could be summarized as favoring the development of products that provide *greater productivity for more users with less training.* If we consider this chapter's discussion, we can see that the major driver of application architectures is to *achieve the greater productivity for more users by allowing them to easily share information in near real-time, regardless of the hardware and software platform or their geographic location.* The drive to greater productivity has led to the development of technologies that:

- *Increase the range of tasks and types of data processing* that computers can support, such as global positioning systems and search engines
- *Increase the speed with which computer users (human or applications) can communicate with each other,* where these technologies not only include technology that speeds the transport of information between computers, but also support different models for invocation (e.g., event-driven, publish and subscribe).
- *Increase the speed at which developers can provide application solutions* through productivity tools that minimize the amount of code that must be written, where these technologies include capabilities that:

  - Provide high-level interfaces to domain-specific general purpose software (such as graphics or security)

- Can be used across a variety of hardware and software environments
- Foster reuse

Note that as application architecture has evolved to maximize these goals, the task of application development has become more one of configuration than coding, with the result that the process of testing (confirmation) becomes more critical to a project's success. The Agile method of software development (*Agile Alliance,* 2001) was developed by an alliance of software engineers who advocate minimizing the specification and upfront design in favor of small incremental increases in functionality ("sprints") that are rigorously and automatically tested with regression tests. Although as software architects we do not believe that this methodology is suitable for every type of application, it does seem well-suited to the challenges faced in developing applications in an SOA environment.

5.3   Tradeoffs

It's interesting to note that although the past 50 years have seen huge advances in software technology, IT organizations have not become more cost-effective in developing and maintaining large-scale applications—exactly the opposite of what one would expect because the motivation for most innovations was the goal of making the process of developing and maintaining applications simpler. To understand why this is the case, consider how difficult it is to explicitly tell someone how to do something when you and the person you are instructing are not in the same physical location. If you and the other person share a large amount of common knowledge, as in the case of a recipe (e.g., what it means to mix and measure), the instruction can be pretty efficient. But if the individual being instructed does not share your assumptions or knowledge base (as in the case of repairing a motor), the task of explicitly specifying instructions is significantly more complicated. As a result, most applications are written in a context using particular tools, hardware, and so on. Too often advances in software technology have been introduced into the marketplace as if there were a fixed set of assumptions or common knowledge base—as in the case of a recipe—when in fact, it is not that simple.

Instead, the environment in which an application is created and maintained is more like an ecosystem—a complex environment where one should expect repercussions when someone introduces a change. The laws that apply to software are more like Einstein's theory of relativity. To restate the principle of *conservation of complexity,* if a computational problem is complex, there is no way to simplify one aspect of the computation without introducing additional complexity in one or more of the other aspects of the problem. If you review Figure 5.10 to examine the effect of the various eras of software on the model of the application, you will see that there has been an increased complexity in one or more of the other dimensions of the model of the application for every reduction in effort. Most methodologies have evolved to provide projects with guidelines as to how best to implement an application in some particular context; unfortunately, that context rarely addresses the full spectrum of the factors used by our model of the application. Adopting an architecture or technology that simplifies one aspect of application development usually complicates one or more of the other aspects of the application model.

5.4   Coming Up Next: The Representation of Meaning

Our goal in writing this book is to sensitize software architects to the full range of topics they should consider in determining the viability of some technical approach to creating an infrastructure for software integration. When considering whether a proposed architecture or technology can deliver the promised savings, you should assess the potential impact on the other aspects of the model for applications and their environment. In this process, you must consider not only the software in place, but also the availability of other technology that can ameliorate the areas that would become more complicated with the proposed solution, as well as the methodology the organization would need to adopt for the architecture to be successful.

In order to illustrate the importance of this type of analysis, in the next chapter we will consider the implications of SOA in the area of communication between man and machine (i.e., what it takes for developers to understand how to interface the services they are creating to the registry and for the registry to effectively communicate the services it has available for use in developing applications). This kind of correlation depends upon the developers understanding the *meaning* of the tags used in the XML schema. At several points previously in the book we have talked about the fact that the data values stored in databases are not sufficiently detailed to allow users to understand the meaning of the data; a set of implicit (although perhaps documented) assumptions is required—for example, the assumption that the time frame for the field SALARY is annual in some particular database. In the next chapter, we will explore why it is so hard to represent meaning; in the process, we will consider some important differences between humans and computers in the way that they process information. We will then consider the types of functionality one might like to see in an XML registry to help address the increased complexity in communication one sees in SOA environments.

Exercises for Chapter 5

1. As we have seen, different application architectures have different properties with respect to the eight aspects of the application model. Depending upon the nature of application you are building, the relative importance of some of these aspects will change. For example, in some cases it makes perfect sense to build a standalone application; in others, a three-tiered architecture would be preferable. Given the current state of technology and software methodology, choose the best application architecture for each of the following applications. Justify your answer in terms of both the application requirements and their effect on the relative importance of the different aspects of the model. Feel free to create figures to illustrate your discussion.

   a. An application that computes the velocity of a plane
   b. A case management system for detecting potential terrorist activity
   c. An electronic trading network between vendors and suppliers
   d. An integrated set of tools for designing commercial heating/cooling systems
   e. An electronic voting system

2. In several chapters, we have emphasized the importance of efficient change management as a key component of the ability to cost-effectively maintain an application. Discuss the various types of changes one should anticipate in choosing an application architecture for each of the applications listed in Exercise 1. For example, one might expect to have to deal with new types of thermostats when designing commercial heating/cooling systems. What generalizations could one make about which types of application architecture are best suited to different types of applications?

CHAPTER

6

The Representation of Meaning

In Chapter 1, we argued that one of the greatest difficulties in large-scale IT initiatives results from the fact that only a fraction of the information required to understand the meaning of data is stored in the files or databases used by applications. The rest of the information may be documented online, but it is typically difficult to access and/or interpret. As a result, flawed specifications are cited as the most frequent cause of project failure. Given the importance of this problem, it is surprising that the industry has made so little progress in improving the representation of the meaning of data, particularly because the failure to do so means that much of what is discovered on one project must be rediscovered on the next. In fact, the inability to concretely capture what has been created or learned means that the bulk of knowledge workers' time is spent in searching for artifacts or information or—even worse from a cost of ownership perspective—re-creating something that has already been created.

Yet representing meaning in digital form is no simple task. In fact, the primary goal of this chapter is to help establish reasonable expectations about what computers can be expected to do in the not too distant future. Most of the limitations in this area can be attributed to differences between how humans and computers process information and our limited understanding of how we humans actually function. We will start with a discussion about what is known regarding how humans process information in order to understand both:

- The full range of information and capabilities a computer system would have to support in order to exhibit intelligent behavior
- Why it is so difficult for us to build such systems

With this background, we will consider the problems encountered in previous attempts to build systems that "think"—the expert systems that dominated artificial intelligence (AI) work in the 1980s. We will then consider how service-oriented architecture (SOA) faces many of the same challenges. In closing, we will suggest one strategy for addressing the risks associated with digital representations of meaning and how this strategy can be applied in developing software architectures that incrementally help us acquire the contextual information required to interpret data.

6.1   On Man and Machine

Humans have long fantasized about machines that can behave like humans. But it is not just the creators of pop culture (e.g., Hal in the movie *2001* or faithful servant R2D2 in the *Star Wars* series) who speculate about these matters. Futurologist and inventor Ray Kurzweil (2005) argues that there is a law of accelerating returns which is "the inherent acceleration of evolution, with technical evolution as a continuation of biological evolution." (p.7) Kurzweil maintains that the effect of this law will be that by the middle of the 21st century we will be able to transform life as we know it. "There will be no distinction…between human and machine or between physical and virtual reality." (p.9) Basing his predictions on the research that is currently being conducted in genetics, nanotechnology, robotics, and neuroscience, Kurzweil believes that "computers will be able to combine the traditional strengths of human intelligence [a 'formidable' ability to recognize patterns due to the 'massively parallel and self-organizing nature of the human brain'] with the strengths of machine intelligence ['the ability to remember billions of facts precisely and recall them instantly']." (p.25)

Kurzweil is clearly right about the assessment of the relative strengths of man and machine (human and computer) and that the research being conducted in genetics, nanotechnology, robotics, and neuroscience will soon provide us with the understanding and tools required to have the *mechanics* of achieving many of his predictions. However, it is not so clear that we are making similar progress in understanding the nature of human intelligence. Unless we want the new man-machine to have to "start over," we will need to capture human knowledge. To represent knowledge we will need to represent meaning.

People and Patterns

There is no reason that we should not have the creation of intelligent, self-learning computer systems as a goal, but it is important for us to understand the full range of capabilities that humans exhibit in their information processing, or we run the risk of producing systems that are merely prototypes—that is, able to function only in an artificial, highly constrained environment. In fact, this is the current state of most AI applications. The major difference between man and machine can be characterized by the statement *Humans are analog; computers are digital.* Humans are inherently pattern-based. Although at the lowest level—that of neurons firing—human information processing may have the on-off attributes of the digital computer, evidence from neuroscience, developmental psychology, and linguistics all indicate that conscious knowledge, or what is called *explicit* memory (Siegel, 1999), contains only a fraction of the information used in making decisions.

> Implicit memory involves parts of the brain that do not require conscious processing during encoding or retrieval….Implicit memory relies on brain structures that are intact at birth and remain available to us throughout life. These structures include the amygdala and other limbic regions for emotional memory, the basic ganglia and motor cortex for behavioral memory, and the perceptual cortices for perceptual memory. (Siegel, p. 29)

What is stored in memory is not the representation of a "thing" but the probability that a pattern of neurons will fire in a particular sequence. The initial impact of an experience on the brain (called an *engram*) can contain many aspects of the experience: "semantic (factual...), autobiographical (your sense of yourself at that time in your life), somatic (what your body felt like at the time), perceptual (what things looked like, how they smelled), emotional (your mood at the time), and behavior (what you were doing with your body)." (p. 28) As a result, two different people will store different patterns of the same experience based on their previous experiences. For example, a person who was severely bitten by a dog is likely to record a very different pattern when a dog jumps on her than someone whose best friend as a child was the family collie.

Moreover, memories are not static—they change over time in a process that researchers call "cortical consolidation." This process "appears to involve the reorganization of existing memory traces, not the laying down of new engrams. In this manner, consolidation may make new clusters of representations, and incorporate previously unintegrated elements into a functional whole."(p. 37) But memory isn't merely a repository of patterns that periodically get reorganized; it is the very stuff that determines what we perceive.

> *The brain can be called an "anticipation machine," constantly scanning the environment and trying to determine what will come next....*Prior experiences shape our anticipatory models, and thus the term "prospective memory" has been used to describe how the mind attempts to "remember the future," based on what has occurred in the past. (Siegel, p. 30)

In short, what we see is a function of what we expect to see based on patterns that have been reinforced enough to be part of our long-term memory. Aspects of our experience in the environment not only affect perception, but also affect and are affected by language. Edward Sapir (1921) and Benjamin Lee Whorf (1956) were two early modern linguists who argued that language and perception were linked. For example, in experiments that included color discrimination tasks, subjects whose language contained more terms for a particular color range performed significantly better than those whose language did not include terms that characterized those distinctions.

Even if we build a multi-processor equipped with the appropriate sensors to simulate all the various aspects of experience outlined earlier (e.g., semantic, somatic, emotional), there would be the need to incorporate some core formulae to identify fear, pain, good, evil, and the like for various subsystems, as well as some strategy for how information should be consolidated. Although systems have been built to detect physical phenomena like heat, movement, and location, the goal of these systems has been either to report this information to a specific application contained in some apparatus (for example, a missile guidance system) or to present the information in some form to humans, leaving any decision regarding action up to them. In the former case, the initial action (e.g., the firing of the missile) was initiated by a human. To move from these types of applications to a computer system that initiates actions based on judgment calls involving "what it observes" is a far stretch.

Software applications can be implemented to successfully perform pattern-matching, but only if they are highly targeted in terms of semantic domain (e.g., fingerprint recognition, radar systems, emission analysis, etc.). Although these applications may learn (i.e., become more accurate by means of some feedback mechanism), they are not capable of making complex decisions that span multiple domains and that include making judgments.

Meaning and Language

Meaning is a term most closely associated with language. Like memory, language is a multi-layered system where the individual's experience may affect his understanding, making the meaning of even a simple noun like *rocket* relative across speakers of the same language. In fact, one could argue that a good part of the power of natural language comes from its ability to have the same statement mean multiple things. For example, consider the distinction between *syntax* and *semantics*. *Webster's New World Dictionary* defines syntax as "the way in which words are put together to form phrases and sentences" and semantics as "the study or science of meaning in language forms, esp. with regard to its historical change." In the absence of context, differences in syntactic form cause the same words to carry different meanings. For example, grammar textbooks typically maintain the following:

- Declarative sentence order is used to assert facts (e.g., *The girl ate the apple*).
- Interrogative sentence order is used to request information (e.g., *Did the girl eat the apple?*)?
- Imperative sentence order is used to issue a command (e.g., *Eat the apple.*).

However, given a particular context, the meaning that is conveyed by uttering a sentence can be very different from the meaning of the sentence in isolation. For example, if a wife comes up to a husband at a party and says *It's getting late,* her intended effect is not to state a fact, and she probably won't be happy if her husband replies *It sure is.* She would be equally displeased if she walks into the den and asks *Are you going to take the garbage out?* and her husband replies *No*. The meaning of an utterance—its intended effect—is based on the context in which it is uttered, including the roles and relationships of the speaker and hearer, as well as what the speaker believes that the hearer knows or believes. In fact, there is a rich body of work in philosophy called speech act theory that focuses on the relationship between syntax and how language is used (Searle, 1969).

Topic of Interest: How Written Language Differs from Spoken

Written language is simpler than dialogue in that it depends less on the roles between the writer (speaker) and the reader (hearer) and their specific context. However, writers do write for an intended audience that they assume shares a common level of background knowledge. Different types of written documents have different conventions with respect to organization. News stories typically begin with a factual account of an event or an update regarding some event (e.g., *Two weeks before he resigned, Commissioner Starbuck wrote a letter to Governor Pinchpenny outlining his concern about…*). They then provide background information on what happened prior to that update—information that would allow a reader unfamiliar with the event to "catch up" but that can be skimmed or skipped by someone who is familiar with the topic. At this point the story often includes the predictions and/or opinions of authorities or individuals associated with the event or case.

On the other hand, editorials are much more varied in organizational structure. One might start an editorial describing some historical situation that will be used as an analogy. As a result, it can take several paragraphs before the featured topic of the editorial appears, and the major claim or recommendation may appear only at the end of the piece.

Moreover, these organizational conventions in writing may vary across cultures. For example, in English prose writers tend to use time and causation to organize their points, whereas in Chinese it is more common to find a more "circular" type of organization, where a topic is approached from a number of points of view thereby leading the reader to infer the desired conclusion.

Once again, when natural language processing applications have proved successful, it has been because their input and/or function was highly restricted, such as translating technical documents or creating abstracts of news stories. For a computer to "understand" language—either written or spoken—with sufficient accuracy to act in the absence of human judgment, an enormous amount of background information would be required above and beyond what a dictionary and grammar can provide. And as we will see in our discussion of the history of expert systems, specifying that background information is extremely difficult.

Computers and Complexity

Computers have several distinct advantages over humans when it comes to complexity and accuracy. Experimental evidence (Miller, 1956) suggests that people are only able to recall seven items plus or minus two from short-term memory. For more information to be recalled, it must be "chunked" into groups (e.g., the way phone numbers are represented), and for information to pass from short-term memory to long-term memory, there must be repetition and cortical reorganization. Computers have no such limitations. Subject to hardware or software failure and limitations in memory and disk, computers have "total recall" and—equally important—they rarely make errors. A software application may have a bug and produce an incorrect result, but it will consistently produce that incorrect result under similar conditions.[1] People, on the other hand, are inconsistent. Humans can perform a task correctly the majority of the time, but occasionally make a mistake. Although there may be a reason for it (e.g., lack of sleep, poor lighting), one cannot predict that they will always make that mistake under similar conditions.

Leveraging Relative Strengths for Maximum Benefit

The strengths of man and machine are orthogonal: People are good at patterns and generating hypotheses but poor at complexity and accuracy, whereas computers are good at complexity and accuracy, but poor at recognizing patterns and generating hypotheses. As a result, it is not surprising that large projects fail due to flawed specifications because the detailed analysis required for accurate specs requires that people accurately interpret a large amount of symbolic information, including source systems that contain poorly documented data and functionality that is either explicitly

---

1 Sometimes it can be difficult to identify what those conditions are, because in highly networked environments, the cause of an error could be something outside the application; for example, a parameter set on something like maximum disk space during the installation of the operating system.

encoded in an "artificial language" (source code) or implicitly encoded (object code) and unavailable for analysis. But it is not just complexity that makes this type of analysis difficult. It is also because communication between man and machine takes place at the symbolic level.

As we have demonstrated in the discussion of language, symbolic behavior depends on mutually shared conventions and mechanisms for perceiving the world. Because of similarities in physiology, humans have sufficiently similar experiences that allow us to communicate (often with some difficulty) with other humans. However, because much of what helps us understand each other is processed by mental systems that operate without conscious attention, it is unlikely we will be able to build systems that can reason like people until we have a better understanding of neuroscience and a model of the principles that govern survival. If we are to maximize the benefit of computers to society in the meantime, we must be sensitive to this "cognitive mismatch" between man and machine. Therefore, *we are more likely to be successful in building software systems if we focus on creating software environments that bridge the gaps in relative strengths by assisting humans in dealing with complexity rather than trying to build systems that emulate what we don't yet understand about ourselves.* In fact, this is exactly what the evolution of software has done, by providing programmers and users with layers of abstraction that allow them to deal with computers at an increasingly abstract level, ignoring details of hardware, operating system, and programming environments.

The Challenge Facing SOA

Service-oriented architecture, augmented by the power of the Internet, promises to be a long-term solution to the problem of interoperability because it enables heterogeneous applications to communicate at the logical level. However, the success of this communication depends on a common representation in XML, which in turn requires a common understanding of symbolic tags and the relationship between tags. Given humans' limitations in dealing with complexity, we will need systems that can help developers learn and manipulate XML schemas accurately. In short, we will need to build software environments that represent meaning in order to correlate information across domains. In the following section, we will examine some historical attempts to build knowledge-based systems and the factors that limited their success. We will then examine how system software designers are addressing the problem in dealing with these issues with XML.

6.2   Earlier Attempts to Represent Meaning

In the 1970s and 1980s, people thought that artificial intelligence (AI) would be the source of our most powerful applications by the end of the century. Some of the most promising of these early initiatives involved attempts to create systems that emulated human performance independent of any understanding of neuroscience. Some of the most impressive work was done in the area of *expert systems* or what came to be called *knowledge-based systems*. One could say that many applications are expert systems in some particular domain (e.g., inventory management, human resources). Once they are configured to determine the desired behavior, when they are invoked with the appropriate data they do the "right thing." The architectural difference between an application and an expert system was the degree to which the behavior of the system could be driven by data. System software like database management systems or communication packages provide their administrators with a command language or interactive tools that let them configure the product for a specific environment. For example, in the case of a DBMS product, that language is the DDL (data definition language) that allows the database administrator to define the schema for a particular database.

The goal of expert systems was significantly more ambitious than that of system software in that they were designed to be *domain-independent*. While system software has a limited semantic domain (e.g., system administration, data access and storage, graphics), expert systems were an attempt to build a generic AI platform for reasoning. As such, they provided the developer with two types of definition languages:

- A language for representing the knowledge that defined the domain, such as the objects and relationships that defined what was pertinent to geological exploration or problem detection for customer support. (In system software, this information would be implicit, such as the fact that in a relational database the pertinent objects include tables, attributes, joins, domains, etc.)
- A language for defining a desired action when some pattern was found in the input data, such as if the system finds this pattern of facts about a particular core sample, then it should signal "Drill here!"

The knowledge base was typically represented by a data structure called a *semantic network*, which can be visualized as a directed graph like the one represented in Figure 6.1, where the nodes represent entities or concepts and the links represent relationships. A *rules* language was used to allow developers to specify the desired behavior, where a rule had a structure of *pattern => conclusion or action*.

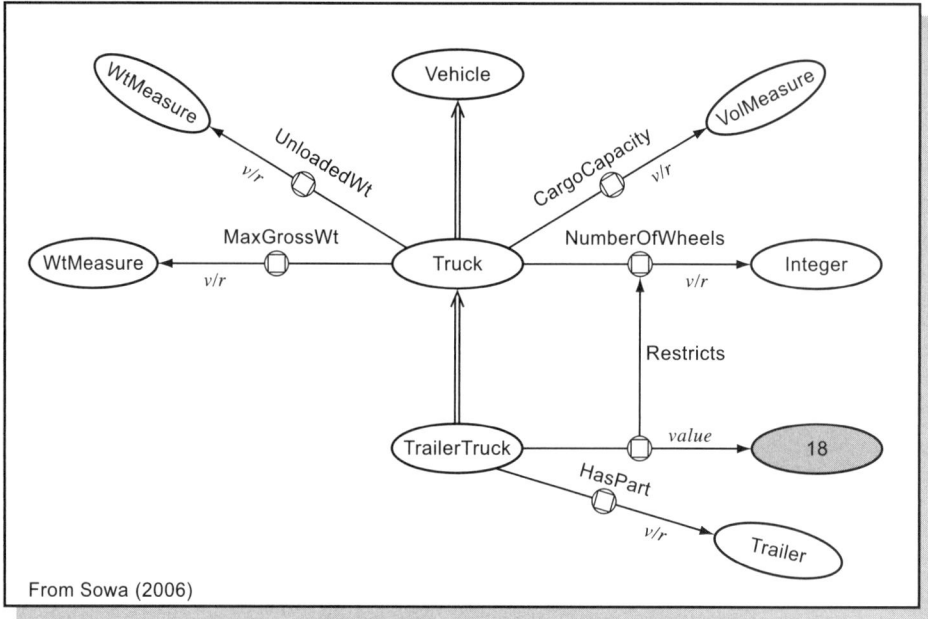

From Sowa (2006)

Figure 6.1 Example of Semantic Network in KL-ONE

The term *ontology* is used in philosophy to refer to the study of existence—a study of what "is." In computer science, the term *ontology* is used to refer to a knowledge base—a "universe of discourse" consisting of a set of objects and "the describable relationships among them." (Gruber, 1993 p. 2). There are a number of published ontologies available, such as Cyc, a common sense ontology from Cycorp, which has been populated and extended by knowledge engineers for over 20 years (www.cyc.com), and DMOZ (the Open Directory Project, www.dmoz.com), which leverages over 35,000 volunteer editors to maintain the largest, most comprehensive human-edited directory of the Web (McGuinness, 2003). Ontologies are often represented as semantic networks and include generic rules about things like inheritance (e.g., if entity X is linked to entity Y by an *is-a* link, then X can be attributed all the properties associated with Y). The vision of the comprehensive ontology builders, like the researchers that developed Cyc, was to provide a rich enough knowledge base that it could be used by multiple expert systems so that developers only had to specify the rules that defined the desired behavior.

Although there were point successes—for example, Schlumberger built an extremely powerful system for the analysis of core samples when drilling for oil—expert systems were not widely adopted for two reasons:

- The expressive power of ontologies made them too complex to easily understand.
- Experts often don't know what they know.

Expressive Power and Complexity

In Chapter 3 we examined the four major meta-models used by database technology—hierarchical, network, relational, and object-oriented. All but the relational meta-model explicitly represent relationships using pointers; in some cases the relationships are themselves objects that carry labels/attributes. In terms of expressive power, the richest of these meta-models—and the one that mostly closely approximates the way humans characterize information and that most closely resembles semantic networks—is the object-oriented data model. The object-oriented data model supports:

1. Multiple means of accessing the same entity; for example, the ability to include Chelsea Clinton's mother as a member of the class of people constituting Chelsea's family, as well as a member of the groups *female mammals* and *authors of books*. As illustrated in Figure 6.2, in directed graphs, these are instances of a labeled link called an *is-a* relation.

2. The ability for an entity of type X to contain one or more instances of the same type of entity; for example, the engine of a car is a component that itself contains components. As illustrated in Figure 6.3, in directed

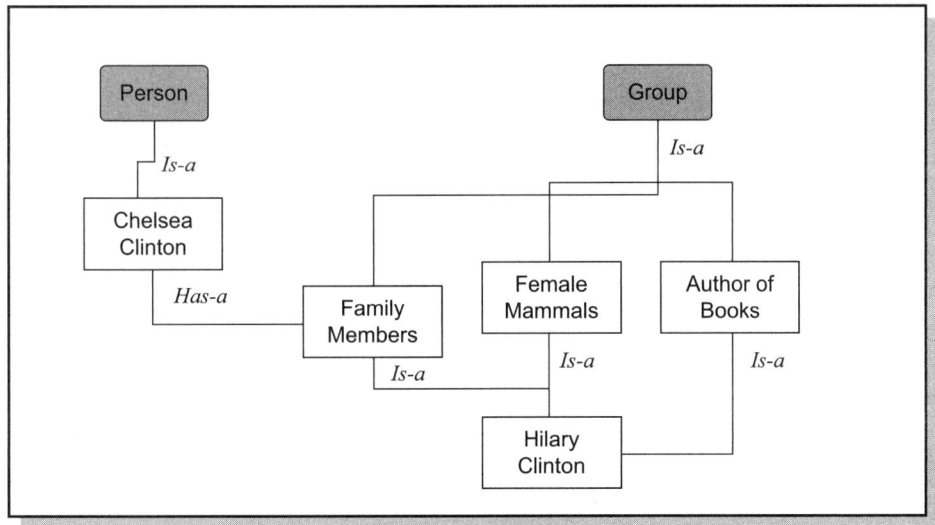

Figure 6.2   Membership in Multiple Groups

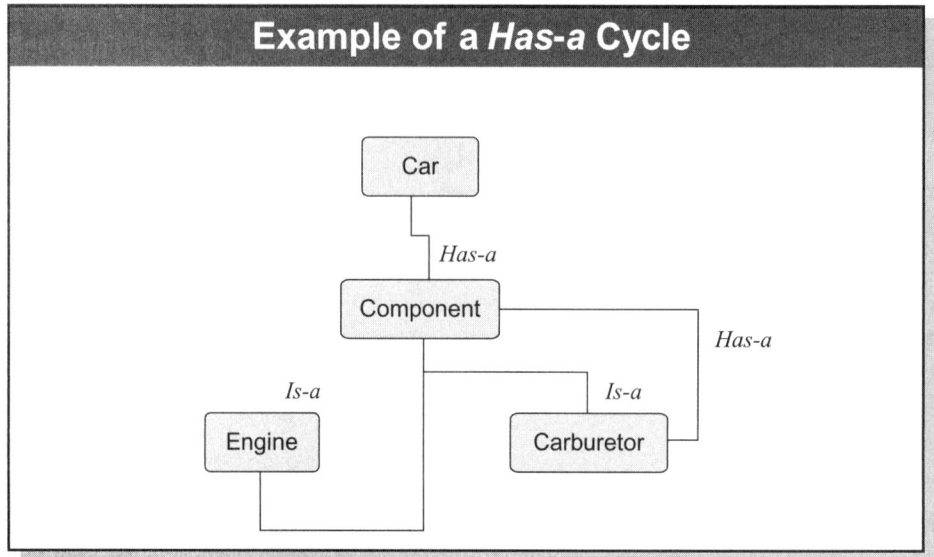

Figure 6.3 Example of a *Has-a* Cycle

graphs, this situation is represented by a cycle where one or more *has-a* links creates a cycle that causes an entity to point to itself.

3. The ability to support inheritance, that is, the ability to infer attributes based on different types of links; for example, the ability to assume that Hilary Clinton is warm-blooded because she is a human, which is (in turn) a mammal. In this case, an *is-a* link carries with it the ability to infer that the entity of the type X inherits all the *has-a* properties from any class to which it has an *is-a* link.

4. The ability to support special cases of inheritance where a subclass does not inherit a property of the class of which it is an instance; for example, female seahorses do not have babies.

Note that the network data model shares attributes 1 and 2 of the object-oriented, but not 3 and 4.

However, despite the fact that these two meta-models offer a superior means of representing semantics, neither network nor object-oriented database technology has been widely used; neither supplanted relational systems (or even the older hierarchical systems) in production applications, although object-oriented concepts have been extremely influential in the design of software. There is no computer-related reason for this. Object-oriented databases can be very efficient if the schema is well-tuned for the application. In fact, object-oriented database management systems have been successfully deployed in the area of telecommunications, an industry that is characterized by some of the largest databases in the world.

The major reason for the limited success of these meta-models was the difficulty people had using them. Once one moves beyond examples like the preceding ones, data models based on these meta-models become extremely complex. Moreover, it is not just the database designer of network or object-oriented schemas who needs to understand the relationships; anyone programming against these schemas has to have the same knowledge, as well as anyone who needs to maintain the application. While people can become conversant with very complex systems over time, it takes not only repetition, but also some form of subconscious consolidation ("cortical consolidation") for information to become part of long-term memory. This kind of effort might be justified if the information learned could be used across organizations and projects (as in learning the principles of mathematics or chemistry), but it is less justifiable in the case of a database used by a handful of applications in a particular company. As a result, IT organizations tend to use less powerful, but significantly simpler, systems.

Determining What an Expert Knows

The problem with expert knowledge is not just that it is complex, but that it is modulated. An experienced practitioner of radiology can look at an X-ray and make a judgment call about the presence and/or absence of a tumor and, if present, its risk of being cancerous. It is not clear that she could express the principles she applies in a knowledge definition language, even if the nodes had associated graphics. Likewise, the sequence of actions that a plumber takes to repair a leak may vary depending upon the location and severity of the leak.

As a result, it became obvious fairly quickly that experts were not going to be able to specify the information needed by expert systems because it would take an inordinate amount of time first to learn the conventions of the system and then to figure out what they knew and specify it to the system. The industry solution was to train a new kind of engineer—the *knowledge engineer:* an individual who was well-trained both in the system and in interview techniques. But even then the task of correctly capturing the information was error-prone and time-consuming. As a result, most expert systems in use today are custom applications that use proprietary structures rather than being based on one of the generic types of development platforms that were offered by vendors in the 1980s.

Topic of Interest: Neural Nets

A neural net is a type of network data structure used by applications that learns by changing the weights assigned to the nodes or arcs in the data structure. Although it sounds like this type of structure might be intended to represent neural mechanisms, it does not. Figure 6.4 shows "a typical neural net, whose input is a sequence of numbers that indicate the relative proportion of some selected features and whose output is another sequence of numbers that indicate the most likely concept characterized by that combination of features" (Sowa, 2006)

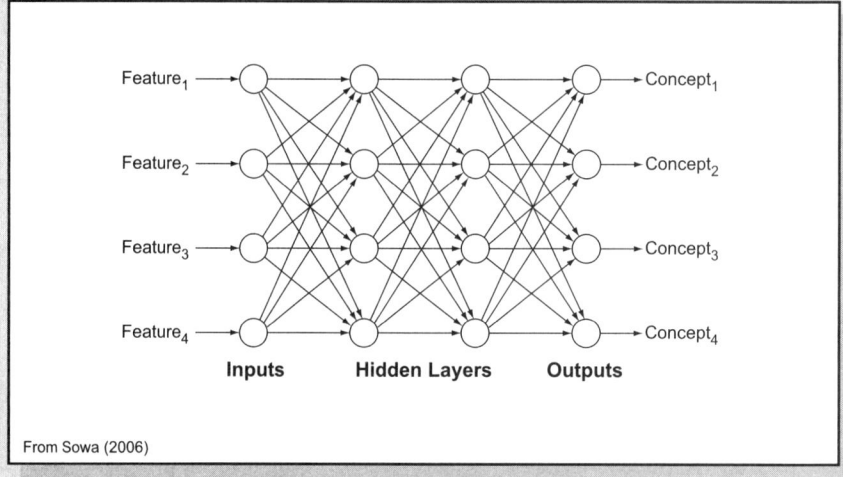

From Sowa (2006)

Figure 6.4 Concept of Neural Net

Sowa offers the following explanation of how these data structures can be said to learn:

> In a typical neural network, the structure of nodes and arcs is fixed, and the only changes that may occur are the assignments of weights to the arcs. When a new input is presented, the weights on the arcs are combined with the weights on the input features to determine the weights in the *hidden layers* of the net and ultimately the weights on the outputs. In the learning stage, the system is told whether the predicted weights are correct, and various methods of *backpropagation* are used to adjust the weights on the arcs that lead to the result.

6.3   The Representation of Meaning on the Web

Despite the limited success of earlier attempts to use the network and object-oriented meta-models, once again there is a large group of software engineers who are advocating the use of a network meta-model—namely, those that believe that ontologies are necessary to correlate information stored in XML across domains. OWL (Web Ontology Language) is a dialect of DAML (DARPA Agent Mark-up Language) that allows developers to specify ontologies for use with web services. OWL was developed as part of the efforts of the W3C (the World Wide Web Consortium), an international group of researchers who, similar to the researchers who work on Cyc, strive to develop a universal ontology. The charter of W3C states the following:

> The goal of the Semantic Web initiative is as broad as that of the Web: to create a universal medium for the exchange of data. It is envisaged to smoothly interconnect personal information management, enterprise application integration, and the global sharing of commercial, scientific and cultural data. Facilities to put machine-understandable data on the Web are quickly becoming a high priority for many organizations, individuals and communities.
>
> The Web can reach its full potential only if it becomes a place where data can be shared and processed by automated tools as well as by people. For the Web to scale, tomorrow's programs must be able to share and process data even when these programs have been designed totally independently. The Semantic Web Activity is an initiative of the World Wide Web Consortium (W3C) designed to provide a leadership role in defining this Web. The Activity develops open specifications for those technologies that are ready for large scale deployment, and identifies, through open source advanced development, the infrastructure components that will be necessary to scale in the Web in the future.
>
> The principal technologies of the Semantic Web fit into a set of layered specifications. The current components are the Resource Description Framework (RDF) Core Model, the RDF Schema language and the Web Ontology language (OWL). Building on these core components is a standardized query language, SPARQL (pronounced "sparkle"), for RDF enabling the "joining" of decentralized collections of RDF data. (W3C, 2001)

Before we discuss the technical challenges faced by the Semantic Web, let's consider why this activity is seen as necessary.

The Benefits and Limitations of XML

As discussed earlier, XML is a relatively simple, text-based convention for representing data and metadata that uses explicit tags to demarcate the beginning and end of entities where the "*<tag-name>*" is used to indicate the beginning of the definition of an entity of type *tag-name* and "*</tag-name>*" indicates its end. Aside from the use of angled brackets and a few other conventions for indicating such things as bulleted lists, there are no other semantic constraints on what can be represented in the language. Relationships between entities can be specified in one of two ways: 1) by including the definition of one entity within the definition of another, much like REPEATING GROUPS were used in a COBOL copybook or structures/classes were referenced in C/C++; or 2) by providing a value-based path between the two entities (e.g., much like one would do in a relational database, but in this case, the URIs are the values used to link entities).

From a computer's point of view, these attributes are perfect for interoperability across the Web. The ability to read and write text-based data is ubiquitous—it transcends differences in hardware, operating system, systems software, and application. However, XML does little to solve the longstanding problem between man and machine. Unless there is some explicit way to define the meaning of the tags used in XML data definitions, we are stuck where we've always been—requiring that humans (who are error-prone, able to articulate only part of what they know, and have a pretty limited capacity for short-term memory) become conversant with a symbolic representation independently created by some other set of humans whose understanding of the world is likely to differ in some way.

As illustrated in Figure 6.5, the goal of the Semantic Web is to address this problem by providing a set of sufficiently explicit semantic networks that can be used not just to ensure the consistent representation of meaning but to allow applications to dynamically determine how to gather data to fulfill a user's (application's) request—a capability that will be critical if we strive to achieve what Kurzweil calls "the Singularity."

With the Semantic Web, an ontology would serve as a point of reference for coordinating and reasoning about information stored in XML. Even though there are a wide range of efforts underway to define and maintain domain-specific XML schemas for different industries (e.g., healthcare, finance, music), most organizations augment these standard schemas with tags that represent information that is important to their internal systems and processes. In theory, these "private" definitions and the data associated with them pose no problem to interoperability because if another application doesn't use the tag in question, it will ignore the data. Of course, there is nothing to guarantee that the other application may not also use the same tag in its internal extension to XML, but perhaps with slightly different semantics for the data values. The goal of the Semantic Web is to provide a single point of reference that could mediate between XML representations.

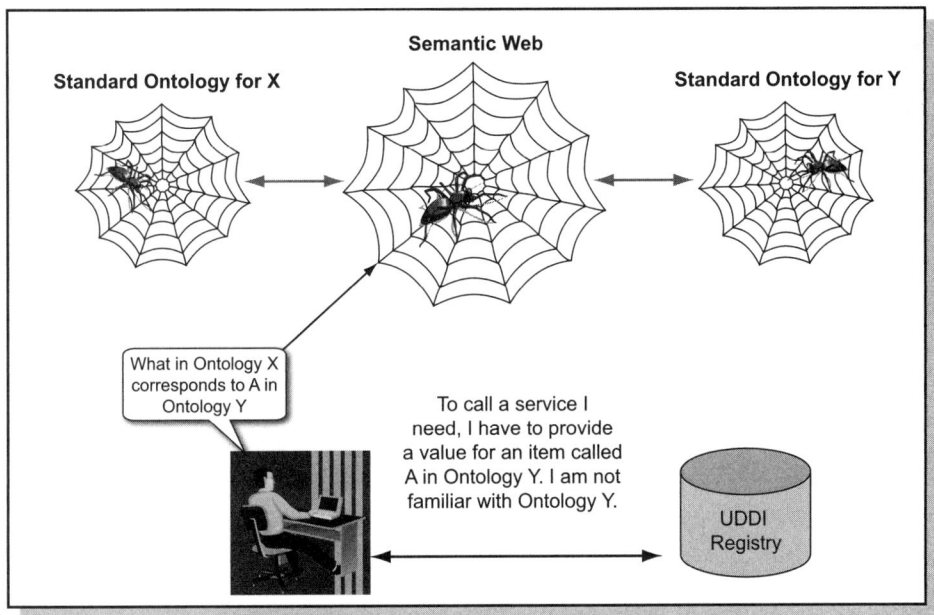

Figure 6.5 The Vision for How the Semantic Web Will Work

There is no doubt that the World Wide Web Consortium faces a better chance of success than any other standards group in the history of software for a number of reasons. First, the combined power of the Internet and the Web provides an unprecedented environment for allowing groups of people to collaborate in near real-time regardless of their geographical location and time zone. Second, to realize the potential value of the Web, it must be easy to enable applications to communicate. Yet the Semantic Web faces the classic dilemma of any standard:

- Either standard ontologies must be designed, implemented, available before an organization XML-enables its applications, and be sufficiently complete to eliminate the need for "private" tags, or
- In the process of XML-enabling their applications to conform to standard industry schemas, organizations will create internal extensions for the schemas that at some later point must be modified to conform to standard ontologies—or ensure that their extensions become part of a standard ontology.

6.4 Trends

If we review Figure 5.10 (reproduced on the next page) illustrating how the major trends in software have affected where the percentage of effort was/is spent in developing and maintaining applications, we will find several patterns that are worth noting.

First, the only area where effort has been consistently reduced has been in computation—the area of writing algorithmic code. As more and more of the functionality in an application has come to be handled by system software, the amount of algorithmic code that must be written to implement a new application has been reduced dramatically. Conversely, the relative amount of time spent on confirmation (i.e., testing and acceptance) has increased for the following reasons:

- Testing becomes more complex because the development team does not have access to all the source code; as a result, tests should be designed to address all the interface points between internally developed code and third-party products so that it becomes easier to pinpoint where a problem exists.
- As third party products—starting with operating systems—issue new releases, there is a domino effect in terms of the need to run regression tests before putting any application utilizing that platform into production. Note that some open source "products" like Perl and Python contain internal regression tests.
- As applications run on multiple platforms across a network, the sheer task of configuring a test environment that mirrors the production environment can be time-consuming.
- Finally, as discussed before, in SOA environments regular regression testing may be necessary on a continual basis to detect any adverse effect of adding a new service to the environment, and even then it will only recognize a problem "after the fact."

Likewise, for developers working in nondeterministic architectures like SOA, it may also be important to pay more attention to context (data integrity) and constraints (error-checking) because the application cannot guarantee that a service has not been changed or adversely affected between execution runs. However, the biggest increase in the percentage of work required in SOA environments is in the area of configuration, which involves correlating/integrating the transaction-level interfaces of existing applications to the XML schemas and the ontologies that may be used to define the relation between them. In fact, in highly heterogeneous environments that

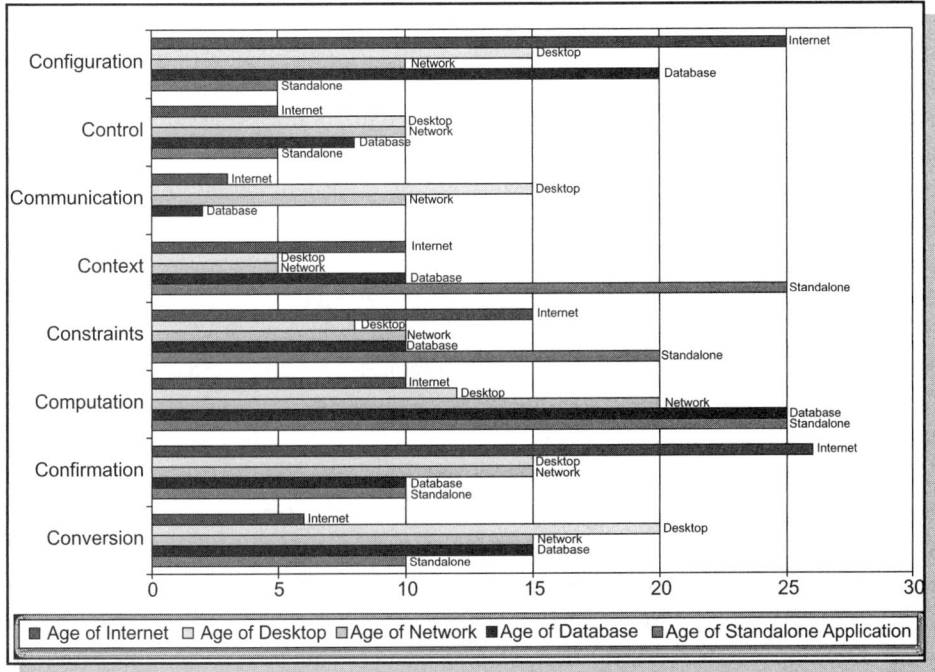

Figure 5.10 Age of the Internet

include technology that spans decades, it may be possible that the increased amount of effort required in configuration could offset the time savings achieved in the other four areas—control (i.e., effort spent in coordinating job execution), communication, computation (less code required due to reuse), and conversion (maintenance).

6.5 Tradeoffs

Two aspects of the configuration required to implement SOA are highly similar to largely unsuccessful projects undertaken in the past:

- The task of designing one or more standard XML schemas sufficiently rich to handle all the application processing needs for an industry (as opposed to schemas that handle common transactions) is very similar to the attempts to define an "enterprise data model" during the early years of client-server networks.

- The task of defining ontologies to enable aligning XML standards faces the same challenges encountered by the developers of expert systems.

Although the Internet enables standards groups to collaborate more effectively across geography and time, there have been no major breakthroughs in terms of technology or methodology to suggest that the results of this work will be any more successful than these earlier initiatives. That is not to say that there will not be successful implementations of SOA in certain environments that can support extensive investment, but that it may be difficult for organizations with constrained resources to undertake these initiatives.

Finally, another reason that the effort required for configuration continues to increase is that, as we will see in Chapter 8, *An Overview of Integration Technology,* there has been only limited success at the data level to reduce the level of effort across projects. As a result, system integration in most organizations is achieved through a hodgepodge of handwritten code and third-party products that, like applications, can span decades of technology. As a result, if one did sufficient research to create bar charts that illustrated actual expenditures along the eight areas of effort in the application model—as opposed to the relative efforts—we would see significant increases in expenditure across all areas. In short, IT may enable companies to be more efficient, but despite the evolution of productivity tools, IT has not become more efficient—or companies would not be spending 50–80 cents of every IT dollar on maintenance, nor would it constitute an organization's largest capital expenditure.

Relative Importance of Accuracy

We value computers because of their speed and accuracy. If the application architecture we are using is nondeterministic (like SOA) and requires complex configuration, we run the risk that there will be bugs in the application that may not be discovered until something fails. Depending upon the application, this may not matter. For example, say that an online bookstore is incorrect about having an item in stock or doesn't quote you the lowest price in the case that it provides access to other bookstores. Or an online search engine fails to discover an important article because of some bug in its ontology alignment. In either case, there is no significant damage. (In the case of the researcher, he is likely to find a reference to the missed article when he reads other material.) However, if it is critical that an application be accurate—for example, a missile guidance system or a transportation logistics program—the bug could be deadly. As a result, if you are chartered with designing an application, you must both decide the importance of accuracy (i.e., tolerance for inaccuracy) and understand the risks associated with the application architecture you adopt and products or services that you use so that you can mitigate these risks by creating more internal checks to detect inconsistent information and/or by performing more thorough testing or more careful monitoring.

Topic of Interest: Risks of Embedding Third-Party Software

The following story is based on our actual experience at an enterprise software company. In building a new release for a productivity platform for data integration management, the company needed an internal, object-oriented database system. Because there were several object-oriented DBMS products on the market, the company decided to "buy" rather than "build." One of the requirements was that the product could run on three flavors of the UNIX operating system—Solaris from Sun Microsystems, AIX from IBM, and HP/UX from Hewlett Packard—because we had customers running on all three. After evaluating the top three vendors, we settled on vendor X and proceeded to embed its product in our new release.

Some time after our new release was shipped and in production in the majority of our customers' IT organizations, vendor X issued a new release that included support for a new release of HP/UX from HP. The regression tests showed no problems so this new release was incorporated into our next update of the product. Several months later customers that were using HP/UX reported serious performance problems. Our development tools were running up to 30% slower than before. After an intensive search, we isolated the types of database activity that were causing the slowdown and reported it to the vendor. But vendor X had hired a new CEO who had decided to change its business model to support the Internet. In the process, they decided that they would no longer time their releases to issue support for all three operating system concurrently. Due to the fact that they had few customers using HP systems, HP/UX was the last in line to be released. Therefore, it took an inordinate amount of time to get vendor X's attention. In fact, the only way we got their attention was to get some of our customers who also happened to be some of HP's biggest customers to call vendor X's CEO and say that HP would provide vendor X with assistance. Upon research, the two companies found that vendor X's product had been making an undocumented subsystem call that had been re-implemented in

(continued)

the new release of HP/UX in such a way that it was extremely inefficient when used in this way. From HP's point of view, it was not a bug because its product had not been used in accordance with documentation. However, because this particular function call permeated a large amount of vendor X's source code, it would have required that a portion of its product be redesigned, something that vendor X was not able to do at that point in its business.

The result was that our company had to port to another object-oriented DBMS product and write some internal support for a feature (i.e., versioning) that the new vendor didn't support. In the meantime, we recommended that our HP customers back out of the new release, which required that we support the old release longer than we had intended. Given the other product enhancements we were committed to, it took almost a year and approximately $1.5 million to make the change.

6.6 Coming Up Next: Metadata and Change Management

As long as the focus remains on building software systems that emulate humans, we are likely to continue encountering the types of problems described in this chapter (i.e., software platforms that are not widely used because they are too difficult to configure and convert [maintain]). A better strategy emerges if we remember that the technical artifacts that have been most successful are those that served to augment humans' capabilities, not replace them. Glasses help us see better, automobiles let us go farther faster, lasers let us cut more precisely, on-board navigation systems help us get there as efficiently as possible; these tools contribute information and/or advice that affect our decisions—they do not make the decisions for us.

The prognosis for achieving the "Singularity" is not good if we continue to focus on initiatives that seek to make computers operate without human intervention when the success of such systems depends upon the ability of software developers to specify complex rules for configuration "from scratch." Building systems that simplify the task of understanding the information that is already in a software environment is the first step. In the next chapter we will consider the importance of metadata—data about data—in helping us reach this goal.

Exercises for Chapter 6

1. The model for an application and its environment provides a means of characterizing the major areas of functional activity required to design, implement, and maintain an application. As we have seen from the discussion in this chapter, the level of effort required in each area will vary significantly depending upon the following:

   - The nature of the application being implemented, in terms of both its functionality and its performance requirements
   - The number and types of legacy systems and applications to which the new application must interface
   - The volatility of the organizational environment that will use the application

   Each of these topics in turn can involve a large number of considerations—so many, in fact, that it is almost impossible to create a single checklist of required functionality that would be equally suitable for all cases. For example, characterizing the application requires understanding:

   - *The performance requirements*—Acceptable speed, number of concurrent transactions and/or users, need for continuous access, etc.
   - *The user community*—Types of users, characteristics of each class of users, absolute numbers, access rights, etc.
   - *The knowledge of the required functionality*—For example, if an application is based on a third-party ERP, module, the effort required to design the new application is significantly different than if the application is being internally developed.

   For you to be an effective software architect, therefore, it is important that you be able to use your understanding of the different challenges associated with each of the 8 Cs in the application model to allow you to prioritize the most important functional requirements for a particular application. The following exercises are intended to make you think about the challenges that must be faced in different application scenarios. Structure your answer as a well-written analysis, the type of document that you might create if you were a consultant writing a statement of work in which you wish to demonstrate your understanding of a prospective customer's needs in order to win against competitors. Consult Appendix A for tips on writing, and feel free to use the Internet to research industries or application vendors.

   a. A manufacturer of medical equipment has acquired a competitor. Each organization uses its own materials resource planning (MRP) application, one of which runs on a mainframe and was written internally in COBOL using flat files; the other uses an MRP application from Oracle running in a UNIX client server environment. Management decided to consolidate both applications using a client-server–based MRP module from SAP.

b. In order to receive Homeland Security funds from the federal government, state healthcare agencies need to provide weekly updates regarding reported cases of infectious diseases to the Centers for Disease Control. In addition, they need to provide an alert within 24 hours of learning of an incidence of any one of a list of particular infections (e.g., bubonic plague). To obtain this information, the state agency, whose own system is based on a COBOL IMS system, must collect information from clinics and hospitals throughout the state, which use a variety of packaged and internally developed applications for tracking patient information.

c. An insurance company offering property and casualty coverage (e.g., car and home insurance) wants to build a web browser–based means of allowing its customers to file claims and/or check on the status of claims. The PPC application for the company is based on a COBOL IMS system.

d. A large manufacturer of engines has grown by acquisition and has five data centers in various locations supporting different manufacturing sites throughout the world. Although all five centers are using the same MRP application, at the current time they have no means of exchanging information about inventory levels. Audits have indicated that the company is losing over a million dollars a year ordering parts from vendors that they could have more cheaply exchanged between sites, so it wants to implement an application that will allow the timely and efficient exchange of inventory between plants.

2. Another important skill for the software architect is the ability to choose a technology or architecture that is well-suited to the requirements of the application being built. Given the current state of technology (as represented in our previous discussions), which of the following technical architectures are best suited to the applications described below: DBMS-centric, middleware-based, or SOA. Use the model for the application and its environment to justify your answers.

   a. A web browser–based application that allows a customer to check on the status of a shipment

b. A trading application for use by stockbrokers
c. A logistics application that minimizes travel time for scheduling service calls
d. A financial application that automates the generation of daily, monthly, quarterly, or annual reports regarding the revenue and profitability of different business units

CHAPTER

7

Metadata and Change Management

Almost every major technical innovation in software has brought with it the promise of greater programmer productivity through reuse enabled by system software products. In one sense, these products have succeeded because they have significantly reduced the amount of time—and code—required to create more and more powerful applications; however, most often the reuse is restricted by the semantic domain of the system software product—that is, applications may share graphical objects (e.g., screen layouts, icons, etc.) or the same database—and most of the time this sharing happens only within development groups that are restricted to either the same business unit (e.g., marketing) or the same application (e.g., an enterprise data warehouse) rather than groups that span the enterprise. There are a number of reasons for this situation, such as internal rivalries between groups, concerns about job security, and minor differences in required functionality, which are hard to coordinate across groups that are coping with different schedule demands. However, technically one of the biggest challenges to effective reuse is a means of allowing a developer to find out what is available to reuse. The service registry in service-oriented architecture (SOA) provides a mechanism for this type of discovery, but it faces the same challenge as previous advances in software technology—namely, the fact that it is better suited to the development of new components and applications than the applications and software components that are already in use because multiple "translators" would be required to interface each application to the registry.

In short, organizations will never reduce the time and costs associated with configuration, confirmation, and conversion until they find a cost-effective means of discovering and *recording* a description of what they already have in a manner that allows that information to be searched and analyzed as effectively as business users make use of the information stored in data warehouses. Clearly, some means of acquiring the metadata that at least partially defines the data in files and databases will be an important part of the discovery process. In this chapter, we will argue that:

- The concept of metadata should be expanded to include both the configuration data used by system software products and a description of the information captured in the logs of these products.
- Storing this information in a queryable environment would greatly improve an organization's process for change management, driving down the costs of configuration and conversion.
- Even in the case that the preceding information could be automatically captured, the correlation of metadata across products and applications remains problematic.

- The biggest challenges in reuse are organizational rather than technical.

7.1   The Role of Metadata in Data Management

The Relationship between Metadata and Data Models

Metadata is most narrowly defined as *data about data,* but it would be more accurate to say that metadata is the set of statements or data structures that a programmer uses to configure and interpret the behavior of software, where those statements conform to some data definition language (or a GUI that itself conforms to some DDL). Without metadata it would be impossible for either a program or a person to determine the "meaning" of a sequence of bits. In the age of the standalone application there was almost a one-to-one correspondence between the file definition and the way data was stored on disk. Although more than one program might utilize a data file, they all shared the same file definition so the concept of metadata wasn't particularly interesting. But there was no electronic means of capturing the fact that two file definitions referred to the same data—for example, the fact that in a university environment a file containing registration information would have some of the same data fields as the file used by the controller's office for billing (e.g., student name and student ID).

The goal of database technology was to provide data security and integrity by having the access to all data managed by a single software component (i.e., the data manager). The process of designing a database required both a logical view of the data (in order to understand both how it was used and how to reduce unnecessary redundancy) and a physical view that corresponded more closely to how the DBMS would implement the data structures used to store and access the data. As a result, two types of metadata emerged—the *logical* and the *physical*—to reflect the two levels of design required to configure a database management system for use in a particular environment. Before you can configure a DBMS to represent data, you need to know what data you want to represent and how it is related. A logical data model represents that information, and there were several languages or graphical conventions that data modelers could use, for example the ERA model described in the Topic of Interest.

The physical data model determines the way a DBMS actually stores and accesses the data in a particular database. Recall that there were four major types of physical data models used by DBMS technology—hierarchical, network, relational, and object-oriented. Once the data modelers in an organization understood what data and data relationships they wanted to represent, the database administrator (DBA), who understood the data definition language used by the DBMS, would design the

> **Topic of Interest: The Entity-Relationship-Attribute (ERA) Model**
>
> The ERA model has only three basic concepts that are used to define everything else in a database—entities, relationships, and attributes—where:
>
> - Entities correspond to objects or what we call nouns in natural language; that is, they refer to people, places, or things.
> - Attributes characterize entities and can refer to either the properties of the object itself (e.g., a value indicating the *length* of the object) or a property that is used to characterize another entity (e.g., a value used to associate a particular instance of one object to another, as *department-number* might be used in the definitions of both *department* and *employee*).
> - Relationships explicitly define the links between objects; for example, that *d-num* in *employee* refers to the same information as *dept-no* in *department*.

physical database using the logical data model as a starting point to create the set of DDL statements that would configure the DBMS. The task of creating the physical database design (or the *schema* for the database) required information in addition to the logical design—for example, an understanding of how various applications would access the data, estimates about the relative volume of different types of entities, and the frequency of execution of queries and/or programs. For example, in the environment of a financial services organization, it is important to know that the number of banking transactions would be greater than the number of accounts. This information about usage and the volume of data was necessary because, depending upon the data model and capabilities supported by the DBMS, the physical data model could differ significantly from the logical data model.

For example, consider the case where a public university faces an ongoing decrease in the percentage of funds that it receives from the state, a situation that the president and provost seek to remedy by increasing the number of foreign students admitted. In an effort to analyze the effectiveness of their international recruiting efforts, the president and provost want a semi-annual report organized by country that tracks the number of applications, the number of students admitted, and their subsequent average GPA. The data modelers might design the logical data model to subdivide students into U.S. and international, and then subdivide the international students by regions. However, if the university uses a DBMS based on the network data model where pointers must be traversed to get to a record of interest, the DBA might opt to ignore the distinction of international region in the physical data model for performance reasons (e.g., because the president's report only has to be created twice a year and could be computed during off-hours, while day-to-day access to a particular student's record would be a much more frequent occurrence that might need to be performed in real-time).

Topic of Interest: Meta-Model vs. Data Model

In epistemology (the branch of Western philosophy that explores the history and nature of knowledge), the prefix *meta-* conveys the meaning *about (its own category)*. *Metadata,* therefore, means *data about data,* while the term *meta-model* refers to a model of a model. In the predecing discussion, we can also refer to the hierarchical, network, relational, and object-oriented data models as meta-models because they serve as a *model of a model.*

The Role of Metadata in Migration

In the case of smaller organizations or departmental databases, a project manager might choose to have the DBA design the physical database description without requiring the definition of a logical data model. However, as with many shortcuts, there was a downside to this practice. For example, if the organization later opted to migrate to a DBMS technology that used a different meta-model from the original DBMS used to implement the database, the new DBA—who was often a different person from the original DBA—would have to perform the same data analysis as the original data modeler to create a logical model and usage information that he or she could use in creating the physical design for the new DBMS system.

This example brings up an important point about change management. Unless an organization wants people to have to rediscover what previous employees have already learned, it must document what is discovered about every data source, or to quote the old saw, *if you don't learn from history, you are destined to repeat it.* Most database products provide some means of exporting schema information and often keep versions of this information as part of documenting the decisions made during the process of development. Even if the format of these reports is proprietary, electronic metadata capture is superior to manual documentation for two reasons. First, it is more likely to be correct—that is, correspond to the way the application or database is actually implemented—because manual documentation is usually drafted after the design has been "completed," at which point it is often difficult to accurately recall everything that should be documented. Second, text files and spreadsheets require interpretation and translation, which can be an extremely error-prone process when the data model or schema definition is extremely complex. (Recall that earlier we referenced one company where the report containing the definition for a single IDMS database was 400 pages in length and another where a COBOL file definition was 100,000 lines in length.)

On the other hand, as we will discuss later in this chapter, even though most development platforms capture and can export relevant metadata, it is not easy to capture all the metadata one needs for efficient change management. For example, in the scenario outlined previously, the DBA in charge of migrating to the new DBMS platform needs three types of metadata to be able to efficiently design the new physical data model and migrate the data:

1. The logical data model, so she doesn't have to repeat this type of data analysis in creating the new database design

2. The physical data model of the database that is being replaced, so she understands how the data is organized under the original DBMS in order to anticipate duplicate records

3. The relationships between the two

As indicated previously, DBMS products typically provide utilities for the second type of metadata, and database design and CASE tools provide the first and often a subset of the third. If the field and attribute names in the physical definition of the new database are the same as those used in the original database, one could write a program (or use a product) to compute the source-to-target mapping. Otherwise, this work has to be performed manually and can take weeks if not months. Note that if the database to be replaced has been in production for a considerable time, it will be important to know if the physical model has been modified, and if so, if the change has been reflected in the logical data model.

Note that we have been talking about how metadata can be used to streamline the replacement of DBMS technology, but an equally important problem is understanding how the interrelationships between databases could be affected by a proposed change to one of the data sources. The ability to rapidly perform this kind of impact analysis depends upon the third type of metadata described earlier—the metadata that relates data values across databases or data stores. As we will see, in some cases this may not be easy to automatically capture.

7.2   The Expanding Scope of Metadata

Metadata from System Software

Up until now we have been talking about the metadata that describes the data used by applications, but there are other types of metadata that can be used in the development and maintenance of IT systems—namely, the information used to configure system software. For example, consider the system administration tools that are provided by an operating system; they are driven by a set of commands that operate against a set of internal data structures (i.e., a data model) that represent such things as disks, users, directories, authorization (passwords), and peripherals. Likewise, much like a database manager in a DBMS, the system administration tools for system software include a set of commands that can report on the data that has been associated with the entities referenced by this data model. The same is true of all system software, such as a graphics, communication, or middleware product. Although DBMS and data integration products have extremely simple and explicit data models that contain little semantic content, the data models used by system software are semantically richer, but more constrained. For example, a graphics package might be extensible in that it allows a developer to create a specialized graphical object along with a set of functions to manipulate instances of that type of object, but access to and control of that new object must be defined in terms of the native objects and commands supported by the package. The reports generated by system software can be seen as analogous to the results of a database query that produces a flat file of data, while the logs kept by these products can be a valuable source of dynamic metadata. The fact that these reports use a proprietary format makes it no different from the export of metadata from any other application in a proprietary format. However, tools like PERL from UNIX make it relatively easy to parse data files for desired information.

The Role of Metadata in Heterogeneous Applications

By the age of the desktop, it was generally accepted that the vision of "open systems" that was popular during the age of the network was not going to be fulfilled. The mainframe wasn't going to die, and the IT systems used by large organizations were going to be both heterogeneous and distributed. As a result, one of the most strategic applications of the 1990s was the data warehouse, an application that provided management and marketing with a set of analytical tools for "slicing and dicing" key data drawn from the IT systems used to run the day-to-day operations. *Business intelligence* (BI) was one of the first of many types of heterogeneous applications that became possible during the age of the network. BI was initially geared at providing business users with a historical view of an organization's performance (e.g., how many snowboards were sold in Venice, California, in the month of May). Later, as companies began to use middleware and the Internet to allow applications to communicate in near real-time, heterogeneous applications for functions like supply chain management or customer relationship management became popular. However, the data warehouse allows us to highlight the bulk of the challenges one encounters in the representation of the metadata that describes data integration.

In contrast to previous strategic integration initiatives like migrating to a new type of DBMS technology, the data warehouse required continuous updates or feeds whether in batch or real-time. The result was that organizations began to realize that data integration could no longer be treated in a "one-off" manner. When migrating to a new application or database environment, it didn't matter whether a company used a tool or handwritten code to move the data because the source system (and associated data integration software) was going to be "retired" after the project was completed. However, the data warehouse implementation team had to create data interface programs not only to load the data warehouse, but also to refresh it. They also had to update those programs when the source application changed (or the users of the warehouse wanted new data), as well as monitor the data interface programs when they ran to ensure that the users were dealing with accurate information. For example, if some natural disaster occurred that shut down a data center that hosted one of the feeds on Monday, the data warehouse administrator needed some means of knowing that the data in the warehouse on Tuesday morning might not accurately reflect the state of the business. This type of information (e.g., that feed X successfully completed executing at time Y and moved Z records with no errors) is called *dynamic metadata*.

As we pointed out in the DBMS example earlier, the ability to electronically capture the relationships between the logical and physical data models was valuable in the case of migrating to new technology. With the data warehouse, it became critical to capture the mapping between the schemas used by the data sources and the schema for the data warehouse because once an organization depended upon the information in a data warehouse to make business decisions, it was critical that any impact of a change made to one of the operational systems serving as a data source be propagated to the data warehouse in as short a time as possible. For example, if the warehouse was updated on an hourly or daily basis, ideally the change needed to be implemented and tested within that period. The ability to rapidly perform impact analysis depends upon being able to quickly answer questions like "Which data interfaces use the field *employee-code* in the *payroll* database?" Because a large data warehouse may have a hundred or more daily feeds, having the metadata representing the source-to-target mappings stored in a system that supports queries is extremely useful.

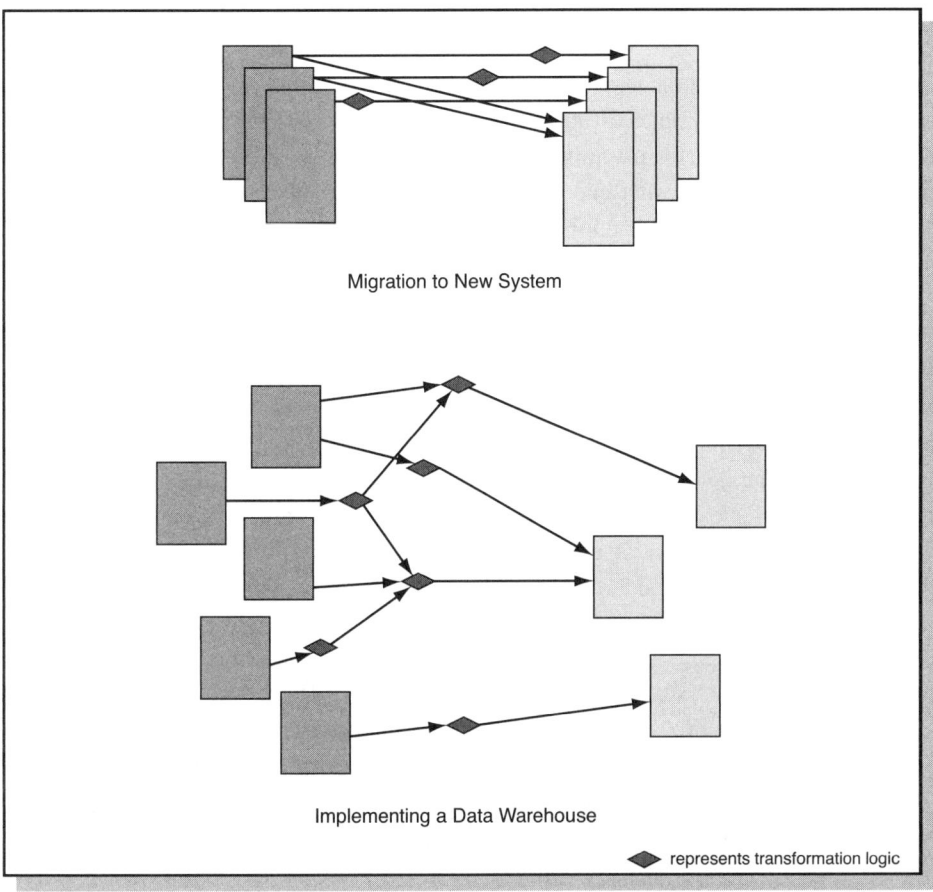

Figure 7.1   Differences in Mapping

As illustrated in Figure 7.1, it is also important to note that the relationships between source and target systems are significantly more complex in the case of a data warehouse than in migrating a single application or database for the following reasons:

- *Heterogeneity and potential overlap of data sources*
- *Different latencies in the data*
- *Complex data transformation requirements*

Heterogeneity and Potential Overlap of Data Sources

The data sources for a data warehouse often reside on different hosts under different technologies and sometimes different types of applications. However, sometimes data must be consolidated from equivalent applications, as in the case of a electronics manufacturing company that had 42 incompatible materials resource planning applications due to its growth by acquisition. As a result, the data modeling and data analysis required for a large data warehouse are typically much more complex than for other types of applications, because the data analysts must understand not only the schema for a particular data source and that used by the warehouse, but also how the schema for that data source relates to those of the other data sources: Do they share common fields? If so, is the format the same (e.g., telephone numbers with dashes versus telephone numbers with periods)? Are the semantics the same (e.g., is salary represented in dollars or dinars)? What do you do if two fields are supposed to contain the same information but have different data values (as in the case where a life insurance policy and an automobile policy for the same customer contain a different address. Which data source should be considered the *database of record* for this data element?)?

Topic of Interest: What Data to Trust

In any large organization, multiple databases contain the same information such as address. However, depending upon the industry, the data values for the common field in one application are more likely to be accurate than the same data in another. For example, in an insurance company, the customer address in the auto insurance file is more likely to be up to date than the value stored in the file for life insurance policies because customers tend to buy cars more frequently than they take out life insurance policies. As a result, in most data warehouse projects, one of the business rules that needs to be created for common data fields must specify which data source should be used as the *database of record.*

Different Latencies in the Data

In a global organization there are no "off hours." Likewise, one business unit may close its books on the 15th of the month, while another closes at the end of the month. Depending upon the nature of the information being consolidated, the data warehouse designer may need to stage the data (that is, store it in temporary tables) until all the data needed for the update has been gathered. As a result, the scheduling and monitoring of data warehouse feeds can itself become a fairly complex task.

Complex Data Transformation Requirements

To consolidate data in such a way that it is meaningful, a developer needs to understand not only that the fields in different data sources are related, but also how they are related. Often one must also transform the data values for one of two reasons:

- *To provide data at the desired level of granularity*—A single application like a financial trading system may process millions of transactions a day, but this is not the level of data that the users of a warehouse want to see in order to understand the *trends* in a business. Rather, the values are more likely to be "rolled up" from more atomic values—for example, totals by store, by region, by product, or averages.
- *To represent comparable data in a semantically consistent way so that it can be combined or compared*—For example, before one can compute total salary expense, all the subtotals of salaries from each of the data sources must be represented consistently—for example, weekly, monthly, or annually.

Sometimes these transformations are simple, but they often can become quite complex. For example, consider the case where a large multi-national corporation has five purchasing systems and wants to build a data warehouse to see how much of what items they are buying from each vendor in order to negotiate better discount rates. Because the same vendor may have different vendor IDs in different countries, it will be necessary to compare names, and perhaps even consult some external service to determine whether an entry in one system refers to the same vendor as another entry in one of the other source systems. Moreover, because this determination will need to be made every time the warehouse is refreshed, the most computationally efficient way to determine which warehouse record to update would be to keep a look-up table that correlates how each vendor in the source systems corresponds to the representation chosen for that vendor in the warehouse. This functional logic needs to be associated with the appropriate source-to-target mapping(s) to minimize the amount of time required to respond to change so that new developers understand how the source and target databases are related.

As illustrated in Figure 7.2, you might want to apply logic or transformations at one of three points in the execution of a data interface:

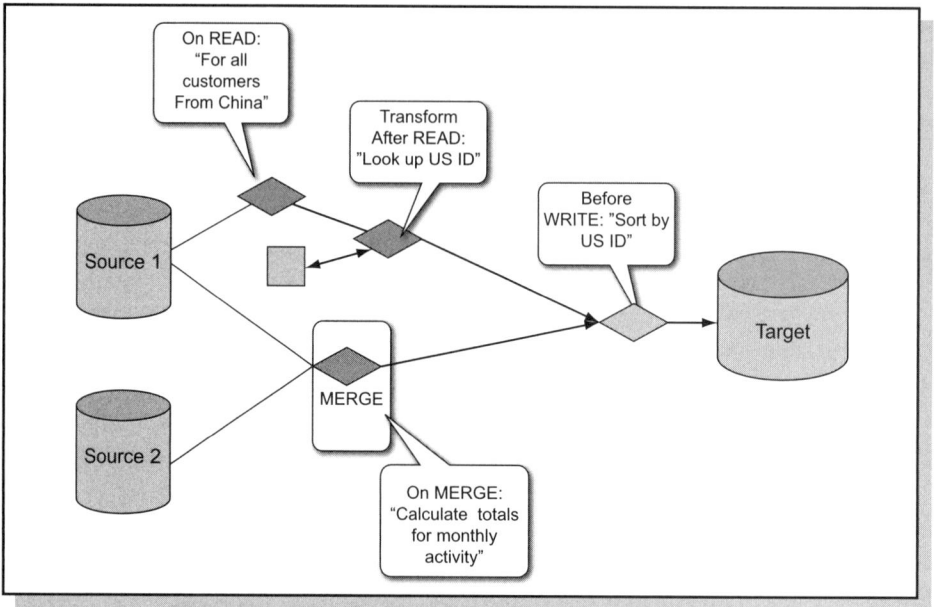

Figure 7.2 Places Where Transformations Can Take Place

1. *When reading the data*—For example, if you have a sequential file of customers around the world but only want to move information for customers residing in London to another host, it would be more efficient to check each record as you read it from the file and move only the records you want rather than moving all the data and doing the check on the new host.

2. *When merging data from different data sources*—Here one might want to flag an error when there is a record in data source 1 that doesn't have a corresponding record in data source 2.

3. *When writing to a target database*—For example, if you want to keep historical data, you might want to create a new key for each target record that is a sequential number one greater than the last key used for that record.

These examples are fairly simple, but in some cases it may take several pages of code operating against multiple input values to produce the desired value. As we will see, the representation of test and transformation logic is one of the most complex challenges in the representation of metadata. Yet it is also one of the most important because in highly heterogeneous environments (i.e., where the data warehouse brings the most value) well over half the input fields to the warehouse schema may require transformation logic. But before that, it is important to understand that software developers are not the only ones who need access to metadata.

Metadata for End Users

Up until this point, we have only been talking about technical metadata—the information needed by developers to create and maintain the programs that load and update the warehouse. As a result, this metadata references actual field names like CLES-CLMKYE. However, as illustrated in Figure 7.3, the users of the data warehouse are

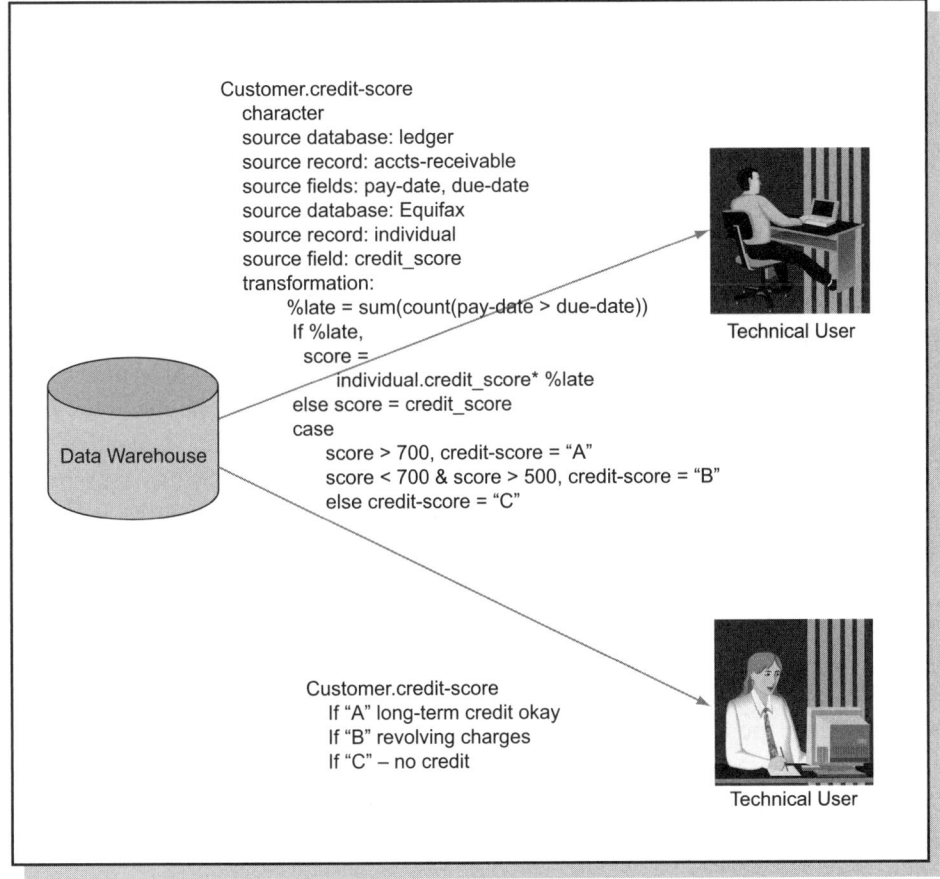

Customer.credit-score
    character
    source database: ledger
    source record: accts-receivable
    source fields: pay-date, due-date
    source database: Equifax
    source record: individual
    source field: credit_score
    transformation:
        %late = sum(count(pay-date > due-date))
        If %late,
            score =
                individual.credit_score* %late
        else score = credit_score
    case
        score > 700, credit-score = "A"
        score < 700 & score > 500, credit-score = "B"
        else credit-score = "C"

Technical User

Data Warehouse

Customer.credit-score
    If "A" long-term credit okay
    If "B" revolving charges
    If "C" – no credit

Technical User

Figure 7.3   Technical Metadata vs. Business Metadata

typically nontechnical and want two types of information: 1) the business metadata or a high-level understanding of what each field in the warehouse refers to (e.g., sales through distributors, direct sales, etc.), and 2) the *data lineage* of a value or how some value was computed (e.g., to answer questions like *How did you get this figure?*). In the latter case, the user wants to know the *data lineage* of the value; that is, which data values were used from which data sources and what was done to those values (and in what order) to produce the value found in the warehouse.

7.3 Data and Metadata

From a computational point of view—with one exception—the major difference between data and metadata lies in the volume. Even with the power afforded by today's hardware, it would not be feasible for a large organization to consolidate all its operational data into a single database. On the other hand, it would be quite feasible to store in a single database the static metadata that defines the software and databases used by a large organization, as well as a good part of the dynamic metadata of interest. (One would need a strategy for archiving the dynamic metadata because the volume of updates to a warehouse can be massive over time.)

The major difference between the data and metadata lies in the need to represent transformational logic. Although complex logic may relate the data values stored in a database (for example, computing profit may take 10 or 12 parameters and involve relatively complex math), the responsibility for "understanding" and performing the necessary logic lies with the application developer and the resulting application. Once the application has been confirmed, the only time someone would need to understand that code would be if a developer needed to modify it (for example, if the tax laws changed in such a way as to affect the formula for computing profit). In contrast, the logic required to correlate metadata descriptions is intended for use by humans in making decisions, whether it is the software developer trying to understand the impact of a change or the business user who wants to know, "Where did this number come from?"

Unfortunately, it is not easy to acquire and maintain metadata suitable for serving both types of users. In order to illustrate this, consider the situation faced by most data integration productivity platforms. Most of these products offer some graphical means of indicating the source-to-target correspondences, but they differ widely in their approach to the transformation of data. In the worst case, they have no support for data transformation, in which case there are two options:

- If they generate code, the developers can modify it by hand
- Programmers need to write and apply transformation logic outside the product in a preprocessing or postprocessing phase

In both cases the metadata contained by the data integration product no longer accurately reflects what happens when the code is executed.

Other products allow the developer to identify the input fields and output fields for the logic and associate the name of a hand-written user function with the appropriate source-to-target mapping. In this case, the product accurately reflects that some computation has occurred using the input field to produce a new value (or validate an old one), but a developer maintaining the warehouse would need to locate and read the code for the user function to understand the potential impact of some proposed change that involved one of the source fields (or—more risky—depend on some documentation captured by the integration product, such as a comment added by the original developer). Other products support wizards that allow developers to graphically string together primitive transformations (e.g., sum, subtraction, concatenation) or smart editors to assist in the creation of some programming language like SQL or Java. This last case provides an organization with the most complete metadata audit trail of what has been done, but requires that any subsequent developer be conversant with the programming language used. Moreover, in none of these cases is the information sufficient and/or appropriate for the business user who wants to know *How did you get this number?*

7.4 Metadata and Impact Analysis

The Vision

Clearly, if an organization had an accurate, centralized repository of all pertinent metadata and the ability to query that repository, it could drive down the costs of configuration and conversion by being able to perform rapid impact analysis in the following types of scenarios:

- *Improved data consistency*—For example, a bank that has grown by merging with other banks might need to change a customer's address multiple times. By investigating its metadata, the bank realizes that it has four databases that contain the field *customer-address—checking account, savings account, loans,* and *credit cards.* Two of these databases are associated with interactive applications that allow the value of *customer-address* to be updated, but only one of those two has a trigger that issues an update to the other three databases.
- *Impact analysis for a proposed change*—An application designer wants to modify a table definition to add a new field to a payroll system in order to start reporting personal days separately from

vacation days. He is worried that this might impact some of the reports generated for management and checks the repository to see. He discovers two reports and sends change requests to the groups in charge of generating the reports for approval.

- *Improved visibility for proof of compliance*—A company's auditors want evidence that the numbers being reported in the financials are accurate. The company issues a query against the repository to obtain the data lineage (including the fact that test and transformation logic has been performed) and presents it to the auditors so they can determine if and where they want to look further.
- *Reuse of knowledge gained across applications*—A manufacturer has grown by merger and acquisition and has five inventory systems in different geographic locations, as well as a data warehouse that IT uses to generate consolidated reports. Now that web services will allow a single installation of a new inventory application to be shared globally, the company wants to consolidate the five applications. The implementation team can query the repository to generate metadata reports that describe the data interfaces that initially loaded and/or refresh the warehouse to understand the following types of information for use in implementing the new web-based inventory application:
  - Which fields are equivalent in the five legacy systems
  - Where and how it was necessary to transform one or more source values to get a consistent representation across the legacy systems

In short, the metadata repository becomes the "corporate memory" of IT for the enterprise so that organizations could, over time, spend less and less on configuration and conversion and more on using technology that could make a significant difference to their operations. Of course, the success of an enterprise metadata repository depends upon the cooperation of *all* members of the IT department, and here one can run into conflicts of interest ranging from which group "owns" the repository (and thus has more power) to job security (e.g., in the case that fewer staff is required to maintain legacy systems).

The Metadata Repository

Over the past 20 years a number of quite powerful repository products have been available on the market, and consulting organizations like that of David Marco (2000) have developed a life-cycle methodology for the implementation and usage of the enterprise metadata repository. As illustrated in Figure 7.4, the earliest products—for example, the Platinum Repository (originally offered by Platinum Technologies and later acquired by Computer Associates)—provided three major types of functionality:

- The ability to automatically import metadata from a broad variety of software products, predominantly database management systems and CASE tools but also ERP products like those offered by SAP and Oracle
- Editors that allow the organization to create a common shared data model to which it can correlate the imported metadata and (perhaps) use as the data model for new development or the development of a data warehouse
- The ability to query and generate reports for the purpose of impact analysis and documentation

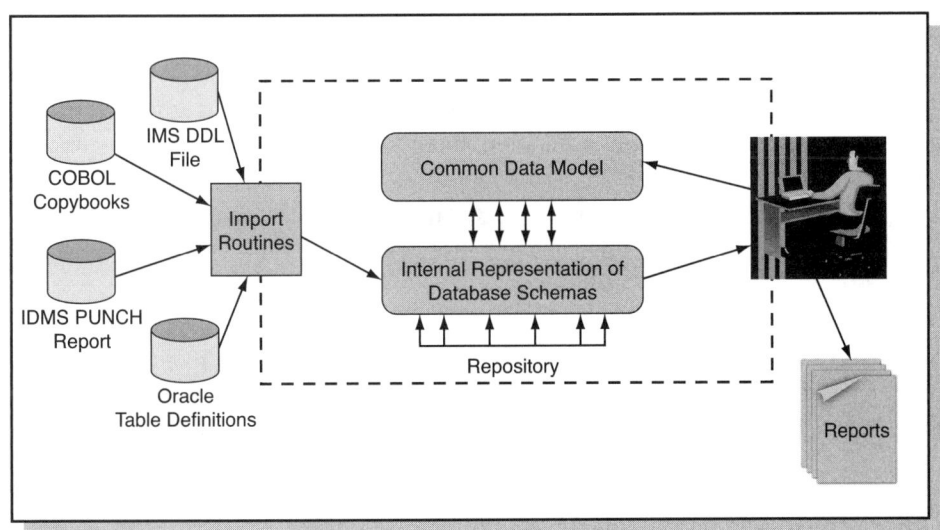

Figure 7.4   Metadata Repository

Later functionality included support for creating and maintaining metadata for the business user along with the capability of synchronizing metadata definitions so that if a change was made to one of the schemas, it was automatically reflected in related schemas when possible (and flagged if not). In actuality, because many changes are more complicated than something like a simple change to the format of a field, there were only a limited number of cases where synchronization could be handled without human intervention. However, the real value of this functionality was the impact analysis that told developers where to focus their attention.

Repository products typically had very simple meta-models that customers would use to design and implement their data model for representing metadata. As a result, every customer's configuration of a repository product was unique. This fact both limited the new functionality that could be offered by the repository vendor and was a deterrent to the development of common industry data models that could facilitate the exchange of information (e.g., in the case that a bank acquired another bank and needed to import the customer account data from the acquired bank).

Initially many of these products were developed and marketed by start-up companies that were trying to fill a functional gap that existed between DBMS vendors who—as suggested earlier—had a vested interest in keeping it difficult to migrate to a competitor's product. However, in large part because of the reasons outlined in the following section, very few organizations committed to building an enterprise metadata repository, and most of these small repository vendor companies were acquired by larger vendors like Computer Associates or Allen Systems Group to augment their other enterprise productivity product offerings. Because many of these companies had grown through acquisition, their product offerings could not communicate with each other so they used the repository product as the "backbone" for an integrated product offering. Companies like Allen Systems Group did a very good job of this integration.

The Reality

Most large organizations own a repository product, and many use them successfully on an enterprise basis for strategic applications like a corporate data warehouse. However, few if any of them have fully achieved the functionality previously described for three major reasons:

- The repository team focused on the wrong task.
- Too much integration was required.
- The time to benefit was judged to be too long.

The Repository Team Focused on the Wrong Task

Too often the repository team focused on defining and enforcing an enterprise data model rather than a metadata data model that would facilitate change management. In

Chapter 5, we discussed why many efforts to define an enterprise data model failed—the complexity of the task, management opting for COTS applications over internal development, and so on. But there is a cultural problem with tying the development of an enterprise data model to the implementation of an enterprise metadata repository: It is too often seen as an impediment to the other technical staff responsible for implementing and/or maintaining other applications. Either they have to wait until the design of the data model is ready or they have to consult with the data model team if the data model doesn't meet their needs. In either case, the communication typically takes a number of meetings and/or memos, and it's the application developer who gets penalized if the application is not operational on time.

An alternative approach might be to see the repository as a productivity tool from its inception, allowing the different development groups to use it to import schemas, specify data models, define mappings, and the like. With this approach, the team responsible for designing the data model would incrementally acquire the metadata that defines how the company actually uses its data rather than how they think the company should use its data, and would have the information they needed to justify any proposed changes (e.g., improved performance, better data integrity, etc.). Likewise, they would be able to accurately detail the level of effort required to implement that change.

Few organizations have taken this approach so it is not clear how effective it could be; the benefits would appear to be twofold. First, it is more likely that the technical staff on other projects would see benefit from the repository and feel that the needs of their application/database were being addressed by the common data model. Second, these short-term benefits would help ensure continued funding of the repository initiative.

Too Much Integration Was Required

As discussed, there is an enormous amount of metadata available from the system software and applications in use in a large organization. However, to mine this information a large number of interfaces must be written to import the metadata into the repository, because there is no widely accepted metadata interchange standard and many products are not "self-aware." (Although they may generate reports describing the contents of their internal data stores, they were not designed to allow users to query or traverse this information.) As discussed in Chapter 3, in the case of legacy COBOL-based systems, the metadata is difficult to interpret and may not accurately reflect the data that is actually stored in a record.

The Time to Benefit Was Judged to Be Too Long

As we have said before, organizations invest in software because they want to use it in as short a time as possible, and IT budget decisions are based in large part on the operational needs of the organization (e.g., increasing revenue, detecting fraud, cutting costs). Because it is hard to anticipate the projects or enhancements an IT organization might need to undertake in the future, it is hard for repository projects to provide specific estimates of when an organization will achieve a particular level of savings. As a result, the case for a repository initiative is often not as compelling to management as "the next new thing."

Topic of Interest: The LISP Workstation

Metadata capture would be much less of a problem if system software were designed to be *self-aware*—that is, to capture changes made to its internal database in such a way that it could make this information readily available to developers in a way that would foster reuse. The LISP workstation was designed with just this capability in mind. LISP (which stands for *LISt Processing*) was originally designed in 1958, and is one of the oldest programming languages in existence. Linked lists were one of the primary data structures used by LISP; in fact, source code was stored in the same manner as data. This not only allowed the language to run interpretively, but also allowed researchers at MIT to create a programming environment that was *self-aware*. This system software was subsequently licensed to two hardware providers (Symbolics Inc. and LISP Machines, Inc.), both of which manufactured and sold LISP workstations. The operating system on the LISP workstation kept an internal repository regarding every piece of code loaded onto that machine. Whenever a programmer created a function on a LISP machine, the system software immediately added that function to the internal repository so that if any other programmer encountered the function and wanted to know about it, she simply had to place the cursor on the name of the function and indicate with a key sequence which of the following information she wanted to see: *who-calls* (for impact analysis) to see what other functions used the function in question, *called-with* to get documentation on the parameters one should use when invoking the function, or the source code. Because of this and because a programmer could test a LISP function interpretively (i.e., without compiling it), the LISP workstation

---

was an enormously productive programming environment, and many proponents hoped that LISP might become a commercially viable language.

Originally a LISP workstation cost somewhere in the range of $60,000, which was $15,000 to $20,000 higher than the first UNIX-based workstations. However, it was not just the price differential that made the LISP workstation lose to UNIX—it was price coupled with other factors, such as the performance, limited support for source code control, the failure of artificial intelligence to deliver on its promise of the fifth-generation computer (the "thinking" computer), and the fact that UNIX was open source.

Service Registries

Up until this point, we have been talking about metadata as it applies to our understanding of how a computer is representing a set of data values. As illustrated in Figure 7.5, in the traditional environment, a data model was tied to a particular installation of some system software product and was two levels removed from the data itself.

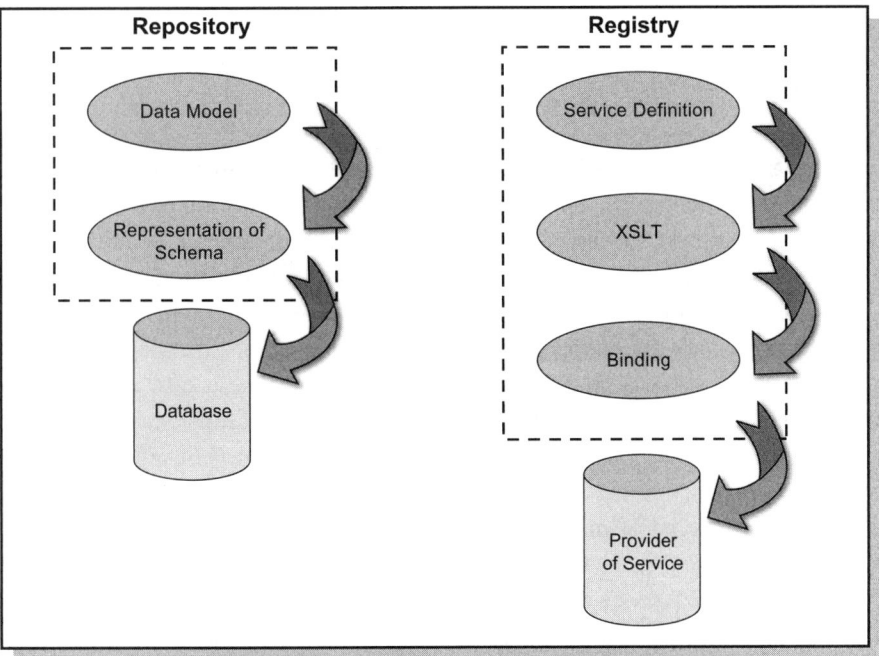

Figure 7.5 Levels of Indirection

Service-oriented architecture adds another layer of indirection by requiring that all services be defined in a common language, regardless of the particular language used to interface to that program or function. Universal Description, Discovery, and Integration (UDDI) is a language that defined a "protocol for publishing and discovering metadata about Web services, to enable applications to find Web services, either at design time or runtime" (Wikipedia, 2007). The Web Service Definition Language (WSDL) in turn is "an XML format for describing network services as a set of endpoints operating on messages containing either document-oriented or procedure-oriented information" (W3C, 2001).

Topic of Interest: The Data Model for Describing a Service

Each service definition in the registry takes the form of an XML document expressed in a dialect of XML called Web Service Definition Language (WSDL). There are two major types of information in a WSDL definition—information that defines the service at the logical level and information about how to bind that logical definition to an actual network protocol. The logical information includes an entry called *port type* that identifies the category under which this service should be "filed" in the registry. In this way a single logical entry can be associated with multiple bindings in the case that the service is available from a number of providers.

As you see from the Topic of Interest, the data model for defining a service includes a number of new concepts, the most notable of which is the concept of *binding* and the specification of the class of services under which this entry should be stored. This is analogous to the concept of a logical data model of a database that corresponds to but is not isomorphic with the physical data model. However, because the goal of SOA is to provide a metadata-driven means of integrating applications, the metadata includes information about how to bind the logical definition of a service to a concrete network protocol and message format to define an endpoint for the actual invocation of the service. As illustrated in Figure 7.6, this leads to two levels of representation for each service.

The other type of information contained in a WSDL is a definition of *port type*—that is, a logical name that defines the classification under which an XML registry should store the service definition.

However, as discussed earlier, a number of aspects of managing an SOA environment are not addressed by these standards. As a result, XML registry vendors like

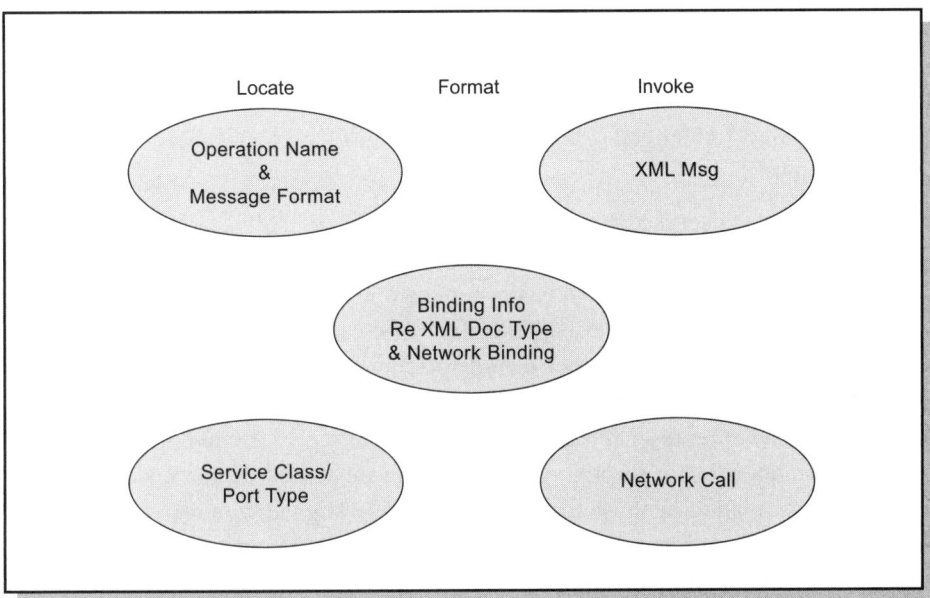

Figure 7.6   Role of Binding in WSDL Service Definition

Systinet also provide tools that allow their customers to not only define the "vocabularies" they will use to organize and provide access to service definitions, but also establish rules of "governance" for the addition and/or replacement of services to the registry.

XML Standards Initiatives

Thanks to the Internet, web services, and the concept of service-oriented architecture, metadata is center stage, with XML as the extensible, hardware-independent interchange format. Large groups around the globe are contributing to an increasing number of XML standards groups, including:

- The Dublin Core Metadata Initiative, "an open organization engaged in the development of interoperable online metadata standards that support a broad range of purposes and business models" (see www.dublincore.org.)
- The W3C, which has designed the Resource Description Framework (RDF) Core Model, the RDF Schema language, and the Web Ontology Language (OWL)

- Groups working on functional XML languages like BPEL (Business Process Execution Language)
- A large number of groups working on industry- or subject-specific XML schemas (e.g., HL7 for healthcare, CML for chemistry, MNML for music)

In Chapter 2 we discussed how the business model of software vendors worked against the success of open systems during the age of the network because if successful, these standards would make it easier for customers to migrate from one software product to another. Because the standards described earlier are more likely to be used for new types of applications rather than displacing old, there is a strong impetus for their adoption. However, there is still considerable risk because their success is so dependent upon the representation of meaning. In fact, given the complexity of representing meaning, it is not surprising that the software standards that have been most widely adopted tend to be those that are more closely aligned with hardware and protocols for communication rather than those that deal with content and meaning. XML standards depend upon large numbers of diverse groups coordinating the meanings of arbitrary tags (e.g., length in musical notation as opposed to length in mathematical notation), the type of initiative that has historically failed. However, there are at least three reasons to believe that in this case, these standards may be widely adopted, namely:

1. *There is a huge desire for them to work.* No one who has ever used the Internet can deny its power and the benefits it can bring. Whether it's the ability to communicate in near-real-time with friends and family or to access materials from the world's great libraries while sitting in your room, the Worldwide Web has transformed the world—for better and for worse.

2. *Service oriented architecture is additive (evolutionary) as opposed to disruptive (revolutionary).* Earlier attempts at interoperability depended upon the adoption of a single intermediate language (e.g., SQL, CDIF [CASE Data Interchange Format]) whereas SOA assumes that there may be local dialects and supports a level of indirection (i.e., the binding) that can accommodate them. Although it may be necessary to create translators to move between the dialects (for which W3C provides another dialect of XML, XSLT [XML Schema Language Transformation]), the fact that a translation was performed and information about what was done in the process is documented in the registry is a vast improvement (and

much more effective for change management) over earlier architectures where support for "user functions" was more like an afterthought.

3. *Both hardware and software vendors stand to make a huge amount of money if they do work.* As discussed before, despite the fact that they supported standards initiatives, large software vendors did not push for their adoption when it meant that it would be easier for customers to "mix and match" installations of their products (e.g., the ability to license SQL Server instead of DB2 to provide more capacity in an organization using DB2, much like you might buy a disk from Seagate rather than Dell). In this case, the vendor could lose business, but the Worldwide Web opens up huge markets for new types of software products that will create a pull for the sale of more hardware and networking technology.

As a result, web services and XML will become two of the industry's pervasive standards. Of course, the law of the conservation of complexity still holds, so although SOA provides a robust architecture for efficiently building heterogeneous applications, it does not eliminate complexity. Either programmers must encounter long, error-prone learning curves to understand the differences between different XML schema definitions or a new class of tool must be developed to help automate that process—namely, the ontology editor.

Ontology Editors

In most early adoptions of SOA, organizations are choosing to bind service definitions at design time, in which case the developer can puzzle out whether a particular port type contains the service he needs and verify that the correlation of tags across XSDs makes sense. However, the W3C also anticipates that some binding could be dynamic (i.e., bound at the time of the application's execution), so that each time an application requests a particular service, it might invoke a different implementation of that service. In this case, in the process of executing, a program would dynamically consult the registry to find the most suitable service and invoke it. It is reasonable to expect then that as the scope of applications grows, an ontology (or semantic network) like the Semantic Web would be used in the process of locating the appropriate service. The Semantic Web is based on a data model called the Resource Description Framework (RDF), a variety of interchange formats that are formally defined in the RDFS (RDF Schema) and OWL (Web Ontology Language). In this case, to capture the metadata audit trail that described the execution of a composite application an ontology editor (or some next-generation metadata capture product that included this functionality) would need to be able to export a description of how a portion of the Semantic Web was traversed.

7.5 Repository, Registry, or Both?

XML also supports a standard for mapping between an XML document using one schema into one using another—XSLT (XML Schema Language Transformations). When coupled with this capability, some organizations might think that their change management problem has been solved. Rather than worrying about establishing an enterprise repository initiative, they'll just get a handle on their metadata when they implement SOA. But this strategy will not work because—as you know by this point in the text—there is no "blank slate" where IT organizations are involved. Unless it is to be used for standalone applications, new technology must be integrated with the old, and few mission-critical applications are XML-enabled. Therefore, if SOA is to deliver on the promise of reuse, translators must be created to invoke any legacy application as a service.

In short, although SOA provides an extensible and efficient architecture for integration, it actually adds to an organization's existing integration burden. As a result, it becomes even more imperative that an organization develop and adhere to some automated strategy for metadata acquisition. However, if this strategy is to be successful it must be evolutionary in two respects. First, it must be able to be incrementally deployed; that is, it should both bring value immediately to any development initiative and over time contribute to the development of corporate standards for data representation, governance, and so on. Second, it must either 1) be extensible with respect to the acquisition of metadata from new types of tools or technologies or 2) facilitate its own replacement by providing the ability to flexibly export the metadata it maintains. We will come back to these ideas in Chapter 9 once we have discussed integration technologies in the next chapter.

7.6 Trends and Tradeoffs

The tasks of configuration and confirmation continue to increase in complexity as software developers use system software to more rapidly build applications to address the needs of highly distributed users in heterogeneous computing environments. The metadata specified in the process of configuring these productivity platforms contains information that could reduce effort in three of the areas across the application model:

- *Configuration* by helping developers discover how data is used and what code/services are available
- *Confirmation/correction* by helping characterize the expected behavior so that tests can be designed to both comply with and violate those expectations
- *Conversion* through providing rapid impact analysis to determine the impact of making a proposed change

However, due to the heterogeneous nature of both organizations' computing environments and the choice of productivity platforms available for system development, the challenge in developing a metadata acquisition strategy is that in many ways it is as complex as the task of data integration.

SOA is a metadata-driven architecture that seeks to provide a platform-neutral means of maximizing the reuse of software assets, while enabling the efficient and cost-effective exchange of information across organizational entities. In order to maximize the reuse of the operational systems currently in place in SOA environments, it will be critical for organizations to be able to solve the problem of metadata integration in spite of the challenges outlined in this chapter. Otherwise, they are likely to not only face increased maintenance costs, but also incur serious risks in their ability to detect and correct system defects that could have serious consequences for their operations.

7.7   Coming Up Next: Integration Technology

Now that you have the background to understand the types of integration challenges you are likely to encounter in different IT environments, we are in a position to evaluate the strengths and weaknesses of different types of integration technology.

Exercises for Chapter 7

1. A number of visionaries would like a metadata repository to be "active" so that if someone made a change to one schema, it would be automatically reflected in any schema to which it was related. What are the problems associated with implementing this functionality? Are there some cases where it simply cannot be done? Are there some reasons that one wouldn't want this functionality? Describe what you think would be the best compromise, that is, the functionality that you think would be most helpful to an organization.

2. A branch of the military has used an integration tool that captures a full metadata audit trail to create approximately 300 translators to interface 75

contracting applications to an electronic procurement package. They have been informed by the vendor of the procurement package that the new release will be based on Oracle and have a different schema than the old. Describe how you might use metadata to streamline the update of the interfaces to the new release.

3. Auditors are encouraging organizations to put in place IT controls that prove that their IT systems are operating and/or being used in compliance with their documented business processes. Often this documentation will require proving that a certain series of actions have taken place in a particular sequence across a number of systems. For example, consider the case when a company terminates an employee. The following applications must be updated before human resources releases permission for a final paycheck to be cut: the email account must be cancelled, any passwords associated with applications or machines removed, security badges/keys/etc. returned, changes to healthcare insurance made (cancel or COBRA), and the payroll system updated to reflect the termination and amount of the final check. Discuss various options for automating the creation of a report or a sequence of reports that proves that the updates took place in the order listed earlier.

CHAPTER

8

An Overview of Integration Technology

To someone reviewing the table of contents for this book, it might seem strange that the chapter dealing with integration technology occurs so late in a book that is focused on software integration. However, too often people try to evaluate architectural solutions and integration technology without really examining *what* they are integrating. A sound integration strategy must consider the functionality not just of the new application or environment, but of the computing environment in which that new technology is being implemented. As a result, it was important for you to understand the strengths and weaknesses of the technology that dominated previous periods so that you can accurately determine the applicability of different integration technologies to different types of environments. In this chapter we will once again start with a historical view of the evolution of integration technology because many (if not most) products were created to address a particular set of requirements that were important at that time. However, we will pay particular attention to the strengths and weaknesses of the technology with respect to metadata capture and auditability during every period because the ability to perform impact analysis is critical to reducing the cost of both configuration and conversion.

Now that it is widely recognized that many of the problems facing IT cannot be solved without an enterprise approach to integration, it is common to see vendors advertising a "one stop serves all" solution even if the functionality that comprises that solution (often the result of a series of corporate acquisitions) isn't fully integrated. In the last half of this chapter, we will use this understanding to enumerate the characteristics of an ideal integration platform so that you can use this model as a framework in evaluating both the best mix of products to meet the short-term integration requirements for some application and a strategy for a long-term solution for enterprise integration.

But before we undertake this discussion, it is important to remind you that this is not an exhaustive study of software integration because the topic would require a discussion of technologies developed over a period that spans more than half a century and hundreds (if not thousands) of products. Moreover, as discussed by writers as diverse as Toffler (1970) and Kurzweil (2005), not only is the rate of change increasing but the body of knowledge is increasing exponentially. In fact, the differences in what humans know—even in a specific field like software technology—could someday make us as specialized as the cells in a body. One of the areas in software technology that is changing the fastest in terms of products and terminology is the area of integration, in large part because it is still relatively early in its *hype cycle*. (See the following Topic of Interest.) As a result, in reading the following material, focus on the architectural characteristics and the pluses and minuses of each, because this knowledge will help you assess the strengths and weaknesses of "new" solutions that come to market after the publication of this book.

Topic of Interest: The "Hype Cycle"

Most industries are regulated with respect to the products or services they provide. Manufacturers have to demonstrate that their products meet safety standards, lawyers have to pass the bar exam, drugs have to be approved by the FDA, and so on. The case is not so clear with software. Although particular types of products can be certified as complying with standard interfaces or meeting particular benchmarks, there are no functional requirements or standards that are analogous to the safety standards for physical products. Because of this, there are no penalties for a vendor selling faulty software. In short, there are few products to which the statement *caveat emptor* (Latin for *Let the buyer beware*) applies more than the acquisition of software. This situation is exacerbated by what the Gartner Group labeled *the hype cycle* in 1995—the excessive exuberance that society exhibits with the introduction of new technology and the subsequent disappointment experienced when the reality falls short of the promise. In Chapter 10, we will discuss how the business model of several key industries benefits from the hype cycle, thereby making it unlikely that this situation will change.

8.1 Age of the Database: Co-exist or Migrate

By the time relational database technology became commercially viable, organizations had already made a significant investment in systems using a hierarchical or network data model. As computer scientists began to explore how to best introduce relational database systems into the mix, they settled on one of two approaches:

- Leave the existing databases in place and design a hybrid system that allowed the three types of DBMS products to work together.

- Develop productivity tools to help automate migration from hierarchical- and network-based systems to relational DBMS platforms.

Although the latter approach was more successful, we will briefly consider the former because some current technologies face many of the same problems that these products encountered.

Heterogeneous Database Management Systems

Database management products based on the hierarchical and network data models were extremely efficient for the operational applications they supported, but provided no easy way to generate the reports needed by management. When some business unit needed information from one of the databases, it would submit a request to IT and sometimes have to wait weeks or months to get access to the information it needed because of the backlog of work in IT. The ability to use a language as simple as SQL to access the data in a database was one of the greatest advantages of relational database technology. As a result, in the mid-1980s database researchers began to explore the possibility of building a type of heterogeneous database management system. As illustrated in Figure 8.1, the concept behind a multibase (also called a federated database) was to use a relational DBMS to loosely couple other databases regardless of the data model upon which they were based. In this way, existing applications could run as written, while a relational query manager would serve as the front end to facilitate management reporting.

In normal operation, a relational query manager uses a combination of table definitions, information about how those tables were actually stored (e.g., pointers and indices), and relational algebra to *decompose* the query issued by a user or application into a set of subqueries. Once these subqueries are executed (often in parallel), the relational query manager merges the results to produce the desired table. In a multibase, the query manager required two other capabilities:

- The ability to recognize when a subquery required data from a remote system and/or another co-resident database system
- The ability to send and receive messages from that remote system or invoke a co-resident independent database

Initially, database researchers envisioned federated databases that could perform updates as well as consolidate data from different systems, but updates also required additional capabilities. For example, recall that the term *transaction* refers to a series of updates to a database that should be treated as atomic by the DBMS; that

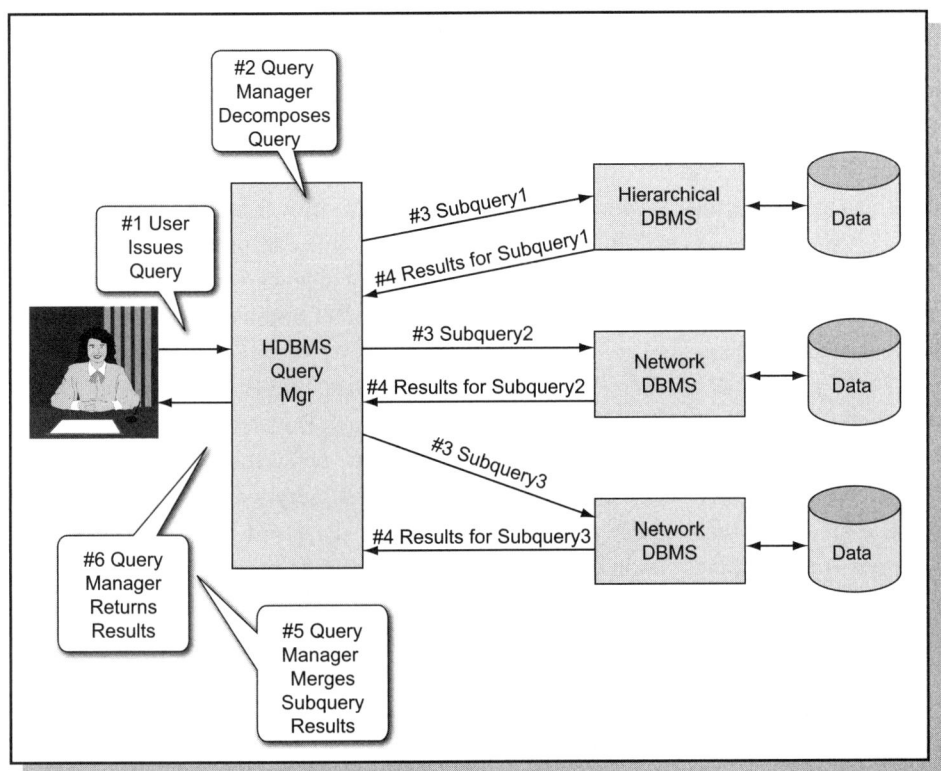

Figure 8.1   Architecture for a Heterogeneous DBMS

is, all of the updates must complete successfully or none of them should be performed. In a standalone DBMS, this functionality could be achieved in a program
through the use of three commands: BEGIN WORK, COMMIT WORK, and ROLL-
BACK. But in a heterogeneous DBMS, a transaction could entail updates to databases
residing on different hosts, where the question became what to do if one of the hosts
was offline.

   To solve this problem, database researchers proposed the concept of a two-
phase commit, which required creating a software component that coordinated the
behavior of all the data managers that governed records affected by the transaction. In
the first phase, the coordinator would issue a *commit-request* to each data manager,

after which it would perform the updates within the scope of an open transaction. At the start of a heterogeneous transaction, the coordinator would issue a BEGIN WORK command to all the data managers and request the desired records; once access to all the necessary records was obtained, the coordinator would make all the updates. If the coordinator received no errors, it then issued a COMMIT WORK command to each data manager; otherwise it would issue a ROLLBACK. But this approach would not always work, as in the case that the coordinator failed in the process of issuing the *commit* commands. In this case, one or more of the data managers would be waiting for the commit command and never receive it, blocking other applications from access to those locked records.

A number of companies like IBM, Control Data, and Burroughs successfully developed heterogeneous DBMS products or prototypes. But, with one exception that we will discuss below, the major shortcoming that prevented their adoption was that they were too hard to configure. For the heterogeneous query manager to work, it had to have a schema that correctly correlated all of the data from multiple operational schemas—in short, a common data model. Moreover, in the process of designing this common data model the development team had to address how to handle differences in the representation of common data elements, which required transformation code. As a result, even if successfully implemented, heterogeneous databases were extremely brittle, making conversion/maintenance very difficult.

The one product that was commercially successful with a similar type of architecture is a product called FOCUS from a company called Information Builders Incorporated (IBI). IBI sells FOCUS as a 4GL report writer that can access data from a wide variety of legacy mainframe products. Like the heterogeneous database management systems discussed earlier, it takes a significant amount of time to configure FOCUS. Moreover, its runtime components are compute-intensive and often require hardware upgrades. However, once that investment is made, it provides functionality that otherwise requires the use of multiple products today, so it remains viable in IT shops with substantial investments in legacy mainframe systems.

Code Generators for Migration

Code generators were another type of data integration product developed during this period. These products were intended to help automate the migration from hierarchical and network-based systems to relational systems and utilized the techniques and technologies used by the COBOL report writers developed in the last half of the 1970s. COBOL report writers provided developers with an interface that allowed them to define the format of a desired report using the names from a COBOL copybook to

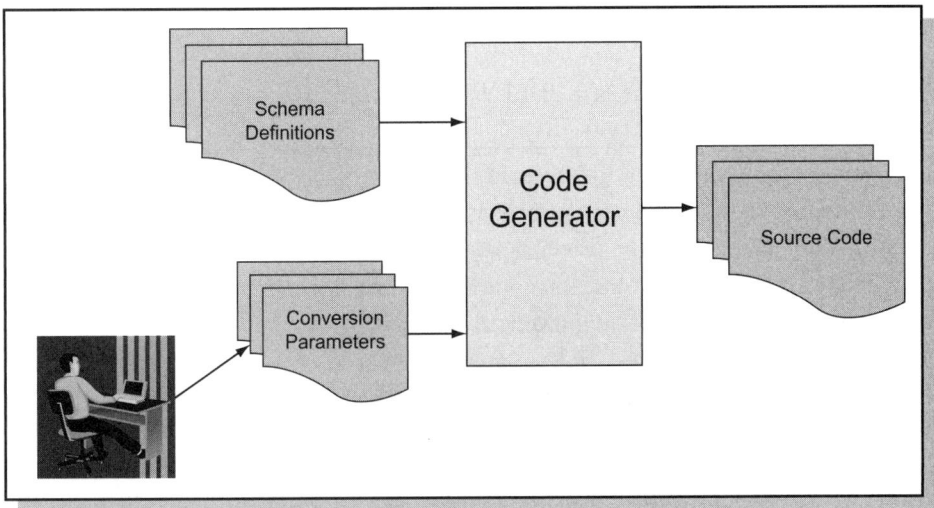

Figure 8.2   Architecture for Code Generators

refer to the desired data values in the report. Once this report definition was completed, the report writer would use this definition along with the copybook to generate the source code for the COBOL program required to produce that report, which the developer could edit if additional functionality was needed. The most functionally robust and successful of these migration products was produced by Carleton Corporation (a company that was later acquired by Oracle).

As illustrated in Figure 8.2, the code generators for migration used three types of input:

- The native schema definition for the source database
- The schema for the relational database that was to serve as the target
- A control file written in a proprietary language that allowed developers to indicate not only how they wanted to correlate the data, but also how they might want to transform it in the process of the migration

The output of these products was usually COBOL source code that performed the desired migration. (Carleton later released a version that produced C code.) The major drawback to these products was that often the code that was produced was very hard to read and therefore almost impossible to debug in the case that the program failed, a situation that was not infrequent when the source data was stored in COBOL files or IMS databases where the use of REDEFINES often led to inconsistencies in the data.

Topic of Interest: The Volatility of the Software Market

Compared to other industries, there is a low barrier to entry for starting a software company. Some products may require a complex environment for testing (for example, an integration product that provides interfaces intended to run on the mainframe), but a software entrepreneur doesn't have to own this software to develop the product. As a result, it is relatively easy for smart people to found a start-up software company, but it is hard for them to compete with large companies over time unless they were "first to market" and became the market leader or have some unique intellectual property.

When the *hype* around the introduction of a new technology begins to cool, market consolidation follows—smaller companies are acquired by larger companies that want to either fill a functional hole in their product offerings or buy a competitor in order to acquire their customer base and maintenance revenue. The existing customers of a software company that has been acquired by a competitor often face an unplanned integration problem as they are gradually forced off the acquired product when the acquiring company announces that it will stop support.

Likewise, in order to participate in new hype cycles, companies often repackage ("rebrand") existing products under new names. Often these secondhand goods are presented as part of an integrated solution, when in fact, a customer would face a huge integration challenge should it buy the "total" solution. As a result, if you are confused by the large number of products in the marketplace, you are not alone. That is why it is important to understand the "provenance" of a software product as part of assessing its applicability to the technical challenges for which it is being proposed.

The State of Metadata Capabilities

The behavior of both heterogeneous DBMS and code generators was driven by metadata that described the relationship between source and target systems; however, this information was not captured in a form that could be exported. The lack of this functionality is not surprising in the case of code generators because these products were intended to assist organizations in migrating from legacy DBMS environments. But it is also important to realize that in the 1980s few people in the industry could appreciate the difficulty that organizations have today in replacing mission-critical applications or the amount of money organizations would be spending on configuration, confirmation, and conversion.

8.2   Age of the Network: Co-exist and Consolidate

As stated earlier, it was during the age of the network that companies came to accept that their IT systems were likely to remain heterogeneous. This realization led to two types of integration initiatives—the data warehouse and enterprise application integration.

Data Integration and the Data Warehouse

The next major advance in integration technology occurred in reaction to the realization that the open systems initiative was not going to result in widespread interoperability. Management finally accepted the fact that their IT systems were likely to remain heterogeneous and distributed, but they were still looking for a way to benefit from the superior reporting capabilities of relational DBMS products. At this point relational database technology had matured, there was a relatively large base of programmers with relational skills, and the cost of a relational DBMS running on a UNIX platform made it feasible for departments to purchase and maintain their own relational systems. For these reasons, by the early 1990s the data warehouse emerged as one of the most strategic applications of the decade, and one that remains important in most large organizations today.

The data warehouse provided a solution to a major contributor to the backlogs of work for IT, management's unending demand for new types of reports. As the cost of relational database technology and hardware decreased, many departments chose to build their own data warehouse. By providing departmental data warehouse development teams with flat file dumps of the information required for these reports, IT could focus on the mission-critical applications that ran the business rather than crafting specific report applications. This strategy was effective for meeting management requirements while minimizing the impact on IT schedules. However, the result was that the process of software development became more decentralized as various departments added staff and budget to build their own warehouses. This decentralization enabled departmental purchases of software products, which has in turn contributed to the spiraling costs of configuration, confirmation, and conversion.

The development team in charge of the data warehouse faced four major challenges:

1. Understanding the nature of the data available in the source systems and using this information to design a data model that made sense to business users and could serve as the schema for the warehouse. Although this was a relatively easy task in the case of a data mart, it could constitute a lengthy undertaking in the case of an enterprise warehouse. In fact, some software vendors and consulting firms began to offer industry-specific models (e.g., for banking, retail) as product offerings to help reduce the time required for this process.

2. Specifying the mapping between the fields available in the data sources and the attributes in the warehouse schema.

3. Implementing the batch programs required to initially populate the data warehouse.

4. Implementing the programs required to refresh the information in the warehouse.

According to Bill Inmon (1996), one of the leading visionaries of this type of application, the tasks associated with data integration could take up to 80% of the time required to implement the warehouse.

Four data integration technologies emerged to meet these needs:

- ETL (extract, transform, and load) products
- Gateways
- Data profiling tools
- Data quality tools

ETL products. ETL products provided data warehouse developers with a user interface that allowed them to graphically indicate both the mapping between the source and target databases and the transformation logic to be performed on the data values prior to populating the warehouse. In the case that the logic was too complex to be specified with a GUI, ETL products allowed users to attach user functions to mapping specifications. The output of using these interfaces was an interface specification in the form of a SQL statement that served as input to an engine that would perform the data manipulation required to fulfill the specification. ETL products utilized an embedded RDBMS to process the data; as a result, they are said to have an engine-based architecture.

This architecture provided ETL products with several advantages:

- First, it made them easy to install and use because they were loosely coupled with the systems constituting the data sources by means of flat files (and later gateway products), each of which presented the data as if it were the information from a single table.
- Their GUI made them easy to use.
- The embedded engine offered two important benefits:
  - During development, the engine could run in interpreted mode allowing developers to interactively examine the output of each step in the process to ensure that the data looked correct.
  - Because all data had to pass through the embedded engine on its way to the warehouse, it was easy for the ETL product to capture dynamic metadata about number of records moved, errors encountered, and so on.

However, as illustrated in Figure 8.3, there are downsides to the engine-based architecture, the biggest of which is that when large amounts of data were being consolidated, the ETL engine could become a bottleneck in the process. The other is that ETL products typically could only process the files from one data source at a time. When a warehouse required data from two data sources, the developer would have to

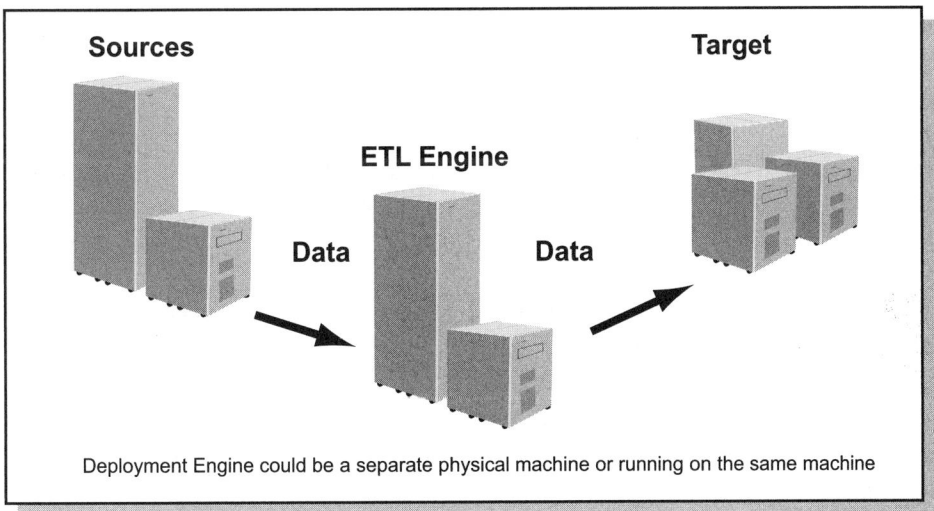

Figure 8.3   ETL Architecture

create three ETL jobs—one to read each source and populate *staging tables* (i.e., tables to hold the intermediate data) and a third job that used the staging tables as input and issued SQL commands to sort and merge the data from the two sources to produce the appropriate target table(s). All this I/O could lead to significant computing overhead.

In fact, Teradata, a manufacturer of a highly parallelized relational DBMS that runs on pro, recommends an extract, load, and transform (ELT) process that immediately writes the data to staging tables within the Teradata database so that all subsequent data manipulation (i.e., data transformations, sorts, and merges) takes place within the Teradata engine. At the height of the hype cycle for warehouse tools, there were 12–15 vendors of ETL products, but after industry consolidation, as of 2007 there were two major vendors—Informatica and IBM (formerly Ascential).

Gateways. ETL products varied significantly in their ability to interface to legacy mainframe environments. Although a few actually generated COBOL code that ran on the mainframe, it was frequently necessary to write additional code that ran before or after the generated extract program, such as code that "flattened" files that contained REPEATING GROUPS and the like. For this reason, a large number of IT organizations found it easier to simply provide the warehouse implementation team with flat file dumps. However, this meant that ETL vendors couldn't provide the full "data lineage" of the data values in the warehouse. Over time, a number of *gateway* vendors like Striva and Attunity appeared that provided data warehouse developers with a relational interface to nonrelational data sources. These products are components installed on the host machines for nonrelational data sources that provide access through either SQL or ODBC and a metadata audit trail back to the data source. Once installed, this type of product eliminated much of the support required from the individuals maintaining the data sources. At least one of these companies did extremely well as the competition between ETL vendors grew; in fact, because of its successful partnering strategy, Striva became a strategic acquisition for Informatica as Informatica sought to establish itself as one of the two dominant vendors in the ETL space.

Data profiling tools. Understanding the data contained in a data source is also a complex undertaking, due to both the complexity of their underlying schemas and the way new data is introduced over time. As a result, even the users of an operational system only know a fraction of the information required to understand the source data sufficiently to build a data warehouse. In building data warehouses there is even more of a learning curve because the data warehouse team often has no experience with the source databases. To fill this need, a number of *data profiling* products appeared (such

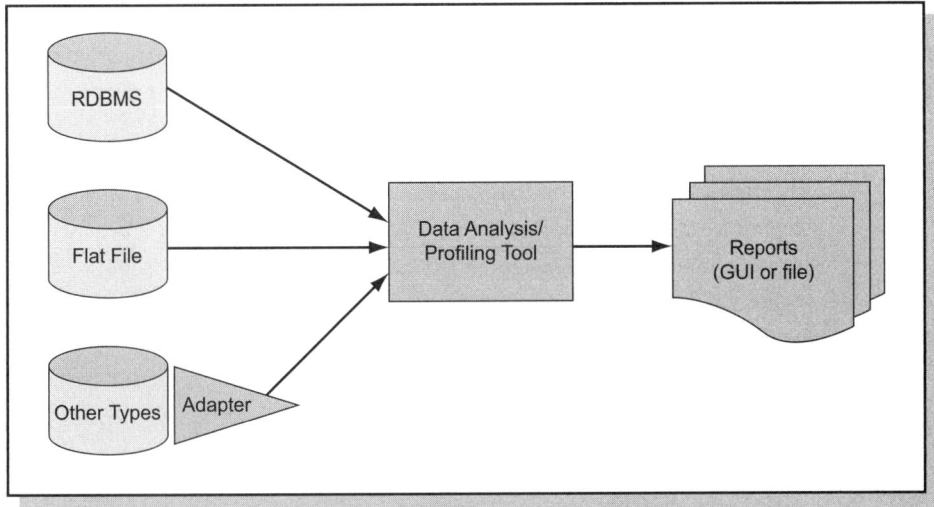

Figure 8.4   Data Profiling Product

as Axio from Evoke or Profile Stage from IBM/Ascential). These products scan and analyze the data that actually occurs in a database. As illustrated in Figure 8.4, data profiling products require that each sequence of records they examine have the format of a relational table (i.e., where each record consists of the same number of the same sequence of fields). Profiling products can operate with or without a formal definition of the input table, because they are able to predict field boundaries by patterns in the data. They are also able to compare the contents of one input file with that of others.

Profiling products generate reports that contain information on such things as:

- The format and content of fields; for example, the fact that a field contains two-character values that correspond to the abbreviations for the states, or that a field consists of a number ranging from 1 to 5
- The frequencies of different values in a field; for example, the fact that in 9,315 records a field contains the letter *M*, in 7,322 records it contains the letter *F*, and in only 1 record it contains the letter *G*
- Determinations of which field(s) serve as primary keys (e.g., those where every value is unique across the records) and relationships across multiple files or tables (e.g., where what appears to be a primary key in one file occurs, possibly with duplicates, in another file that has a different primary key)

Although the data warehouse was the major motivation in the creation of data profilers, data profilers are useful in a number of situations where developers have limited information about the contents of a database or file, for example:

- Third-party consultants or outsourcers who have limited contact with the staff maintaining the data sources
- Law enforcement agencies that seize computer files and have no cooperation from the owners of the data
- Organizations that receive files from external organizations—for example, an online auto auction that needs to process the DMV information from each of the states or a financial services provider that wins a 401(K) account from a competitor and receives the employees' investment information on tape

Data quality tools. Data in production databases is inconsistent or incorrect for a number of reasons—applications being designed in parallel, typos during data entry, growth through mergers and acquisition, and sometimes because there are simply different ways of representing the data (e.g., *IBM, I.B.M.,* or *International Business Machines*). Other data integrity problems occur because of external factors, such as when a company changes its name or divests itself of a business unit. Data quality products were originally developed by data services companies like Harte Hanks or Acxiom that often sell services to "clean" a company's data files or provide "information of record" on businesses and their offices.

Data quality products typically have rich algorithms for "fuzzy matching"—using a set of rules or specifications to determine whether two data values or two sets of data values refer to the same entity. For example, they are able to determine that a record containing fields with the values:

John Smith
713 Box Ln
Austin, TX 78703

probably refers to the same individual as one with the data values:

John Q. Smith
713 Box
Austin, Texas 78703-3456

These products assign ranks in the process of matching and allow developers to con-figure the products to define thresholds of certainty so that above a certain threshold of certainty, the product counts a comparison as a match, below a certain threshold the match is rejected, and within some range the potential match is reported to a human for a decision.

Data quality products can be used for such tasks as:

- *Standardizing names and addresses*—The latter can be very impor-tant in bulk mailings because the post office charges a lower rate when addresses are in a standard format.
- *Eliminating duplicate records*—for example, the John Q. Smith and John Smith example given.
- *Determining household relationships*—for example, recognizing that two customers live in the same household so you can send only one mailing, as in:

John Smith	Jane Smith
713 Box Ln	713 Box
Austin, TX 78703	Austin, Texas 78703-3456

Data Quality and the Data Warehouse

Data warehouses often need to consolidate data based on fuzzy matching. For exam-ple, consider a company that has five purchasing systems because it grew by acquisi-tion. Management might decide to build a data warehouse to track a consolidated view of the company's purchase orders in order to negotiate discounts with vendors based on volume. Because it is highly unlikely that the vendor identifiers will be the same across the five purchasing systems, new vendor keys will be required for the data warehouse and a key correspondence table created to enable the programs that update the data warehouse to correlate the records in the source systems with those in the warehouse. The company probably would not have undertaken the project if it didn't believe that the different business units were using some of the same vendors, so in build-ing the key correspondence table they will need to compare such things as vendor name and address to determine if they have previously created a new key for this vendor.

Software companies typically have higher profit margins than services com-panies so as the data warehouse market grew so did the importance of making data quality products from companies like Harte Hanks and IBM commercially available.

> **Topic of Interest: The Amount of Data Transformation Required**
>
> Different types of applications have different levels of variability in the way data is represented. For example, financial transactions are fairly standard—an invoice will have identifying information about the company sending the invoice, the person or company to whom the invoice is being sent, the date upon which the invoice is being sent, and an itemized list of the items covered by the invoice (each entry of which will have a quantity, a part number, a description, a per unit price, any discount, and a total for that line item), the subtotal, applicable taxes, (potentially) shipping, and a figure representing the total due. Although there may be differences in the language used to describe a part or in currency to represent monetary values, these differences can typically be addressed by a simple translation or mathematical conversion on a per field basis. Thus, it is not surprising that financial institutions and financial applications have some of the most effective intra- and inter-organization integration.
>
> The configuration of other applications is much more variable due to a greater variability in business practices that can affect what data is required and how it is represented. For example, a bill of materials database might contain vendor information in one MRP application and not in another. In consolidating from systems containing these types of differences, up to 50% of the data values (or more) may require transformation, and the logic required to resolve the differences in data representation can run anywhere from one to several pages to describe. As a result, the failure to have a standard means of representing functional logic constitutes a huge gap in the ability to capture the full metadata audit trail for integration that would be required for integration products to be interoperable.

The Role of Metadata in the Data Warehouse

Building data warehouses made the value of metadata clear to the nontechnical user because in most cases the values stored in data warehouses represent summary information—that is, aggregate values about groups of transactions rather than data about specific transactions. But summary information is only valuable if it is accurate, so data warehouse users often want to know how the values in a warehouse were computed (i.e., the data lineage of those values).

As a result, most ETL vendors emphasize the importance of the metadata they capture. What they capture is indeed an important part of what is needed to represent data lineage, but it has two major limitations that are illustrated in Figure 8.5. First, unless they offer their own integrated gateway products, the metadata captured by ETL products have no means of capturing the actual fields that were accessed in nonrelational data sources or verifying that nothing has been done to the data values in those fields prior to their being passed to the ETL product. In the case that an organization does opt to use gateway products in conjunction with an ETL product, it is possible to capture this information for the purposes of audit and impact analysis, but that requires the creation/purchase and maintenance of a repository (which could simply be a database stored in one of its RDBMS products) and a set of interfaces to automate its population.

A more important gap in the metadata captured by ETL products derives from the frequency with which test and transformation logic must be hand-written outside the ETL engine. Consider a legacy data source where all dates are compressed using a proprietary algorithm in order to save space. Accessing the legacy data source

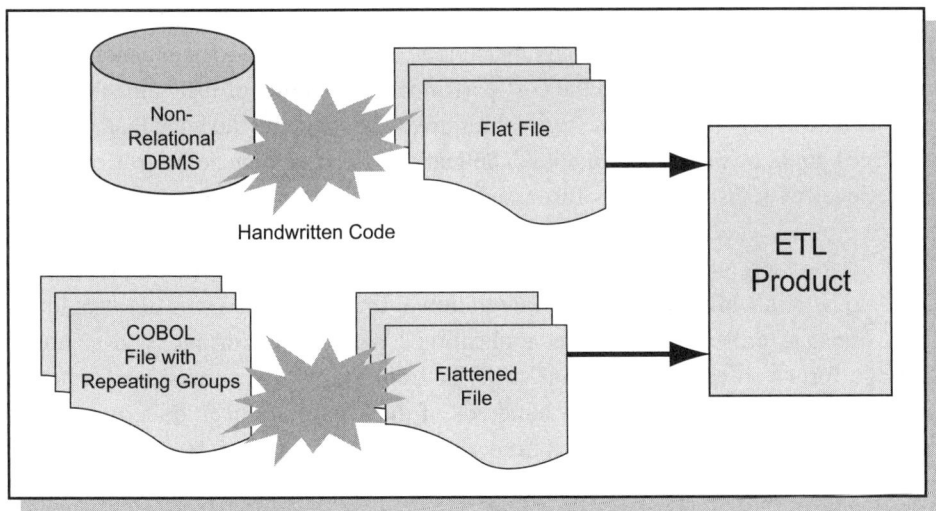

Figure 8.5   Gaps in ETL Metadata Capture

requires a hand-written program to access the data, invoke the proprietary routine to "reconstitute" the representation of dates, and write the data back out for use by the ETL product.

Finally, as discussed in Chapter 7, ETL products—like almost all other data integration products—have a limited ability to document the test and transformation logic that occurs within the context of their product. ETL products typically include a rich library of basic transformation capabilities that can be invoked from their graphical user interfaces. However, because it can be extremely time-consuming to use this type of interface to define complex test and/or transformation logic, most developers will use the option to insert user functions written in SQL or some other programming language. The fact that some function has been called is of limited value to the definition of the business metadata required for the nontechnical users of the warehouse and an area at risk for malfeasance. (Think of a user function that funnels fractional cents into a bank account in the Caymans.)

Enterprise Application Integration

Organizations began to realize the cost of integration relatively early in the age of the network as they tried to understand the data relationships across applications in the process of designing a common data model. As long as organizations depended upon proprietary applications, it wasn't clear how the situation could ever improve, and as IT organizations became more distributed geographically, it became harder to find the downtime to synchronize data through batch jobs. However, when organizations began to favor COTS applications and the cost-performance tradeoffs of local area networks (LANs) and wide area networks (WANs) improved, there came the hope that standard interfaces could be developed to allow applications to communicate in near real-time at the level of transactions. As discussed in Chapter 4, middleware and enterprise service products emerged to fill this gap.

However, another type of integration technology is required if an EAI solution is to be efficiently maintained—integration at the data level. Typically data interfaces translate either between the application's native API format to a standard message format (often expressed in XML) or from that standard message format to the application's native API. Often hundreds of these interfaces can be required. For example, consider the case of the electronics manufacturer that grew by acquisition and as a result had 42 incompatible MRP applications installed at different sites across the world. If each instance of an MRP application had to support a total of 10 types of message formats (e.g., five interfaces for messages sent and five for messages received), then 420 data interfaces would need to be created and maintained, and this is only one type of application used by the company. By the time all the necessary interfaces were created there might be 1000 or more data interfaces on 50 or 60 hosts. Although it might not be particularly difficult to write any particular interface by hand, it could be extremely difficult to determine which ones should be changed to accommodate some change in an application or business policy, a situation that makes the conversion (maintenance) of these applications very costly. Without an integration infrastructure that could perform impact analysis, programmers often make what they think is an isolated and safe change to an interface, where some adverse impact on a loosely coupled application goes unnoticed for some period of time. This situation can in fact result in the same kind of mistakes we saw in the age of the standalone application when data would become out of sync in two files, e.g., causing the Social Security Service to continue to send benefit checks after an individual had died.

Adapter Technology

As noted before, often organizations will purchase COTS applications from different vendors. Because COTS applications have published APIs at the level of the transaction, a number of vendors sought to offer "adapters" to simplify integration in these situations. Crossworlds (now part of IBM) and Attunity illustrate two different approaches to delivering this type of solution. We will examine the architecture for both of these approaches in more detail as part of illustrating the data challenges faced in EAI.

Two Examples of Adapter Technology

Plug and play adapters. Crossworlds wanted to automate transaction-level integration across COTS applications from different vendors. As illustrated in Figure 8.6, Crossworlds offered a hub-and-spoke architecture for integration, where the hub was a server that coordinated the communication between applications. The spokes represented about 60 business processes that were grouped into three major application areas—customer relationship management (CRM), enterprise resource planning (ERP), and supply chain management (SCM). Off each of these spokes were vendor-specific adapters for each of these business processes, where each adapter translated between the application-specific format and a vendor-neutral representation used by Crossworlds's internal processing. The general idea was that the customer would buy the basic platform and the set of adapters required for the application modules it had installed, and integration would be "plug and play."

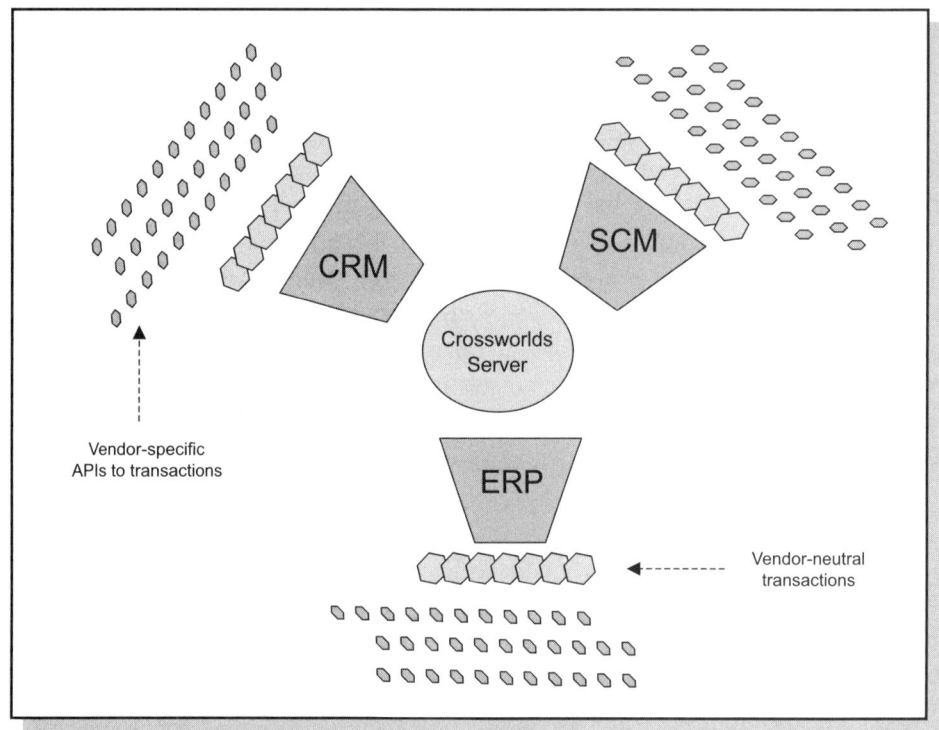

Figure 8.6 Crossworlds Plug and Play Adapters

Although other application and integration vendors have had success offering targeted plug and play adapters to move between their software and other applications, these interfaces are *point to point*; that is, each set of adapters was specific to two specific applications, that of the vendor and that from one other type of vendor. Crossworlds's mix-and-match approach proved harder to implement and support, with the result that after some management problems, the company was acquired by IBM. The technical reasons for Crossworlds's limited success resulted from the failure to understand three aspects of the problem space:

- This architecture did not address the process of differences in semantics and format in the representation of data values. Once again, the electronics manufacturer can serve to illustrate the complexity of this problem. The 40-plus incompatible MRP applications were based on products from only five vendors, but their configuration and the conventions for the representation of data were specific to each installation. In addition, most COTS products include the ability to store customer-defined fields that are often critical to the customer's business. Recall that one vendor's MRP application had over 3000 tables in its database. There was simply no way for Crossworlds to anticipate or account for these differences in implementation. As a result, if a company opted to use Crossworlds's adapters, it faced writing hundreds if not thousands of transformation functions by hand.

- The number and/or complexity of required adapters proved larger than envisioned. As discussed before, it takes considerable effort for large organizations to upgrade to a new release of a mission-critical application because they must not only test the installation of the new release with the releases of the other products in use in their environment (e.g., the operating system and communications products), but they usually also have to run hundreds of regression tests to prove that no bug has been introduced that adversely affects the data. As a result, even a single company can have multiple releases of the same application in use across different business units, and frequently (even in this day and age) the releases are not compatible with respect to their API, functionality, and/or embedded products. As a result, Crossworlds faced massively complex test and configuration issues in the development of its products.

- Finally, Crossworlds did nothing to address the need for interfaces to legacy and proprietary applications based on COBOL files and/or hierarchical or network database technology. As a result, it offered a partial (as well as problematic) solution to the problem of data integration for EAI.

Given the severity of the problems outlined, you might wonder how this could happen; that is, how a group of people can found a software company, develop a product, and even take the company public with a product that falls so short of solving customers' problems. Part of this situation is due to the hype cycle and part is due to the fact that there are serious problems with the way many organizations make their software purchasing decisions (a topic that we will consider in greater detail in Chapter 9). People do not set out to fail; they often simply don't understand what it takes to succeed. As discussed previously, in the area of software this is usually because they arc operating with bad specifications; that is, they have a limited understanding of the problem space. In fact, the major purpose of this book is less to advocate a particular type of technology or architecture than to give you the background you need to anticipate the technical challenges a new technology or product will face, because this is not something that falls within the skill sets of most business users.

Standards-based adapters. As illustrated in Figure 8.7, Attunity is an example of a vendor that took a less automated but more successful approach by providing developers with adapters that used a standards-based API (ANSI SQL-92) but provided access to a broad array of sources. In this way, it allowed the developers to decide the best way to deal with data transformation requirements and installation-specific differences—as well as how (or whether) to implement a metadata strategy.

In addition to offering support for accessing data by interfacing to both 1) mainframe databases like IMS or Adabas and 2) transaction monitors like CICS and Tuxedo, Attunity offers adapters to hybrid environments like C-ISAM, a set of C-based routines for accessing ISAM files, and D-ISAM, a version of C-ISAM with better indexing, as well as the ability to interface to various changed data capture environments.

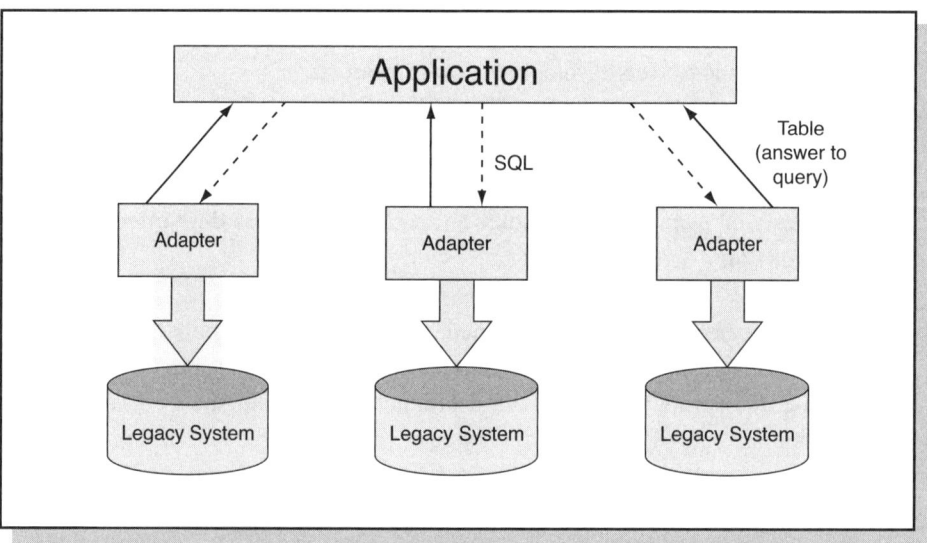

Figure 8.7 Standards-Based Adapters

The state of metadata capabilities. By providing the ability to import schema definitions from the systems to which they interface, standards-based adapters are able to help their software partners and developers provide a more complete metadata audit trail, and by leaving the question of how to capture the metadata that describes data transformation up to the developers, they do not introduce "gaps" (or black boxes) into the data lineage of data values. Standards-based adapters don't totally eliminate the complexity of data interfaces, but they are straightforward to use and can automate an important part of the data integration process.

Topic of Interest: Using Marketing Material for Technical Analysis

Part of what makes the evaluation of software products difficult is that it is hard to determine whether a product has all the functionality you require or whether it will perform adequately before actually using it to implement the application. You can talk to references who will give you anywhere from 30 minutes to an hour of their time to hosting an on-site visit, but references may be somewhat vague about the specifics of their environment because they consider some information to be confidential. You can require a proof of concept (paid or free), but this is only valuable to the extent that you design that proof to test the items about which you have critical concerns. For either of these two efforts to provide valuable information it is important that you have a clear understanding of what the product purports to do, and here you are dependent upon two types of information—marketing collateral and technical white papers.

Unfortunately, from a technical perspective marketing material is often misleading. A good part of this material focuses on the business problem and business value of the type of software product being sold. But this material usually includes a list of the technical problems that one encounters in solving the problem, and this information will provide clues about whether the product is robust or not. The more specific the description of the problem—and the more white papers offered as part of documenting their solution—the more likely the company has technology to address it. The trick is to look for what the vendor doesn't say as a clue to where the

(continued)

areas of weakness lie. Therefore, reading the marketing material for a number of vendors of the same or similar types of products can help you compile a vendor-specific list of questions or concerns that you should pursue before purchasing the product. In fact, by combining this list with an analysis of an organization's current and future challenges—a topic we will discuss in Chapter 9—you put yourself in the best position to make a sound decision.

8.3   Age of the Desktop: Relax Controls

From the point of view of data access, the applications that emerged during the age of the desktop were pretty straightforward because they were either based on an embedded relational database management system or supported some sort of comma-delimited format for data exchange. What these applications did complicate was the *control* of the IT environment by:

- Increasing the scope of tasks associated with configuration, security, and system administration of computer systems within large organizations
- Greatly increasing the risks of the misuse of data by:
  - Making it easier for individuals to—intentionally or inadvertently—compromise confidential information
  - Allowing the creation of private copies of "official" information that was later used even though out of date

Although the vendors of PC operating systems have begun to add capabilities to support more control over authorization and access, the bulk of PC users in large organizations have significantly less well-defined processes for the use of data in the context of the PC environment than in the mainframe environment.

The most important legacy of the age of the desktop was the blurring of boundaries between IT and the typical office worker. As noted before, as late as the 1980s, senior managers did not use keyboards—they had secretaries and assistants who used word processors and computer terminals and provided them with reports. By the end of the 1990s that attitude was passé; in fact, familiarity with and the effective use of electronic communication is now considered a necessary skill for anyone who wants to climb the organizational ladder. Although this trend was exhilarating for the individual worker, it has attacked the very foundations of the IT organization. For over 40 years, IT had been held accountable for defining the processes and controls for employing computer technology in such a way as to minimize error, maximize uptime, and ensure security. With the widespread use of the PC, these processes could be compromised by an intern with a laptop.

8.4 Age of the Internet: Publish and Subscribe

It is human nature to either overestimate or underestimate the amount of effort required for some task based on one's experience. After decades of considering computers the province of the "supersmart," the relative simplicity of using early applications on the Internet allowed people to be so impressed by the power and reach of the Internet's capabilities for transport and display that they significantly underestimated the difficulty of using the Internet as the basis for a business. With some exceptions like Amazon and eBay, a majority of the early B2C (business-to-consumer) businesses failed in large part because they did not appreciate the technical challenges of data integration. In fact, in some respects ebusiness applications are probably almost as dependent upon efficient data integration as those in telecomm in terms of the volume of concurrent users and the numbers of data systems to which they must interface.

As a result, the web-based applications that are most successful are those that allow users to do one or more of the following things at any time of the night or day without having to physically change locations:

- Efficiently search huge amounts of textual information to find documents of potential interest
- Find and communicate with other people who have similar interests
- Obtain accurate information about things that require access to an extensive amount of specialized information (e.g., get driving directions from Mapquest)
- Comparison shop and place orders and/or bids for objects or services
- Obtain hands-on technical support from remote call centers (e.g., with applications that allow remote users to take control of your PC)

However, web-based applications are still seriously lacking in certain types of customer support, such as when there is a bug in updating a website. For example, one of the authors of this book ordered a new laptop from a company that was able to build, ship, and deliver the product in less than a week. However, she was unable to register for a free software upgrade although the documentation about the product available online said that she should do it upon receipt of the equipment. When trying to register her "service ID," the website responded that the model she had purchased was not eligible for the promotion even though the packing slip listed it as one of the items included in the purchase. After almost an hour of listening to the same set of messages while on "call waiting," the technician found a note in his email that said that—despite the information on the website—it would take 2 weeks from delivery for the purchase information to be entered into the system managing the promotion. This experience was annoying but did not offset the convenience of being able to purchase the computer online. However, what it does illustrate is how far our techniques for developing web service–based applications are from what would be required for mission-critical applications like information sharing for the purpose of detecting terrorist activity.

The age of the Internet has greatly increased the complexity of integration along a number of dimensions:

- Increasing the types—and amounts—of information that must be integrated and managed. Now text, audio, graphics, and video must be handled as well as traditional structured data.
- Redefining the boundaries of working groups, thereby complicating the task of tracking who should have access to what information. Even in the age of the desktop, the number of people who had programmatic access to the data in mission-critical systems was tightly controlled. However, in today's interconnected but loosely coupled software environments, that group of people may include customers, partners, and thieves.
- The increasing rate of change and the risks of security breaches due to the dynamic nature of the publish and subscribe execution protocol enabled by web services, XML, SOA, and the Semantic Web.

Two new types of integration technology have emerged to meet these new needs, both of which are architectural reincarnations of earlier technology:

1. Enterprise content management (ECM) systems like the family of products offered by EMC[2]

2. Enterprise information integration (EII) tools like those offered by Meta-Matrix and Composite

Enterprise Content Management (ECM)

Few people understand how heavily regulated most industries are. In addition to the accounting rules that govern such things as revenue recognition and product safety standards, there are rules that govern how long various types of documents must be maintained as well as rules about how confidential information is accessed and maintained. The earliest document management systems provided a development platform that allowed customers to document the rules and processes they used to manage different types of documents including information regarding how they were stored (e.g., on tape, in bound books, etc.). Individuals responsible for managing documents would use the ECM product to log their handling of a document. In this way, the ECM product not only helped organizations keep track of where particular documents were, but also provided them with an audit trail as evidence that the documents had been handled properly.

ECM products have grown in functionality to accommodate new technology for the electronic acquisition of different types of "content" (e.g., web pages, graphics, etc.) in addition to textual documents. Although they are not typically included in discussions of integration technology, these products do provide a means of integrating the types of data that drive Internet applications and thus are likely to be an important part of any enterprise integration strategy.

Enterprise Information Integration (EII)

Data warehouses are an excellent way to consolidate information from multiple systems for the purpose of decision support when the data is structured and relatively nonvolatile. But they are not suitable when it is either not clear what information the user might want or not feasible to consolidate all of the potential information into one physical database. For example, in law enforcement, it is possible to characterize the queries that an investigator might want to make (e.g., Has this individual ever been incarcerated, been arrested for assault, lived in Pasadena, etc.), but it is not currently feasible to accurately consolidate all the data required from law enforcement agencies, courts, and penal institutions into a single data warehouse. Ideally the user would be able to issue this kind of request to a dashboard or portal, and the system could dynamically determine where to go to find the answer and return the desired information.

Service-oriented architecture (SOA) provides a good architecture for the actual data access aspect of this type of application, but there needs to be some type of product that helps one correlate the user's logical view of the problem space with the backend data sources. EII products like those offered by Composite and Meta-Matrix are designed to provide this functionality. As you can see in Figure 8.8, EII

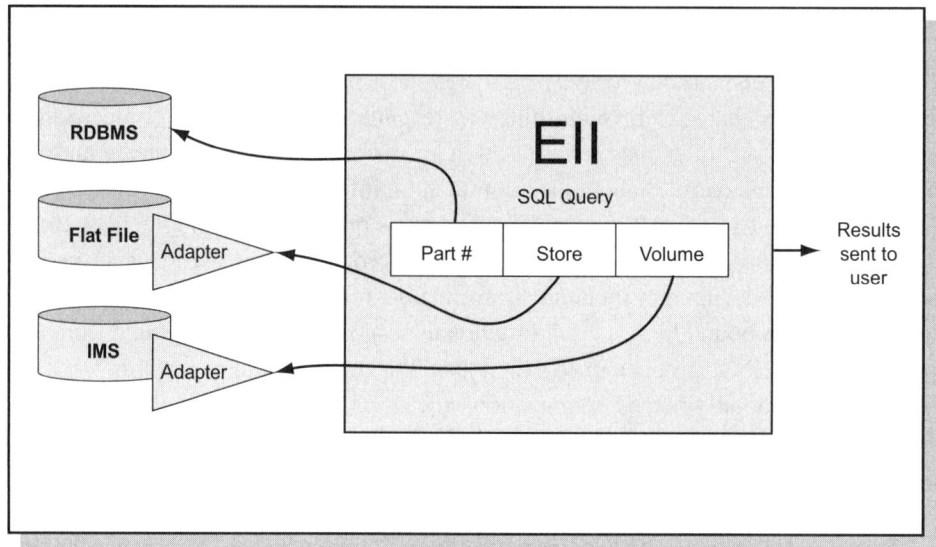

Figure 8.8 EII Architecture

products essentially have the same architecture as the heterogeneous database management systems used in the 1980s. As a result, EII is a good test case for demonstrating how you can use what you know about the history of software technology to determine the set of technical requirements that a vendor must meet for you to either choose a particular type of product or choose its product over a similar product offered by a competitor.

As you may recall, heterogeneous database management systems failed for the following reasons:

- The configuration cost was high because it required both creating a common data model *and* determining the best way to correlate the schemas of the data sources to that model.
- The performance could be slow because of the processing time for network traffic and the potential for performance problems with relational technology.
- The cost of conversion (i.e., change management) was high because there was no easy way to perform impact analysis.
- There is limited support for the transformation of data values for the purpose of consistent correlation.

Several technological advances have helped address these issues, namely:

- There are now gateway products that provide SQL access to nonrelational data sources that reduce the challenges in configuration and support distributing some of the transformations that might be required. Although it is still necessary to design a common data model and correlate between the relational view of nonrelational data sources and that model, the data modelers do not have to worry about understanding the details of hierarchical and network data models.
- The performance of both communications and relational DBMS technology has improved significantly. However, although these advances might help with the first two problems outlined earlier, because of the fact that an EII product is likely to require the use of adapters, you should still emphasize performance in your evaluation of any EII products. For example, in its marketing material and technical white papers, Composite software emphasizes that it has two capabilities to ensure optimal performance:
  - Its internal algorithms perform as much processing as close to the data source as possible. For example, if it realizes that it has to merge data from data sources A and B using field A1 from A and B1 from B, then it will sort on fields A1 and B1 at the point that the data is read from A and B.
  - It develops multiple strategies for retrieving the data and monitors performance during the remote processing so that it can change strategies if performance is slow.

Composite also supports the creation and maintenance of a repository for its metadata on one of several widely available relational systems, allowing customers to issue queries against the metadata for the purpose of impact analysis, thereby enabling efficient change management. Because some of the other vendors of EII do not emphasize these capabilities in their white papers and marketing material, you might suspect that these capabilities could be a deciding factor in your product evaluation. To test this hypothesis you could construct a proof of concept that allows you to compare the performance of products both against your particular volume requirements and against the performance of their competitors. However, in the process of the design of the proof of concept, you should also focus on the specifics of your functional requirements. For example, if in your application domain you will frequently need to merge (i.e., join) data from multiple data sources on different fields, then even the performance of products that distribute processing close to the source may not be enough to eliminate the need for the efficient processing of data closer to the user interface, which might even require the purchase of additional (or more powerful) hardware. Likewise, you should probably assess the complexity of the data transformation capabilities required to correlate the data sources to the common data model to ensure that the SQL-based capabilities are sufficient or that the metadata for the logic of user functions is accessible from the EII repository. Otherwise, there will be too many "black boxes" in the metadata audit trail to perform efficient change management.

As you can see, an awareness of historical precedent can help the software architect prioritize the critical functional requirements to assess whether some product can be successfully utilized in a particular environment (i.e., to help you distinguish between the "non-negotiables" and the "nice to haves").

The State of Metadata Capabilities

The age of the Internet has opened huge possibilities for allowing users to make more informed decisions in a more timely fashion than ever before—*if* organizations can learn to integrate autonomous systems efficiently and securely. As integration has taken center stage, more and more vendors are beginning to understand the importance of a metadata strategy. Your challenge will be to assess 1) the quality and completeness of the metadata that a product acquires and 2) how much of that metadata they are willing to share through export.

Topic of Interest: Metadata and Interoperability

When talking to software vendors, the topic of metadata is a lot like discussing world peace with defense contractors. There is no way that any defense contractor would claim that his company wanted anything but world peace, but the fact is that defense contractors make a lot more money in times of conflict and/or outright war than in times of peace. Similarly, no software vendor will say that metadata is not important, and in fact, a number will tout the benefits that their acquisition and management of metadata will bring. However, as with other types of standards that are tied to more abstract levels of functionality, the fact remains that many software vendors do not want metadata interoperability because it would be easier to migrate off their products and onto a competitor's. As a result, in the short term, an organization's best bet is to develop its own enterprise metadata integration strategy and evaluate all new vendors on the basis of the completeness of their metadata acquisition and export/import capabilities.

8.5 Code Generators for Integration

Software productivity tools have historically focused on reducing the amount of code that a developer had to write by embedding capabilities within a proprietary runtime in order to simplify the task of installing and testing. If a productivity tool produces source code, it often must be compiled, linked, and tested like hand-written code. If the generated code is unreadable, then it is hard to debug if it crashes, but if it is readable then the temptation is for developers to modify it by hand if some change needs to be made, in which case the organization can no longer use the product to enhance or document the code. For these reasons, and because they often take more training for developers to learn how to use, code generators have often not been the tool of choice for data integration when the development team was focused on implementing a particular type of application.

However, the fact that both the viability of SOA and the success of many strategic applications depend upon an enterprise approach to integration, companies are beginning to reconsider the value of code generators as a preferable approach to enterprise integration for the following reasons:

- The benefit of a shorter learning curve for a particular project is offset by the cost of maintaining multiple runtimes and performance degradation due to increased network traffic and/or the overhead of processing by embedded engines.
- The fact that some hand-coding is required with most integration technology offsets the benefits of a shorter learning curve.
- Industry analysts now maintain that integration is so central to IT that organizations should have an "integration competency center."

In general, there are four major criteria for judging code generators:

1. Their extensibility with respect to data sources and functionality

2. The degree to which they support reuse and a rapid change cycle

3. Their ease of use

4. Their ability to deliver acceptable performance

Extensibility

In the ideal world a single product set would support all the data integration and transport needs for enterprise integration, but it is unlikely that this will prove the case in the foreseeable future because the two domains of data and communication are fairly distinct. Communication protocols are much more tightly coupled to hardware, while the challenges in data lie in much less well-understood areas like semantics. It is more reasonable to assess a code generator on whether it can generate source code that can configure and/or invoke communications products rather than generating the source code that actually interfaces to operating systems, device drivers, and low-level communications protocols. In other words, if a code generator is to help drive down the cost of conversion (maintenance) for the enterprise, it should generate native code that interfaces to what is already in place (rather than requiring the use of a proprietary runtime) and minimize the need to hand code user functions to perform test and transformation logic. To meet this last requirement a code generator would have to be configurable with respect to the type of code it generates (e.g., the language generated, the functionality of the code generated, etc.).

Reuse and Efficient Change Management

As discussed earlier, support for impact analysis is critical to reducing the cost of maintenance and depends upon both the automatic acquisition of a full metadata audit trail and the ability to treat that metadata as data that can be queried, imported, and exported. With these capabilities, developers facing the need to change some value can quickly determine what other data values in the enterprise are dependent upon that data value and whether one or more data interfaces must be modified. Likewise, they will also have the ability to discover the test and transformation logic that has been used in other data interfaces and reuse specifications and/or previously generated code wherever possible rather than creating an equivalent capability. Ideally, the code generation should allow them to "copy and paste" the metadata specification for the desired logic rather than having to re-create it in order to maximize reuse and consistency.

Ease of Use

Productivity software is geared not only at reducing the amount of code that must be written by hand, but also at minimizing the amount of specialized knowledge required of users, whether that knowledge is low-level and hardware-specific (e.g., *big endian/ little endian*) or tied to an understanding of data models (e.g., hierarchical vs. object-oriented). The fact that code generators require more training is probably the largest historical reason that organizations have opted to use products that require proprietary runtimes instead. Runtime-based integration products provide the developer a graphical interface for the purpose of configuration and then use the information specified by the developer to configure proprietary runtimes. Although this strategy can increase long-term system administration and maintenance costs as well as adversely affect performance, it reduces the vendor's liability and simplifies testing because the customer has only three points of reference—what the data looked like before it entered the runtime, the parameters created through the GUI that describe what should happen to the data in the process of executing the runtime, and the data as it appeared as it exited the runtime.

In contrast, code generators produce source code rather than feeding parameters to a runtime. Although this approach typically performs more efficiently than products with proprietary runtimes and costs less to maintain, it requires that the staff utilizing the product understand how to install and test the code in the execution environment. In fact, the way vendors have addressed this challenge constitutes the major differentiator between these products. Those that want to minimize the amount of specific knowledge required of users are more likely to generate source code that conforms to standards like Java and/or SQL. This strategy reduces the skill set required for developers, but requires all systems to be accessed via that standard or that there be a gateway product installed that can mediate between that standard and any system that does not support the standard(s). Otherwise, a code generator must be capable of generating multiple programming languages/APIs, in which case there must be some technical staff that understand the details of installation and test on the various systems in question. Note that ease in installation and test is diametrically opposed to extensibility (i.e., the fewer the skills of the user the less extensible the product and the more dependent it is on other runtime components).

Acceptable Performance

Determining whether a product will provide acceptable performance is heavily tied to a number of factors that are external to the product itself, for example:

- *The users' concept of acceptable performance*—In the case of determining a potential target in warfare, speed is of the utmost importance; in legal work, it might be acceptable if the user could get a report in several hours or more.
- *The nature of the data and data sources with which it will be used*—For example, if the application requires processing large volumes of data on nonrelational sources, a code generator that required gateways for nonrelational data sources might not perform within what the users of the application consider acceptable.
- *The number and types of data transformations required*—If hundreds of source-specific look-up tables are required and the code generator requires that all transformations take place within a single engine,

then it might be difficult to maintain the look-up tables in a remote location, particularly if they must be updated in the normal course of business (e.g., where new vendors are added on a regular basis).

Two Examples of Code Generators

In this section we will briefly look at two examples of code generators—one (Sunopsis, now part of Oracle Corporation) that is standards-based and the other (ETI Solution) that was designed to be fully extensible to eliminate the need to license or purchase any proprietary runtime or support any standard. Like all other integration technology, both strategies have their strengths and their weaknesses.

Sunopsis

Sunopsis had as a goal to create a single platform/GUI to address all integration activities and leverage the hardware and software that customers already have in place. Like ETL products, Sunopsis is based on an embedded relational engine, but as illustrated in Figure 8.9, it supports a much richer execution protocol by providing the capability to support event-driven and service-oriented protocols in addition to batch. In order to support these protocols, the Sunopsis Active Integration Platform requires a runtime, but this runtime is written in Java and can operate against any relational database or relational gateway.

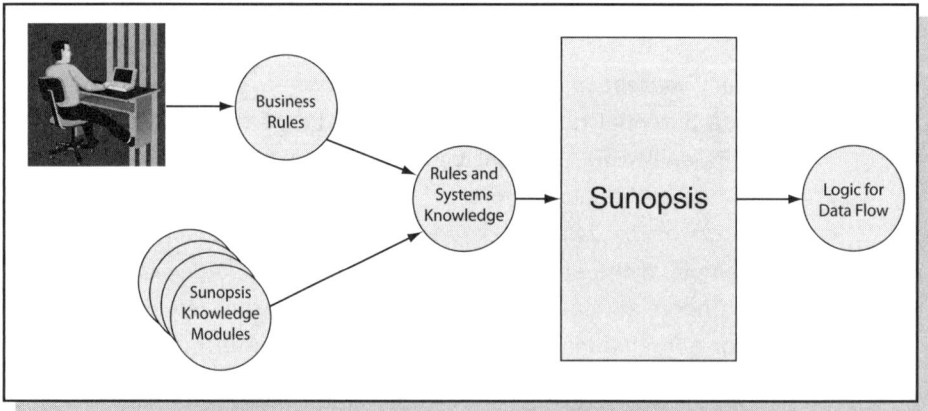

Figure 8.9 Sunopsis Functional Architecture

Sunopsis assumes that the developers using its products are proficient in SQL and provides a GUI that allows Sunopsis to attach business rules to the data mapping. However, it supports an ELT approach where all test and transformation logic takes place within its embedded engine. This approach allows it to provide a full metadata audit trail and to provide rapid impact analysis for efficient change management because all test and transformation logic is performed within its embedded engine. (When a gateway is used, the audit trail is somewhat less complete because one would have to consult/query the gateway product to understand the algorithm that it uses to map between nonrelational data sources and the relational view it presents as an API.)

Ranking Sunopsis against the code generator criteria. In terms of the four criteria discussed earlier, Sunopsis rates high both with respect to its ability to support reuse and impact analysis and with respect to ease of use because SQL and Java skills are widely available at the current time. However, it is somewhat limited in its extensibility because of the need to use gateway products on nonrelational data sources. Likewise the code it generates could accordingly encounter performance problems if it has to access a large number of high-volume nonrelational data sources. Finally, depending upon the nature of the data transformations required on source fields, the requirement that all transformations take place within its embedded engine could result in developers writing transformations outside the product when it is not possible to perform those transformations within the embedded engine or it is too difficult to maintain necessary lookup tables remotely. In these cases, the metadata captured by the Sunopsis development platform has been compromised.

ETI Solution

Like Sunopsis, ETI Solution is a code generator that:

- Is suitable for any type of integration project
- Provides developers with a GUI that allows them to specify test and transformation rules and associate them with the mappings between source and target systems
- Captures a metadata audit trail of anything that happens to the data values from the time it is read from a data source until the time that it is written or displayed

However, as illustrated in Figure 8.10, ETI Solution differs from Sunopsis in the following ways:

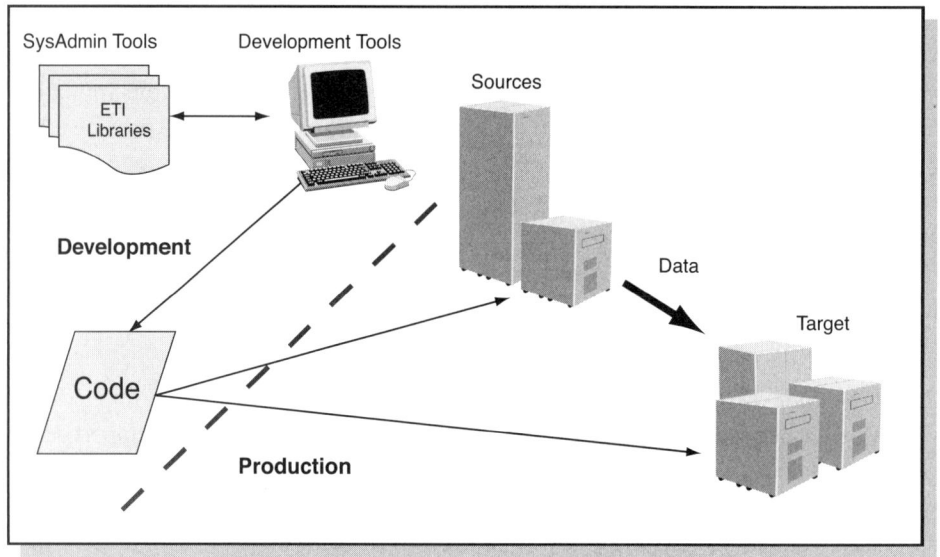

Figure 8.10 ETI Solution Architecture

- ETI Solution requires no proprietary runtime; it uses an extensible data-driven architecture that allows it to generate different types of native code in order to provide optimal performance. ETI Solution stores the information it requires to generate code for a particular environment in a "data system library" not unlike the "knowledge packs" used by Sunopsis, but—as illustrated in Figure 8.10—it also provides system administrators with a suite of editors that allow them to extend and/or create these libraries. As a result, the range of programming and command languages ETI Solution supports is potentially unlimited; for example, it offers data system library products for a broad range of environments including COBOL, IMS, IDMS, Oracle, DB/2, SQL Server, C, C#, and Java, as well as accelerators (i.e., add-ons to libraries) for products like MQSeries and WebMethods.
- ETI Solution's patented Dialogue Coach technology uses grammars to dynamically create menu-driven interfaces for the specification of test and transformation logic. The GUI provided for the specification is suitable for use by someone like a data modeler who may not know how to program against the source and/or target environments

because at any point in the process, the menus contain all the next legal choices. Likewise the sequence of menu choices forms a description of the business rule or transformation logic that makes it accessible to business users. Finally, because the system administrator can create grammars that define organization- or industry-specific dialogues, ETI Solution can eliminate the need for handcoding any user functions to ensure that it will always capture a complete metadata audit trail.

- As illustrated in Figure 8.11, ETI Solution offers a different GUI for all three of the stakeholders in the integration process—the data owner responsible for specifications, the developer responsible for generating and testing the data interfaces, and the system administrator

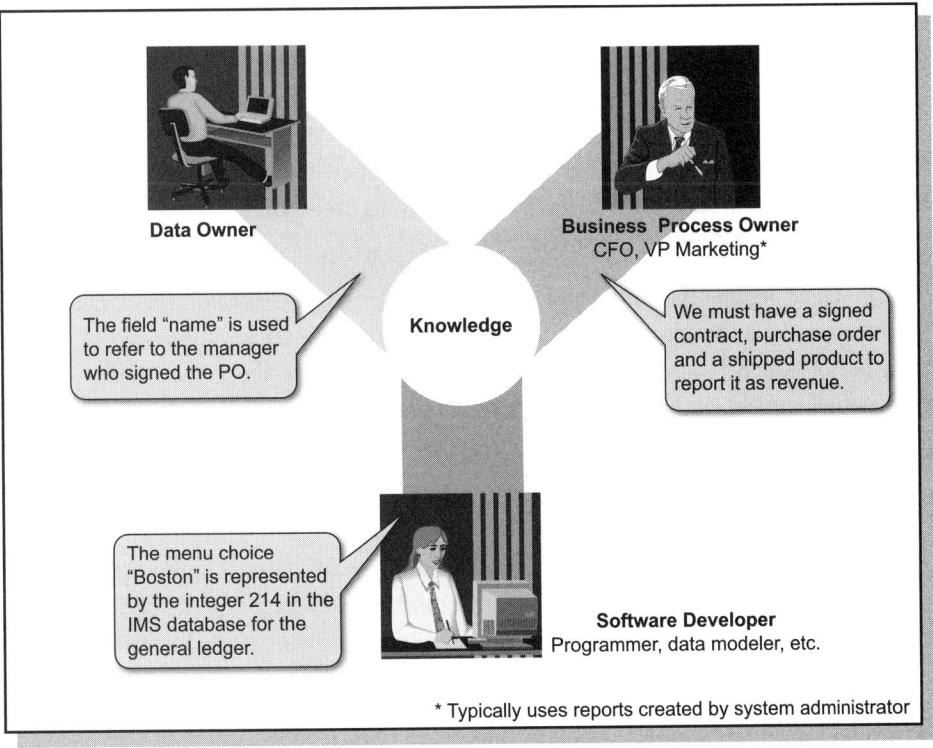

Figure 8.11   The Three Stakeholders

responsible for extending the capabilities of the product including enabling the generation of reports requested by management or business owner. Because the product keeps an audit trail of the communication between the data owner and the developer, the ETI development platform helps to 1) reduce the time required to modify the spec, 2) guarantee that the documentation of the spec matches the generated code, and 3) keep management apprised of the progress of the project (e.g., providing answers to questions like *How many high priority problems have been open for more than 10 days?*).

Ranking ETI Solution against the code generator criteria. ETI Solution scores high on extensibility, performance, and reuse through impact analysis. Because there is no proprietary runtime or gateway product required, the interfaces that it generates run as fast as hand-tuned code, and because there is no need for handcoding, it is able to capture a full metadata audit trail. However, ETI Solution is more difficult to use than a product like Sunopsis for the following reasons:

- The extensibility of the product depends on the system administrator having mastered the material presented in several weeks of training—or being willing to engage someone certified in ETI Solution.
- Cooperation is needed from the individuals maintaining the systems to be accessed for such things as setting up accounts, providing sample Job Control Language, and so on.

Once again, the choice of the appropriate code generator for a particular organization depends upon a variety of factors about the organization's needs, ranging from performance requirements to the level of cooperation the group implementing the solution can expect to obtain.

8.6　The Current State of Integration Technology

It's a volatile time in the integration problem space. A large number of different types of products are already available, and others are emerging at a regular pace—including such things as XML appliances (standalone hardware components whose role is to secure, accelerate, and route XML messages in a service-oriented architecture) and transformation engines (standalone applications whose sole role is to test and transform data values in a service-oriented architecture). There are also an increasing number of options for how to use integration technology as some vendors are rethinking their licensing models to avail themselves of web services to sell their product as an ASP (application service provider).

At the same time, now that industry analysts are advocating that organizations establish an integration competency center, larger vendors are acquiring complementary integration technology so they can be seen as a "one-stop shop" for an enterprise solution. However, to make sure that the products match the marketing, before accepting such a claim, it is important to ascertain that:

- The different product modules are themselves integrated (i.e., that you can move smoothly between them without having to exit the GUI or perform any export/import step).
- The functionality provided by the range of products is not application-specific (i.e, some vendors provide a full range of products for enterprise integration, but the products cited might only be configured for a particular application). For example, if the vendor also offers other data integration or transformation capabilities in its middleware or web-service offerings, but claims in advertising that another of its product lines provides all the integration capabilities needed by an enterprise, it is fair to wonder if it really has an integrated "one-stop shop" offering.
- The product offering meets your critical requirements for both functionality and performance.

Otherwise, the only thing that you have simplified by buying from a single vendor is the purchasing and payment process.

One can expect integration to remain a complex problem. As software technology continues to evolve and new types of capabilities emerge, strategies and products for integration will need to be created and/or modified. As a result, when you choose one integration technology, you should always assume that you may need to migrate to another integration technology at some point. Choosing products with a strong metadata strategy will be important to your ability to minimize your cost in adopting superior technology at a later time. There are three major aspects of the metadata strategy that you should consider:

- The completeness of the metadata that the product captures, such as the ability to version and document the use of the product across developers as well as the information that characterizes what's done within individual sessions.

- The flexibility with which the product allows the user to traverse or query this information. This is extremely important at the enterprise level because of the sheer complexity of the information. It is not just a matter of what the product records, but how you can get to it. For example, impact analysis should apply not only to source-to-target mappings and business rules, but also for things like hosts or developers (e.g., *How many data sources reside on IBM mainframes?* or *How many man-hours have we spent on project X?*) Even if the information required to answer queries like these is captured by the product set, it is of limited value unless it is easy to get to the information.
- Whether this metadata can be exported in a format that can be easily imported into another environment.

8.7   Trends and Tradeoffs

By this point in the book, it should be pretty clear that trends in software are not much different than trends in fashion. Hems can be up, down, or in-between—straight, ruffled, or uneven. Whether you're adorning the human body or storing data relationships, there are only so many options. There may be breakthroughs in hardware and communication technology that make new types of applications possible, but the integration technology that addresses content—the technology that we have been discussing in this chapter—continues to face the same challenges: the symbolic nature of both metadata and data, the need for complex functional logic to correlate data across independently developed systems, the fact that regardless of how data may be represented in memory, it needs to be serialized before writing to disk, and so on.

As a result, it is not surprising that productivity tools wind up using very similar architectures to those used decades earlier for different applications, as in the case of EII products having the same basic architecture as the heterogeneous data management systems built in the 1980s. Whether you are designing a new integration product or trying to determine which vendor has a superior solution, it is important to use the background you have acquired to evaluate the problem space and pay special attention to where earlier products failed to understand how to prioritize the critical functionality required to succeed.

8.8   Coming Up Next: Developing an Integration Strategy

By this point you know enough about the evolution of software to understand the class of challenges encountered in software integration, as well as how software products have tried to automate different types of integration. In the next chapter, we will discuss a methodology that uses the model of an application and its environment to build a stepwise strategy for developing an efficient solution to enterprise integration.

Exercises for Chapter 8

In this chapter, we discussed the major types of integration technology that have been developed to facilitate with the development, deployment, and maintenance of different applications. In the exercises for this chapter, we will ask you to revisit your analyses of the application scenarios in the exercises for Chapter 6 to:

- Refine your explanation of the technical capabilities required for integration technology to be used on the project.
- To determine what *appears* to be the best technology or comabination of technology to use.

We emphasize the word *appears* because determining the best integration technology to use is complex for the following reasons:

1. There are often tradeoffs in choosing one technology over another. Product A may offer benefit X but have drawback Y, while product B offers benefit Y1 but has drawback X1. In these cases, further research is typically needed. With this research it is sometimes possible to choose a superior technical solution. In other cases, it comes down to whether the company wants to make a great short-term investment to save money in the long term, or spend less now and more later.

2. For the purpose of discussion, software productivity products are classified as to the types of applications that they have been used to implement and their architectural features even though products within the same classification can vary significantly. For example, EII products can exhibit performance problems when they have to consolidate large amounts of data from non-relational data sources. Yet the EII product Composite has sophisticated internal runtime logic to address these issues.

3. Products—and product classes—acquire new capabilities over time and since the time that this book was published, new capabilities might have become standard for a particular type of product.

In short, there are no easy answers, and products continue to evolve. Nevertheless, drafting your answers in light of what has been presented in the book gives you valuable experience with the process of this type of analysis.

The scenarios from Chapter 6 are repeated here for your convenience:

a. A manufacturer of medical equipment has acquired a competitor. Each organization uses its own materials resource planning (MRP) application, one of which runs on a mainframe and was written internally in COBOL using flat files; the other uses an MRP application from Oracle running in a UNIX client-server environment. Management decided to consolidate both applications using a client-server–based MRP module from SAP.

b. In order to receive Homeland Security funds from the federal government, state healthcare agencies need to provide weekly updates regarding reported cases of infectious diseases to the Centers for Disease Control. In addition, they need to provide an alert within 24 hours of learning of an incidence of any one of a list of particular infections (e.g., bubonic plague). To obtain this information, the state agency whose own system is based on a COBOL IMS system must collect information from clinics and hospitals throughout the state, which use a variety of packaged and internally developed applications for tracking patient information.

c. An insurance company offering property and casualty coverage (e.g., car and home insurance) wants to build a web browser–based means of allowing its customers to file claims and/or check on the status of claims. The PPC application for the company is based on a COBOL IMS system.

d. A large manufacturer of engines has grown by acquisition and has five data centers in various locations supporting different manufacturing sites throughout the world. Although all five centers are using the same MRP application, at the current time they have no means of exchanging information about inventory levels. Audits have indicated that the company is losing over a million dollars a year ordering parts from vendors that they could have more cheaply exchanged between sites, so it wants to implement an application that will allow the timely and efficient exchange of inventory between plants.

CHAPTER

9

Defining an Integration Strategy

Advances in integration technology are only as valuable as they are applicable. An elegant integration architecture like SOA provides dynamically configurable routing and transport, but is not a viable solution to enterprise integration for an organization if it cannot be straightforwardly applied to integrate the majority of production applications in use today. As we saw in the previous discussion of integration technology, many of the difficulties encountered in integration come more from the large learning curve required for the participants rather than the lack of available technology. In fact, one could argue that most problems in software integration are the result of ignorance, error, and/or failure in communication. Users don't know exactly what they want. Individual developers are usually conversant with only one of the applications involved, and even for that application they are unfamiliar with all the details about the representation of data that they would need to know to integrate it or migrate it. As a result, because one cannot accurately scope what one doesn't know, the process of integration is highly iterative and often extremely inefficient.

The purpose of this chapter is to demonstrate a methodology that will allow you to anticipate where the greatest areas of risk lie in the integration required for a particular IT initiative. In addition to characterizing the types of technical problems a project is likely to encounter, you will learn to factor in how organizational structure, geographic location, and even compensation systems can influence the combination of tools and processes that are most likely to mitigate the risks and ensure a successful outcome. Likewise, you will learn how to ensure that your short-term solution helps the organization reach its long-term goals.

9.1 An Overview of the Methodology

The term *methodology* is used here to refer to a sequence of steps for using the background you have acquired to devise a successful integration strategy that will both help an organization meet its immediate goals and contribute to the organization's future capability to reduce the amount of time it spends on configuration and conversion (maintenance).

There are five major steps in the methodology:

1. Architectural analysis

2. Identification of key areas of functionality for productivity tools

3. Definition of strategy and process

4. Plan for auditability and reuse

5. Criteria for evaluating integration technology

Recommending a methodology that consists of a sequence of steps may seem to contradict the current best practice of using an iterative and incremental approach to software development. However, this methodology describes a set of activities that should take place *before* the development of an application begins, because it is intended to provide guidelines and criteria to the individuals responsible for implementing applications regarding:

- Potential areas of risk
- Strategies to facilitate efficient communication among the stakeholders in the application initiative
- Criteria for evaluation of integration technology to ensure a choice that balances the organization's short- and long-term needs

9.2   Integration Strategy vs. Application Strategy

An organization may opt to standardize on a particular type of IT architecture or infrastructure product, but it is applications that meet some business need that get funded and implemented. Almost every application initiative requires an integration strategy because even a standalone application usually requires an initial load of data and a set of interfaces that allow it to exchange data with other applications in use at the organization. However, as discussed in Chapter 8, although choosing an integration technology that favors a particular type of application might simplify the initial integration required to get the application operational, it can actually add to the integration challenges faced by the organization in the future.

Most organizations have a set of long-term goals for their IT organizations—for example, reducing the number of data centers they maintain, outsourcing some percentage of their work, or improving the efficiency and stability of their operations. If you are responsible for recommending an integration strategy, it is important that you understand these priorities and the level of management support behind them so that you can consider the implications any solution you suggest may have on these long-term goals. In this way you will be able to either:

1. Further motivate your recommendation, in the case that the optimal project-level solution also contributes to the organization's long-term goals; or

2. Be able to clearly articulate the trade-off when the optimal project-level solution is in conflict with those long-term goals, as well as articulate a possible transition strategy to move from the point solution to a set of tools better suited to the long-term corporate goals at some later time.

Historically, management has not insisted that decisions regarding integration technology be justified against corporate IT goals, so over time different projects licensed multiple integration platforms with incompatible runtimes, a situation that has been one of the major contributors to the increasing costs associated with configuration and conversion.

9.3 Architectural Analysis

A Thorough Analysis Requires Multiple Perspectives

In the Preface of this book, we argued that the term *architecture* was a good metaphor for software design because an architect must balance four major considerations in the design of a building—the characteristics of the site on which it will be built, the functional and aesthetic concerns of the client, budget and long-term value, and any constraints imposed by legislation such as zoning. In the case of a software initiative, the management of the organization has a business goal in commissioning the work—for example, implementing a new line of business, creating an electronic trading network, or consolidating multiple data centers. That goal will drive the design of the target solution that will often (but not always) involve the use of new technology. But just as the design of a building is constrained by the characteristics of its geographic site, the design of any integration strategy—which we could call the foundation of an application—is constrained by the organization's current IT environment. Likewise, any integration strategy must not only consider cost, but also a number of human factors that can seriously affect the success or failure of the project—for example, the number of people whose input is required, their geographic locations, whether they have a vested interest in the success (or failure) of the project, and so on.

Accordingly, an architectural analysis of integration has four dimensions:

1. An analysis of the current IT landscape

2. An analysis of what's needed to implement the application in the target environment

3. The human factor—an assessment of the skills, knowledge, and motivations of the stakeholders in the process

4. (Possibly) regulatory requirements that must be met

The deliverable for this stage of the methodology is a description of both the areas of greatest risk and the critical functionality of integration technology acquired to mitigate that risk.

9.4   Using the Application Model as an Analysis Tool

The following section illustrates how you can use the model of the application and its environment outlined in Chapter 5 as a tool for this type of analysis. Figure 9.1 illustrates the three major aspects of implementing and maintaining an application: the platform(s) used in its implementation, the application itself, and the environment in which it exists, (e.g., the applications to which it is interfaced, etc.).

We will use this model as a means for keeping track of the relative importance of each of the eight categories of effort required for any initiative. However, before we proceed to discuss the process of architectural analysis, we will review the major differences between four of the five eras we have used as an organizing principle throughout the book. (We are ignoring the age of the desktop in this discussion because although this period greatly complicated data integration and data integrity, even the most complex desktop applications of that period were single-user systems and thus had a simpler general architecture.) Figure 9.2 illustrates the relative level of effort required to implement and integrate an application during each of the periods.

In the age of the standalone application, the platforms used to configure and control the application were fairly simple—a compiler, Job Control Language, and schedulers. Likewise, both conversion and confirmation were relatively straightforward

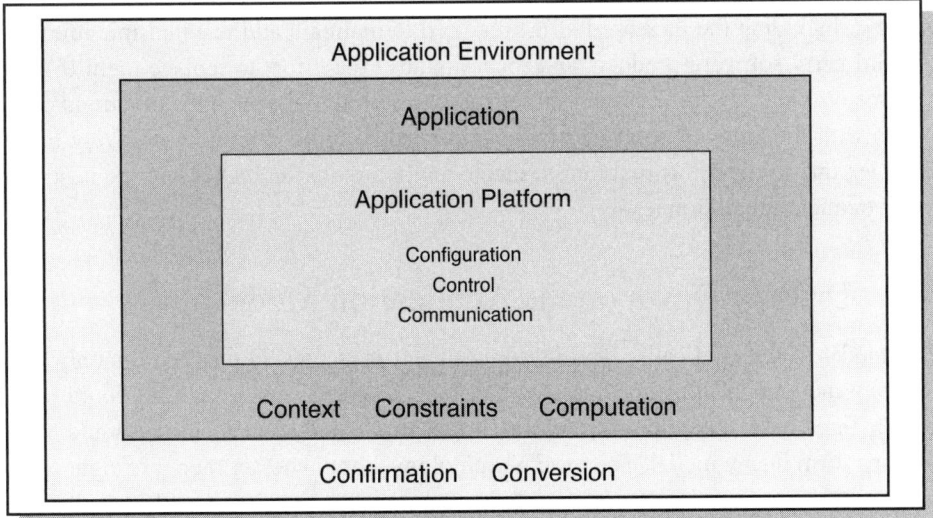

Figure 9.1   The Model of the Application and Its Environment

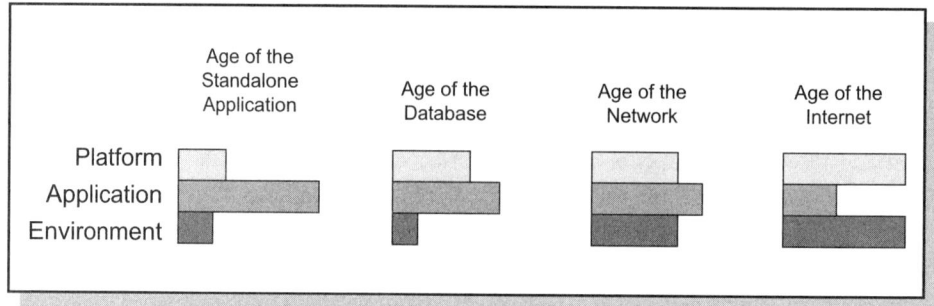

Figure 9.2 Application Development: The Path from Code to Configuration

because programs were "standalone"; that is, they were only integrated with other applications by means of file-based, batch jobs. In the age of the database, the task of writing an application became significantly simpler because the DBMS eliminated the need to write code for reading from and writing to disk. By the age of the network, the effort required to write an application was further reduced because GUI development platforms provided additional increases in programmer productivity comparable to that provided by database technology. However, the efficiency provided the developer was offset by increased effort in ongoing system administration and test, including the increased effort required to maintain and test multiple releases of third-party software products and (occasionally) the effort to replace them if they became obsolete for some reason. In the age of the Internet and SOA, this trend continues with the areas of configuration and confirmation becoming respectively more complex due to the effort required to create and maintain the UDDI and the need for more frequent regression testing.

9.5 Drilling Down on the Application Model

The model of the application and its environment presented in this book is only one of many such models that one could create. The categories and definitions could vary, but the three basic categories—platform, application, and environment—should exist in some form in any model. The exact terminology—and whether there are eight categories or 18—is less important than for you to have a consistent and well-defined model for use as a frame of reference during the process of analysis. Because you will be using the model presented in Chapter 5 as a basis for developing your answers to the upcoming exercises in this book, we will discuss each of the eight areas of effort in the model in greater detail to illustrate the types of things to think about when performing this step in the methodology.

The Platform

Configuration

Configuration refers to any task that must be performed before a developer can begin coding an application and can include any of the following types of activities:

- Gathering specifications from end users of the new application and the users and/or staff maintaining or using the data sources
- Designing a data model
- Designing and implementing a database schema
- Defining a common interface format (e.g., XML schema or a set of APIs)
- Installing and configuring new hardware or software that will be used by the new application (e.g., .NET from Microsoft)
- Creating an XML services registry and defining the processes for how services are to be managed

Notice that many configuration tasks can be performed without the use of software tools, such as designing a data model or specifying procedures for managing services. As a result, in complex application scenarios the area of configuration can be the source of many errors and inefficiencies—particularly when there is the potential for "malicious compliance" (for example, where one set of participants will no longer have employment after the new application has been put into production).

Control

The term *control* refers to the type of execution protocol used for invoking applications. In the age of the standalone application, a combination of schedulers and Job Control Language (JCL) fulfilled this role. In the age of the network, event-driven protocols were added to the mix, where different types of server applications run continuously and can be invoked by some external event. This type of execution protocol requires that the server application be reentrant (i.e., support multiple concurrent users) and often includes the use of message-oriented middleware or an enterprise service bus. In the age of the Internet, a publish-and-subscribe protocol emerged to meet the needs of computing environments where the number and nature of participants (i.e., users and applications) is unknown at the time of design. IT systems in most large organizations use a combination of these protocols, where large (often mainframe) batch applications or system administration tasks are invoked by schedulers, mission-critical applications use an event-driven protocol, and browser-based applications use a publish-and-subscribe model. Event-driven protocols allow heterogeneous applications to communicate in near real-time, but the use of these products increases the level of effort required for control because they entail the purchase, installation, and maintenance of additional runtime software on every host that participates in the communication. In addition, because control requires cooperation among the various groups of people that use and maintain the different source applications, both event-driven and SOA protocols further increase the effort expended in configuration and confirmation (i.e., testing).

Communication

The term *communication* refers to the area of effort that enables secure and reliable communication between hosts, including the purchase and installation of modems, firewalls, routers, and so on. This aspect of an application's platform is one of the most tightly coupled to the details of hardware and is usually embedded in the software that controls execution; therefore it is transparent to most developers. However, it is an important area to consider in developing an integration strategy because it can add significant time and cost to the areas of configuration and confirmation.

The Application

Context

The term *context* refers to the amount of effort it takes the programmer to create and maintain any persistent data that the application requires to operate. As illustrated in Figure 9.3, in the age of the standalone application, the application "owned" the file(s) it used as input because only one application could access the file(s) at a time. If the application ran in batch mode, only one user was allowed access at a time; if the application ran under a transaction monitor, there was still only one application accessing the file at a time, but in this case the application was the transaction monitor. As a result, during this period the effort spent by programmers in establishing the context

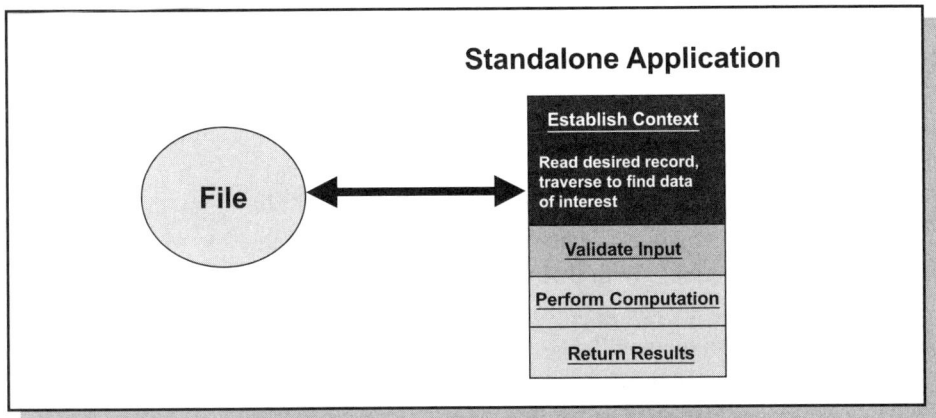

Figure 9.3   Effort to Establish Context

in which the application would execute centered primarily on file I/O and could constitute a significant part of the code.

As illustrated in Figure 9.4, during the age of the database and the age of the network, system software not only significantly simplified the effort required for programmers to establish an application's context, but also improved the capabilities of

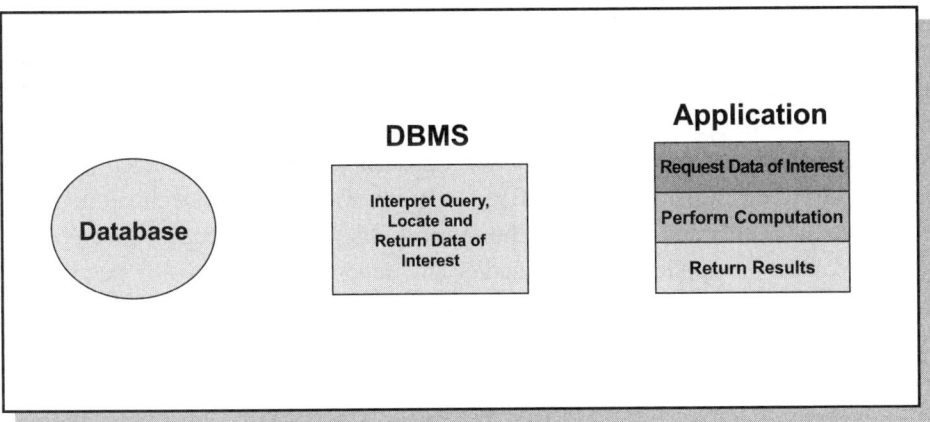

Figure 9.4   Effort to Establish Context in DBMS-Based Application

applications by supporting concurrent users through locking and access control to a common store of data.

It is not clear at this point how SOA will affect the effort required to establish context. There are several different models in use, each serving a different need. In the case of a data service layer, a web service provides access to data, serving a similar role to a DBMS but across database technologies and platforms and potentially incorporating transformation, cleansing, and merging logic into the service invisible to the calling applications. With this type of service, all service calls are atomic (i.e., completed as soon as a value is returned). As a result, there is no need for the service to keep any information about the fact that it was called by a particular application. In fact, the service may not even know which application invoked it. When SOA is being used to enable applications to communicate at the transaction level, invoking a service (such as requesting a quote in an electronic trading network) might require that one or more persistent objects be created and maintained within the service, or some existing application that interfaces to the SOA environment, in order to be able to reference something like a special promotion code. In the latter case, an interaction might consist of several related transactions, in which case the service may need to manage persistent data to be able to recognize when the same subscriber is invoking a related service (e.g., place order) provided by the application.

Constraints

The term *constraints* refers to the effort required to "error-proof" a program to keep it from trying to inappropriately perform some operation. In the age of the standalone application, a constraint might be a boundary condition, such as testing to see if an update would violate some limit like the maximum number of instances that could be stored in a particular array. As applications came to use more embedded system software for everything from databases and graphics to security, much of the low-level logic regarding user values or parameters was handled by the embedded software (e.g., ensuring that a parameter specified for length was a positive decimal number). As a result, the constraints created by the application programmer focused more at the level of calls to the application's API and/or any import capabilities—for example, to ensure that an XML message conformed to the expected schema definition. Here again we can expect that SOA might increase the level of effort, at least in organizations that do not have rigorous test and release processes for the publication of new services.

Computation

Computation refers to the effort a programmer spends in creating and maintaining the appropriate correlation between actions taken by the user of the application (human or electronic) and the objects that the application creates and maintains. In the earliest standalone applications, the programmer was responsible for writing all the code, such as the user interface (whether command-line driven or graphical), the data structures that represented the logical objects manipulated by the user, the data structures used to relate different kinds of objects, and the functional logic that corresponded to each user action. Once application writers began to use a variety of third-party productivity tools to implement applications (e.g., GUI tool-builders, etc.), the functional logic for storing, retrieving, representing, and maintaining the well-formedness of objects was handled by the runtime of these third-party products. As illustrated in Figure 9.5, today the major area of effort in computation is in writing the functional logic that interprets user commands to perform any necessary operations and issue the appropriate updates to the internal data structures, often through calls to the APIs of the embedded software products.

As an example, consider an application that allows architects to create 3D designs. Such a product might include not only the runtime for a 3D drawing product, but also an embedded DBMS for document management (e.g., keeping different versions of drawings and specifications in sync for easy access). Neither embedded

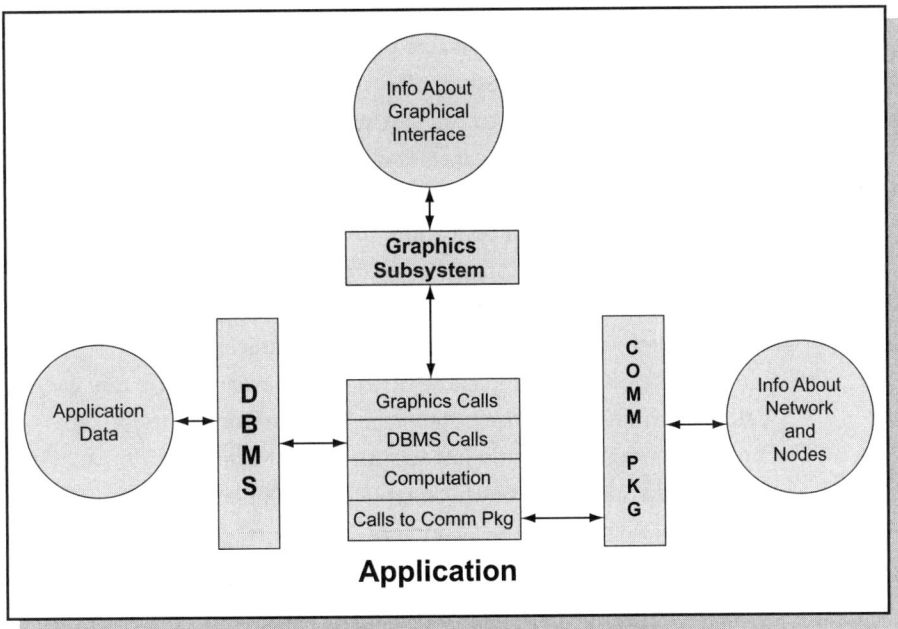

Figure 9.5   Application Programming with Embedded Software

product has any knowledge of the other, so the software developer building the application would be responsible for designing a database schema that would support correlating the graphical object information with the other documentation associated with the project, as well as implementing the appropriate database calls to ensure that the DBMS treated the data appropriately with respect to storage and versioning.

The Environment

Confirmation

Confirmation refers to the effort expended in verifying that the application is working properly, and includes the following types of activities:

- *Test design and construction*—This includes the design of test cases including the data and any related software required to execute the tests. The range of tests should validate that the application acts as expected in both the case that the input is well-formed and the case that it is ill-formed.

- *Test environment design and construction*—In most organizations, testing does not take place on production machines, so this area of activity includes setting up a hardware and software environment on a test machine that is as similar as possible to the one in which the application will actually execute. This process also includes setting up accounts and access rights to the test system so that the appropriate developers and quality assurance staff can execute tests and review the results. If regression tests must be run with great frequency (e.g., when implementing an application in an SOA environment), this process may include developing or configuring a set of tools that can automate the invocation and validation of tests to minimize the amount of time required on the part of the technical staff.

    Note that the complexity of the test environment can vary greatly depending upon the number of hardware and software environments that an application has to support. For example, if an application is designed to run on three types of UNIX platforms (e.g., AIX, AUX, and Solaris), the test environment must be set up to exercise the application on each of these types of platforms.

- *Defining and implementing the test process*—This process includes how and when different types of tests should be performed in the development process. The complexity of this effort is determined not only by the proposed functionality of the application, but also by the application architecture and software used to implement it. For example, standalone applications are easier to test than applications that use an event-driven or publish-and-subscribe execution protocol. In some cases, one might try to ensure that tests are run at defined points (e.g., after checking source code into a source code management system), by creating triggers that automatically invoke the test, and/or by generating reports that indicate when they were run.

Conversion

Conversion refers to the effort required to modify and maintain the application once it is in production. Several different types of factors can affect the complexity of this area of effort, including:

- External factors, such as the number of regulations placed on the business activity supported by the application or the frequency with which the users may want to adapt the application. For example, competition between cable and telecommunications providers is intense, as technical advances like VoIP (Voice over Internet Protocol) and 3GL wireless technology have enabled them to offer alternative solutions to the customer. The companies in this business regularly offer aggressive marketing campaigns that bundle services in different ways to attract new customers with special pricing. Likewise, one can expect some changes in the regulations that govern these industries. As a result, applications that serve these industries are likely to be significantly more volatile than, for instance, an application used by the registrar's office at a college or university.
- The application architecture used in implementing the application, such as an application that runs in batch mode on a periodic basis (e.g., to create the monthly financial reports for an organization). This application not only is likely to be less volatile than one that communicates with other applications in near real-time, but also will provide the technical staff maintaining the application a greater period of time in which to implement a modification.

9.6 A Sample Integration Scenario

Now that we have reviewed the model of the application in greater detail, we will illustrate how it can be used in architectural analysis to identify the areas of greatest potential risk. The following describes a potential application scenario that we will use for this purpose:

> Manco is an international manufacturer of widgets with three data centers. Two of the data centers use a series of three proprietary applications running under COBOL on a mainframe; the third uses a series of integrated ERP products running against Oracle. Manco wants to eliminate the use of the mainframe (and two of their data centers) within the next 30 months by migrating the data in the proprietary systems to the ERP applications at the third data center. At the end of this process it would like to have seven years' worth of data available in the ERP environment, because that is what the company is required to maintain for the purposes of a potential audit. However, within the next six months it wants to implement a data warehouse to provide consolidated materials requirements for use by a new supply chain management (SCM) application from the same vendor that provides the integrated ERP products. For the warehouse project, the company wants to move two years of data. Once the migration from the COBOL-based applications is complete, this data warehouse will be retired because the SCM application can interface natively to the ERP products.

In the following discussion, we will assume that you are a consultant being asked to develop an integration strategy for the initial data warehouse project. As a reminder, the methodology phases are:

1. Architectural analysis

   a. An analysis of the current IT landscape
   b An analysis of what's needed to implement the application in the target environment
   c. The human factor—an assessment of the skills, knowledge, and motivations of the stakeholders in the process
   d. (Possibly) regulatory requirements that must be met

2. Identification of key areas of functionality for productivity tools

3. Definition of strategy and process

4. Plan for auditability and reuse

5. Criteria for evaluating integration technology

Phase 1: Architectural Analysis

Long-Term Goals and Their Potential Impact

Cutting the cost of IT expenditures appears to be a long-term goal for Manco management because it hopes to shut down two of the three data centers within 30 months. If this intent is public knowledge, then it is likely that some of the employees and managers at those centers will be concerned about losing their jobs. In fact, some of the more talented staff may choose to leave. As a result, there is a risk that the employees of these data centers may be less than eager to see the data warehouse initiative succeed, particularly if it is implemented in a way that reduces the risks associated with the migration from the proprietary applications to the ERP system. Given the potential for this type of turmoil, it will be important for you to be sensitive to these dynamics during your interaction with the staffs of all three data centers, as well as discrete and measured about volunteering opinions that could add to the potentially sensitive situation.

Topic of Interest: How Compensation Plans Can Create a Conflict of Interest

Companies spend a significant amount of time devising compensation plans that will motivate employees to focus their efforts on the tasks that management believes are most critical to its success. Occasionally, however, the compensation plans run counter to the company's best interest. For example, in most organizations a manager's power is reflected by the number of people reporting to her or the size of the budget for which she is responsible. Although this strategy for compensation has proved effective in most situations, it creates a conflict of interest between the manager and the organization if success on some project would actually lead to what the manager would consider to be a demotion (e.g., the abolition of his team or data center). As a result, in many cases a manager may appear to support a data consolidation initiative while doing little to ensure its success. Nor is this an easy problem to solve, because even if one devised some type of bonus for the top manager in such a situation, that does little to motivate the managers and employees who work for that manager. In fact, in most data center consolidation initiatives it is so difficult to detect "malicious compliance"

(continued)

that many companies make no attempt to consolidate centers after a merger or acquisition. As a result, devising compensation plans that provide the correct type of motivation across cycles of growth and downsizing is a huge problem for human resources (HR) departments.

Step 1: Assessing the Current Landscape

As indicated in Table 9.1, in building the data warehouse we can expect configuration to be complex (and therefore constitute a risk) because production applications typically have complex schemas. Once the data model for the data warehouse has been designed, it will be necessary to discover how to correlate the equivalent information from the three distinct data sources. Because the SCM application (the "audience" for the data warehouse) will integrate natively with the Oracle-based ERP products and the two COBOL-based environments will be migrated to the Oracle-based environment eventually, it makes sense to adopt the data values used by the Oracle-based ERP products as the representation for the data values in the warehouse. Because understanding how data values should be correlated and/or transformed requires communication across a number of different people at a number of different sites, this process is likely to be error-prone and iterative.

Table 9.1 The Current IT Landscape

Area of Effort	Degree of Risk
Application platform	
Configuration	▲ ▲ ▲ ▲ ▲
Control	▲ ▲
Communication	▲ ▲ ▲
Application	
Context	▲
Constraints	▲
Computation	▲
Application environment	
Confirmation	▲ ▲
Conversion	▲ ▲ ▲

Moreover, because two of the data sources are COBOL files and because COBOL is not strongly typed, these files are more likely to contain inconsistent and/or inaccurate data. One of the most labor-intensive parts of implementing a data warehouse lies in the acquisition, transformation, and consolidation of the data (Inmon, 1996). Because the data stored in mainframe environments is more likely to use numeric codes for symbolic data values than databases that are stored under relational technology, another area of risk lies in the area of constraints—that is, implementing the code that is responsible for checking and transforming data values. Finally, because we expect the process of implementing the data interfaces to be error-prone and iterative, the area of conversion could constitute a risk because developers may introduce new errors in the process of iteratively revising the interfaces.

Step 2: Determining What's Needed to Implement the Target Application

A data warehouse is only valuable if it provides its users with the data they need at the time they need it. As indicated in Table 9.2, the biggest areas of complexity that arise from the requirements of the target environment (that is, the Oracle-based warehouse) are control and communication.

- The data needed to refresh the warehouse comes from three separate geographic locations (the three data centers), so it will be important

Table 9.2   Implementing the Target Application

Area of Effort	Degree of Risk
Application platform	
Configuration	▲ ▲
Control	▲ ▲ ▲ ▲ ▲
Communication	▲ ▲ ▲ ▲ ▲
Application	
Context	▲
Constraints	▲
Computation	▲
Application environment	
Confirmation	▲ ▲
Conversion	▲ ▲ ▲

to ensure that all of the interface programs that refresh the warehouse complete without error before the information in the warehouse is used to determine what to purchase. Otherwise, the business would be making decisions on incomplete data without its knowledge.

- Update of the warehouse is further complicated by the fact that the COBOL files—unlike the Oracle database, which probably maintains "last modified" information—are unlikely to indicate what information has been changed since the last data warehouse load, thereby requiring the creation of some other technique for identifying the changed records, or in the worst case doing a complete refresh of the data from the COBOL-based data centers in every load cycle.

However, the risk associated with these issues is reasonably small because the frequency of these SCM decisions is likely to be weekly or monthly rather than hourly. Thus, allowing a 12- to 24-hour window for remedy of issues would probably be sufficient to address the normal failure of any feed (as opposed to failure due, for instance, to an act of God or war).

Step 3: The Human Factor

Given our earlier discussion, the biggest areas of risk posed by the human factors that affect the project derive from the fact that the project requires an extensive amount of communication from people across multiple organizations, where the majority of those participating might be concerned about losing their jobs and may thus be motivated to do their best. Consequently, Table 9.3 shows configuration and confirmation

Table 9.3 The Human Factor

Area of Effort	Degree of Risk
Application platform	
Configuration	▲ ▲ ▲ ▲ ▲
Control	▲
Communication	▲ ▲ ▲
Application	
Context	▲
Constraints	▲
Computation	▲

Table 9.3   The Human Factor (continued)

Area of Effort	Degree of Risk
Application environment	
Confirmation	▲ ▲ ▲ ▲ ▲
Conversion	▲ ▲

as the areas most likely affected—configuration because of the potential for partial and/or incomplete specifications, and confirmation because these errors are most likely to be discovered during the testing process.

Step 4: Regulatory Requirements

There are no regulatory requirements for the data warehouse project.

Topic of Interest: The Specification Process

In most IT initiatives, three different types of staff must cooperate in order to understand how to design and implement a software solution. Subject matter experts (SMEs) are either the users of mission-critical applications that serve as data sources to the initiative or the end users of the application being developed as part of the initiative. SMEs are typically neither technical nor familiar with the business processes used across the enterprise. What they are familiar with is the information that the individuals in their business unit use to conduct their jobs and how that information entered into and/or retrieved from the software applications is used. Likewise, the developers that maintain these applications have limited knowledge about how these applications function or are used, but have the knowledge about how and when one can interface to them. Finally, there is the staff responsible for and knowledgeable about the target application.

Typically, individuals in this third group are responsible for interviewing the other two types of individuals to define the specifications for the project. In most cases, the information they gather is used to create one or more mapping documents that describe how the data elements in the data

(continued)

sources correlate with the data elements in target applications, in addition to a description of any test and transformation logic required to address differences in the semantics and representation across the two systems. These documents are frequently created using a word processor or spreadsheet product and can run a hundred or more pages in length. Once these documents have been developed, SMEs and the developers maintaining the source systems are asked to review and sign off on the specifications. This is an error-prone process because of both the length of the document and the fact that these individuals usually have a very limited understanding of the target application. Unfortunately, many of these errors are not discovered and corrected until development and test, and frequently the original specification documents are not updated to reflect the correction(s). As a result, it is not surprising that flawed specifications are cited as one of the largest reasons for project failure and that specification documents are of limited value to other projects that use the same data sources.

Phase 2: Identification of Key Areas of Functionality for Productivity Tools

The architectural analysis suggests that this project will be typical of many in that the greatest amount of complexity and therefore the greatest area of potential risk lies in partial or inaccurate specifications. As a result, in determining the best combination of integration technology and methodology, we should look for integration products that not only automate the actual extraction, transformation, and loading of data, but also could provide value in the subsequent migration initiative. Key functionality would include products that:

- Assist in the process of data discovery and the matching of string fields.

  Rationale—The users of source applications are the subject matter experts (SMEs) best suited to determine the logical correlations between the data values represented in the COBOL files and those in a target application, although their success depends upon having an accurate description and understanding of the meaning of the data elements in the target schema. However, they are unlikely to know how the data values in the source are actually represented on disk and whether any changes have been introduced in that representation through the use of REDEFINES to accommodate some other need in the source application. A data profiling tool could not only streamline this process for the data warehousing project, but also be extremely beneficial in the migration project because in that case seven years of data must be moved, making it much more likely that there will be inconsistencies across groups of records in the source files. Similarly, a data quality product would eliminate much of the human intervention required for matching names, addresses, and the like.

- Provide some means of electronically capturing a metadata audit trail for the specification of source-to-target mapping and test and transformation logic in a relational DBMS.

  Rationale—Not only is the area of specification traditionally error-prone, but in this project it will require the cooperation of three groups of geographically distributed people, two of which may be less motivated than the third to complete the project on time. As a result, choosing integration technology that captures the specification information in an environment that makes it visible (through queries and reports) has a dual benefit: It not only helps developers more quickly isolate the source of an error in specification (for example, when a set of data values looks wrong in the process of testing), but also discourages "malicious compliance" by making the progress on developing the specs visible to a wide audience.

- Enable as much reuse as possible in the subsequent migration initiative.

  Rationale—Manco plans to cut its IT costs over the next 30 months by closing two of its three data centers. As a result, Manco management is likely to favor an integration solution that would allow the company to reduce the risk of the long-term migration project by leveraging the work from the short-term data warehouse project. In the best case, it could reuse the same integration products because presumably Marco will have staff trained in their use by that time. However, even the ability to reuse the final (i.e., correct) specification of mapping and business rules would be beneficial. As a result, at the very least any integration tool(s) chosen for the warehouse project should be able to capture and export this information.

Phase 3: Definition of Strategy and Process

Tools are only as effective as the skills of the people who use them, whether they are found in a garage or a workshop; however, in large projects, the coordination of activities is equally important. In the construction of a building the tasks are sequential—the framing and exterior walls must be complete before the electrician is called in, and the electrician must be finished before the drywall is installed. However, as discussed earlier, "waterfall" development methodologies do not work for complex software initiatives. Yet in large integration projects where multiple groups are using an iterative methodology to work in parallel, it can be difficult to accurately assess how the project is tracking to the deadline unless the actual development and test required for the integration is centralized in some way. For this reason, it makes sense to recommend to Manco that the company handle all the actual development and test of the data integration for the warehouse out of a single group using software tools to track as much of the communication with the owners of the data sources as possible.

This approach has the following advantages:

- A single data integration team can work more efficiently with the data warehouse team as changes evolve to the schema for the warehouse, particularly if the integration products being used support impact analysis.
- Centralizing the development staff simplifies the process of setting up access to the test environment and the monitoring of regression tests.
- By having the same set of developers working on all the data integration, they are more likely to notice irregularities in the semantics of data values during unit test.
- Having a single integration team will facilitate providing Manco management with a consistent representation of the status of the integration efforts in particular and the project in general.
- This strategy will also facilitate reuse of business rules and mapping information to streamline the part of the subsequent migration initiative that deals with the same data elements. (See the comments on reuse in the next section.)

Of course, these advantages will be of little benefit without an efficient means of facilitating both 1) the capture of the initial mapping specifications and business rules and 2) a means for tracking the communication between the developers and the subject matter experts. Using a data profiling product should reduce many of the errors in the initial mapping specification, but it will also be important that the mechanism used to specify the mapping and business rules supports the concept of a "living document"—one that can evolve to track and report on the discoveries made during the development process.

Phase 4: Plan for Auditability and Reuse

Auditability

It is impossible to document every action taken by every employee in a company. What accountants look for in conducting their annual financial audit of a company's books are documents that provide evidence that a company's employees are complying with recommended business practices. Prior to Sarbanes-Oxley, this verification concerned itself primarily with financial reports and the documentation that pertained to the numbers that appeared in those reports (e.g., contracts, purchase orders, invoices, bank deposits). Now organizations are being asked to document a broader range of business processes—and provide evidence that employees are following the recommended steps outlined in those processes—in order to demonstrate that management has taken sufficient precautions to minimize (or ideally eliminate) fraud. For example, they may need to document that the individuals who perform the final test and check-in of new source code are not the same individuals who wrote the code or that an employee who has left the company no longer has access to the physical facilities of the organization, the network, or email.

In the process of conducting an audit, accounting firms also seek to validate that software applications perform in accordance with the company's stated business practices by correlating their analysis of a representative subset of paper documents with the financial reports generated by the company's applications for that set of transactions. This strategy was adequate for the days of standalone applications and batch updates because it was possible to capture reports from each application and perform similar correlations by hand. However, this type of strategy has become more difficult with business transactions conducted electronically in near real-time across multiple countries and applications and businesses expected to be operational 24x7. At any point in time a business transaction that must update several systems might be in the middle of its processing, so a snapshot of each system at that time would not reflect a consistent state across the systems. For example, a bank might maintain separate systems for loans and bank accounts. An online customer might initiate a balance transfer from savings to make a loan payment. This involves a multi-system transaction that debits the money from the savings account system and then credits that same amount to the loan system. A snapshot of the savings account and loan systems in the middle of this multi-system transaction would represent an inconsistent state.

Documenting code by hand has never been a successful solution to auditability for the following reasons:

- There is no way to guarantee that the documentation accurately reflects the functionality of the code (or has been kept up to date over time) without inspecting the code.
- The range of documentation required to fully understand the code is typically distributed across a number of documents that may use slightly different terminology (e.g., comments within the source, functional specifications, design documents, etc.).
- The effort required to understand and evaluate this type of documentation is so difficult and time-consuming that the best an external reviewer can do is to say that the documentation exists.

As a result, it has become critical that integration technology be self-documenting and constructed in such a way as to clearly delineate what it can guarantee about its functionality and where there may be functionality that has to be verified independently (as when it allows developers to include user functions that transform data values).

In choosing the integration technology for the Manco warehouse project, it will be important to choose products that will allow the project to not only capture a full metadata audit trail for the purpose of data lineage and impact analysis, but also demonstrate that this documentation is indeed accurate (i.e., that there are no gaps in how the audit trail was acquired).

Reuse

All system software products promote reuse because they eliminate the amount of code that developers need to write by providing them with a high-level interface to a particular set of capabilities that hide the details of interfacing to hardware and operating system(s). In others words, software productivity products allow the programmer to "reuse" the runtime software supplied by the productivity product. However, in the process of using productivity tools, a programmer may create functionality that he or she would like to enable other programmers to reuse. One of the major appeals of SOA is that it promises to provide an infrastructure that will facilitate the reuse of code. In the case of Manco, at the very least one should recommend integration technology that captures an accurate description of all the test and transformation logic applied against the data elements from the COBOL sources because equivalent functionality will be required in the subsequent migration project. (Recall that we have already recommended that the warehouse use the semantics and format of the data values used in the Oracle-based ERP products in order to be able to reuse the specifications that correlate data values across the two projects.) However, an integration product that also allowed one to reuse (or regenerate) the work performed in one project on other projects would be preferable to one that merely provided accurate documentation.

Phase 5: Developing Criteria for Evaluating Integration Technology

The Short View

As discussed in Chapter 8, a large number of data integration products were created to support the needs of a particular application like the data warehouse or e-commerce. Over time, industry analysts and consulting firms began to compile a superset of all the requirements for functionality that they had seen across customers. Their goal was to develop as complete a feature-function list as possible for each class of tool with the result that a list might consist of 50 to 100 capabilities organized into 15 to 20 categories like transformation or disaster recovery. The result was that these feature-function lists began to be incorporated into requests for proposals (RFPs) for the vendors of different types of tools (e.g., ETL for data warehouse, EAI for the type of near real-time enterprise application integration required for applications like customer relationship management). Although these feature-function lists allowed customers to determine which vendor had the most fully functional offering for each product type, they have the following drawbacks:

- They failed to acknowledge that certain types of functionality (e.g., test and transformation logic that references multiple data values, often from more than one record) are required for all but the most trivial integration projects and that a company might be better served by seeking a product that is suitable across application initiatives rather than using multiple products for the same functionality.
- They did not address how to enable an organization to maximize reuse of knowledge and code across different application initiatives.
- They led to evaluation schemes that awarded the contract to the vendor with the most points across the feature-function list rather than

the vendor with the product that had the functionality that would bring the best value to a specific organization with a specific set of requirements over the long term.

That is not to say that these capabilities in feature-function lists may not be valuable, but that they are not of equal long-term importance. For example, the ability to capture a complete metadata audit trail is significantly more valuable than support for multiple date formatting or timestamps that represent fractional seconds because these capabilities could be added as user functions. In contrast, it is difficult if not impossible for a customer to enable a product to capture metadata if a vendor does not support it.

Topic of Interest: When Vendors "Check the Box"

As we have seen throughout this book, software productivity tools were created to address a particular problem or type of application. As the developers of these products become more conversant with the problem or application, they begin to add capabilities that they hope will help differentiate their product from those offered by competitors. For example, over time ETL vendors added capabilities for aggregating data (e.g., computing sums, totals, averages, etc.), performing fuzzy matching (e.g., to determine common customers), and so on. By the time an application area becomes mature and the functional capabilities are well-understood, there can be anywhere from 20 to 50 or more of these feature/functions. Customers frequently use this feature-function list as an evaluation tool to determine which productivity products to purchase. As a result, most vendors will try to add sufficient functionality in every area to allow them to "check the box," a practice that limits the value of these lists unless customers can thoroughly specify the exact functionality they need in each category— something into which they may have limited visibility before the start of the project.

The Long View

In Chapter 5 we introduced a principle called the *conservation of complexity* that maintains that when a computational problem is complex, there is no way to simplify one aspect of the computation without introducing additional complexity in one or more of the other aspects of the problem. Advances in productivity for the programmer have been offset by the need to have access to technical staff with both highly specialized domain knowledge (e.g., data modeling or GUI design) and training in the specifics of how to administer and configure specific productivity products. In large part because integration strategies have so often had a project orientation, there is probably no problem more complex in large organizations than developing an efficient infrastructure for enterprise integration. As a result, there is no optimal answer because there will always be a tradeoff. A long-term strategy will require extra analysis and effort that may add to the time and cost of the initial projects, but without such a strategy the organization's integration problem will only grow in complexity.

If a company wants to eventually reduce the costs associated with configuration, confirmation, and conversion, it must take a long-term view. In general, the best way to reduce IT costs is to establish some criteria that are non-negotiable and are used to evaluate competing integration products and strategies. Some of these criteria for maximizing reuse are obvious:

- *Automated metadata capture*—Because the largest cause of failure in IT projects is tied to incomplete or inaccurate specifications, a strategy that reduces the shortcomings in this process should reduce the cost and risk of future projects. As a result, everything that is discovered about and implemented against any data source should be captured in or exported to an environment that can be queried. In the case that multiple products have this capability, the strategy that captures a more complete history should be favored, even if that means the organization must expend some development effort to import that metadata into a queryable environment.

- *Using as few integration products as possible to minimize licensing, maintenance, and training costs*—Because the configuration of productivity tools typically requires technical staff to have specialized training, the greater the variety of integration products, the greater the number of highly skilled IT staff the organization must employ. Note that to meet this goal will require that the team evaluating the optimal integration strategy for the enterprise perform architectural analysis for more than the immediate project. But this analysis does not require extensive involvement from other personnel, because it is based more on an understanding of the challenges posed by the data sources and the nature of other proposed projects. However, it is often politically advantageous to include the management that would be responsible for the subsequent projects in discussions and/or reviews so they have an opportunity to be part of the adoption process.

Evaluation Criteria for the Sample Scenario

Architectural Analysis for the Long Term

Step 1: The current landscape—In terms of the current IT landscape, the migration project is simpler than that of the data warehouse because there is one less data source involved—the Oracle-based ERP products are already in use by one data center. Likewise, the semantics and the format of the data values for the Oracle-based ERP products are well-defined.

Step 2: The type of integration required for the target application—The integration required for Manco's longer-term strategic IT initiative is similar to the problems anticipated for the data warehouse project, but differs primarily in scale in the following ways:

1. Greater number of inconsistencies in the data.
   Rationale—Seven years of data must be moved before Manco can retire the COBOL-based systems and consolidate data centers. As a result, it is more likely that there will be REDEFINEs that must be interpreted and less likely that the technical staff maintaining the applications will remember what they mean—if, in fact, any of the individuals on the staff were even employees seven years ago.

2. Potential performance problems.
   Rationale—The volume of data that must be manipulated in the migration will be significantly greater because seven years' worth of all the data in the files must be extracted, tested, transformed, and consolidated. This process will be I/O-intensive, could be computation-intensive, and—depending upon where tasks like sorting and merging take place—could constitute a bottleneck that would be cumbersome to an iterative development process.

3. A significantly larger number of test and transformation requirements.
   Rationale—This assumption is based on both the differences in data volume and the greater semantic variability in the data being moved. The

domain of the data warehouse is the set of information related to the financial transactions of purchasing, so the only real semantic variability one can expect is in recognizing when the same type of part is being purchased from multiple vendors, where the values for part number and part description are likely to vary. However, in the migration project the data being manipulated will include the bill of materials (that is, the hierarchy of component descriptions) that describe the products being manufactured, where there will be a greater likelihood that not only the names, identifiers, and data structures will differ, but even the products themselves may differ. For example, not all manufacturing facilities may produce all the products sold by Manco, or they may use different suppliers (with different part numbers) for the same component.

4. Even more stringent requirements for test and audit.
   Rationale—Manco is concerned about being properly prepared for a financial audit, or it wouldn't be moving seven years of data. Testing in these cases usually entails running both the new and old application in parallel and comparing results on key values before cutting over to the new application. For this reason, a metadata audit trail would be even more valuable as a means of providing further verification to auditors that the data was migrated accurately.

Step 3: The human factor—In the migration project, the intent of Manco management is clear with respect to reducing headcount, increasing not only the likelihood of malicious compliance, but also the loss of key personnel because often in such situations the brightest and most capable employees will find other jobs before layoffs become imminent.

The Effect of Long-Term Needs on the Criteria for Evaluation

Two additional evaluation criteria emerge from considering the longer-term migration project in conjunction with the data warehouse—the importance of efficiency in performance and the need to capture the communication between SMEs and the integration developers in some form that makes the results visible to Manco management. The latter criterion comes from the fact that the employees of the two COBOL-based data centers are likely to be more conscientious if the results of their cooperation (or failure to cooperate) is visible to management. For example, if John Jones has more open, high-priority issues than any other SME, he will appear to be either incompetent or uncooperative.

The differences in scale also mean that the following criteria should receive greater weight in the evaluation of competing products:

- The ability to automate the rate of data discovery and to perform fuzzy matching.
  Rationale—These products can significantly reduce the number of iterations required to successfully migrate the data by alerting SMEs to inconsistencies in the data sources before development begins and automating much of the matching that would otherwise need to be done by hand.
- The automated capture of metadata—particularly metadata that describes test and transformation logic—in an environment that supports queries for the purpose of impact analysis.
  Rationale—Even with the help of a data profiling product to pinpoint inconsistencies in the data, the migration project is likely to require a lot of iteration because of the complexity of the schemas in operational applications. Being able to rapidly determine which interfaces need to be modified when an error is discovered will be critical to the timely completion of the project. Likewise, having this information accessible will provide a better audit trail as well as enable the reuse of transformation logic and business rules across other projects.

Candidate Integration Technologies

Both projects would benefit from the use of data profiling and data quality products— a data profiling product to help speed the recognition of inconsistent data and a data quality product to help standardize data values and match symbolic fields like names and addresses when comparing data across the three data stores. In addition to evaluating the various products for core capabilities, two other criteria should be the effort required to integrate these products with the other integration products under consideration and the type of metadata that they capture and export.

In terms of the products that actually extract, transform, and load the data, two types of technology could be used: an ETL engine-based product or a code generator. Although the architecture of a code generator suggests that it would provide a solution that is more computationally efficient (provided that it generates good code), an ETL product provides the benefit of being able to execute data interfaces interpretively, which offers easier debugging because a developer can examine the data at each step in the process. For this reason, both types of products should be considered during the evaluation.

9.7   Coming Up Next: Areas for Further Study

Earlier in this chapter we used the analogy of designing and constructing a building to justify the need to bring multiple perspectives to the task of determining an organization's most pressing integration needs and prioritizing the functional requirements for a successful integration strategy. We then presented a methodology to assist you in determining how to establish a set of criteria for weighting the importance of functional capabilities in the evaluation of integration products. In this process, we used a scenario that focused on the area of integration that deals with content, but the same techniques can also be used to evaluate the best fit for integration technology that focuses on transport. In either case, it is important to realize that multiple types of considerations go into a successful integration strategy, and many of them are not technical but tied to the people and the nature of the organization's business/charter.

No problem is more troubling or more important to IT departments than discovering a cost-effective means of balancing their current needs with the ability to incorporate new technology and gracefully retire outdated mission-critical systems in favor of building applications on new architectures that promise greater flexibility. Developing a realistic—and evolutionary—integration strategy is key to solving this problem. Our goal in this book has been not only to give you an appreciation for the strengths and weaknesses of different types of software technology and application architecture, but also to sensitize you to the fact that some problems like complexity will always be with us and that addressing many of these problems depends upon an appreciation of the differences between humans and computers. In the next chapter we will focus on some of the more interesting challenges facing us in IT in the 21st century and your role in addressing them.

Exercises for Chapter 9

1. Use what you know about the different types of issues one encounters in data integration to draft a request for proposal (RFP) for Manco. Use Appendix A as a guideline for the organization of the RFP.

2. Use the description of the different types of integration technology provided in Chapter 8 to describe the benefits and tradeoffs between using an ETL product and/or a code generator as a solution for Manco.

3. Use the methodology described in this chapter to describe the challenges and criteria for solutions that should be used in developing an integration strategy for the following scenarios:

   • A financial services company has grown by acquisition and has multiple systems for customer account data. The company does not want to replace these systems because the different lines of business have different operating requirements. The company has decided to build a data warehouse to consolidate all customer data into one system and wants to have the first iteration of the data warehouse available within 1 year. There is also an initiative to evaluate, select, and implement a CRM application within 2 years, and of course SOA is on the roadmap for some nebulous date in the future.

- A bank wants to migrate off its old mainframe IMS-based proprietary application to a new UNIX DB2-based application. The CIO wants to have the new application loaded and operational within 1 year, but there are so many critical reporting interfaces to the old application that they can't all be rebuilt within 1 year. The IT department is recommending that the new application become the "master" and feed information back to the IMS "slave" application, which will then feed the reporting interfaces.

- Company A manufactures athletic wear sold around the world. Regional distributors maintain inventory and stock local stores. Throughout the year, Company A switches its manufacturing to season-appropriate clothing. But different regions, especially in different hemispheres, have different seasons. Company A, located in North America, may change from summer clothes to winter clothes just when South America is going into its summer season. The regional distributors get stuck with out-of-season inventory that might be useful to another distributor. The goal of the project is to help the regional distributors share inventory information so they can request inventory from other regions, and to help Company A prepare a more accurate picture over time of what type of apparel is needed when. The regional distributors are not currently network-connected with Company A but have some level of access to the Internet—they can get to a website and download/upload information. Connectivity is expected to improve in the future.

CHAPTER

10

Topics for Further Study

At this point you have the background and skills required to be a valuable contributor to helping an organization define an integration strategy. However, devising the optimal integration strategy for a particular organization does not help simplify the problem in the long term. Our hope is that some of the readers of this book will want to use the knowledge they have gained to improve the use of software technology, either by addressing some of the organizational issues that inhibit progress or by devising products and techniques that are inherently evolutionary—that is, architected to facilitate integration. This chapter provides a brief overview of how one might approach both types of problems.

10.1   Addressing the Human Factor

Throughout the book, we have repeatedly pointed out situations where the customers and providers of IT have a conflict of interest. Software vendors and consulting companies are in the business of making money. As a result, there are a number of reasons that simplifying integration is not in their best interest:

- Reducing the risk and cost associated with migration could adversely affect software vendors' maintenance revenue because it would be easier for customers to migrate off their products. Maintenance revenue is typically the most profitable of all their revenue streams, so this result would have a serious impact on their financial performance.
- A long-term solution that reduced the costs of configuration, integration, and confirmation would not only significantly reduce the market opportunity for consulting firms, but also eliminate the potential for software companies to create point solutions.
- Finally, being "first to market" in technology offerings can provide financial benefits that offset product weaknesses. As a result, software vendors usually take a "check the box" approach to integration by providing interfaces where it is easy, but supporting some industry standard where it isn't rather than focusing on addressing the more difficult aspects of providing functionality that could simplify the more complex aspects of integrating their product.

But it is not only software vendors and consulting firms that stand to lose if the cost of software integration is reduced. Many employees and managers in IT organizations could also be adversely affected. Technical staff with expertise in legacy systems might find themselves out of a job. Managers whose position in an organization's hierarchy is judged by their budget and headcount would be adversely affected by being more efficient unless they were rewarded for it (in which case, the staff working for them are likely to try to sabotage their efforts). In fact, the only individuals who stand to gain from reducing IT costs are those who are *not* part of the IT organization or the organizations that sell products or services to IT. (In fact, even the industry analysts stand to lose financially if the situation were improved.)

Given these conflicts of interest, the only way an organization can hope for matters to improve is for their general managers to become sufficiently comfortable with software technology to:

- Understand enough about the problem space that they are not intim-idated (or misled) by technical jargon and unrealistic claims about the "next new thing"
- Establish compensation plans or contract criteria that ensure the best interests of the various individuals/groups are aligned with those of their organization

One of the best ways to get people to behave in a certain way is to reward them for behaving the way you want and penalize them for behaving the way you don't want. For example, you could consider a technique used in the construction industry by offering incentives to the contractor for completing ahead of schedule and penalties by the day for missing the deadline. Perhaps if project teams had similar incentives they would be more interested in leveraging existing knowledge and technology within the company rather than picking a different technology because they want it on their resume. Similarly, offering rewards to existing employees for mastering new technologies might not only foster more cooperation, but also minimize the loss of knowledge that accompanies turnover in staff. Finally, as noted before, what gets measured gets done. By using the methodology outlined in Chapter 9, you can develop a set of priorities that can be used across all your projects that will lead to long-term cost reduction.

10.2   Examples of Technical Areas That Warrant Further Study

Our major emphasis in this book has been to describe the chronic problems that have led to the failure of software initiatives. However, our focus on what is difficult should not be seen as cynicism about the importance and value of information technology. Instead, the hope is that an awareness of these issues will suggest new ways of approaching the problem space that could in turn lead to new technologies or superior solutions. The following sections outline two such proposed areas for study.

Classifying Applications Using "Physical" Architecture

The three-tiered architecture proposed during the age of the network recommended that software designers isolate the code for applications into a presentation layer, an application layer, and a data layer. At the time, software development methodology favored a "top-down" approach that was well-suited to a sequential design process, where the early deliverables took the form of documents (i.e., functional spec, design spec, and test plan) and the later deliverables took the form of source code and test data. Today's fashion favors such highly iterative methodologies that one—the Agile methodology—argues against documentation altogether.

Both approaches fail to recognize how central data and data integration are to choosing the appropriate software architecture for an application. In reality, different classes of applications not only have different levels of tolerance for inaccuracy or performance, but also differ significantly with respect to their integration requirements. For example, an application that assists a surgeon in visualization during a surgical procedure needs a high degree of both accuracy and speed and—as a result—would benefit from an architecture that hard-coded the interfaces to data sources such as the sensors that report the position of an instrument, rather than one that used a more open integration architecture. On the other hand, a medical application that correlates clinical results for different types of treatment might be better served by a batch application with a highly efficient integration architecture and tools that facilitate rapid integration so that information from a variety of different types of data sources may be evaluated.

In short, one size doesn't fit all. As long as we try to implement all applications using a single application architecture, integration will remain an afterthought—a problem that we try to solve by means of some layer that is independent of the execution protocol and functional requirements of the application. But what if the problem is that we are confusing logical architecture with efficient algorithmic design? Perhaps greater attention to designing the functional subcomponents of an application along their algorithmic requirements might result in application architectures that could be more easily upgraded and modified.

Likewise, it might be helpful to use the application model presented in this book to develop a classification system for different types of applications and use the defining characteristics for these classes of applications to propose a recommended architecture for each. Note that if this work were presented properly, it would be possible to more accurately assess the benefits afforded by some new technology by seeing how broad a range of application types it could serve. Likewise, such an analysis might be extremely beneficial in defining the functional requirements for improved types of system software and productivity tools, which in turn could lead to simplifying the problem of integration.

To understand the potential importance of this kind of analysis, consider the following. Today there is a tendency for productivity products to be designed to meet a particular type of application's need. For example, ETL products were designed to meet the needs of programmers who were developing data warehouses, while middleware products were designed for robust, real-time communication between heterogeneous applications required for applications like financial trading. Yet in both types of applications a significant amount of data transformation is required. Because most organizations consider these applications to be distinct functionally, they have not recognized the similar algorithmic requirements. As a result, they are likely to have used different products and/or groups to implement transformation, with the result that their future costs for integration/configuration and confirmation will be increased. Worse yet, they may be accessing the same data sources from multiple integration products and implementing subtly different transformations within each, resulting in inconsistent results between the data warehouse and the real-time applications.

Products that Manage Configuration Across the Enterprise

How the Use of System Software Decentralizes Knowledge

As discussed earlier and illustrated in Figure 10.1, a broad array of system software products have been developed to enable the rapid creation of different applications that utilize the advances in network, communication, and presentation technology.

Although these products have significantly improved the productivity of the application programmer, that productivity has come at the cost of complicating the tasks of configuration and confirmation. In fact, one could argue that the use of these products has been a major contributor to the ongoing increases in the costs associated with these two efforts.

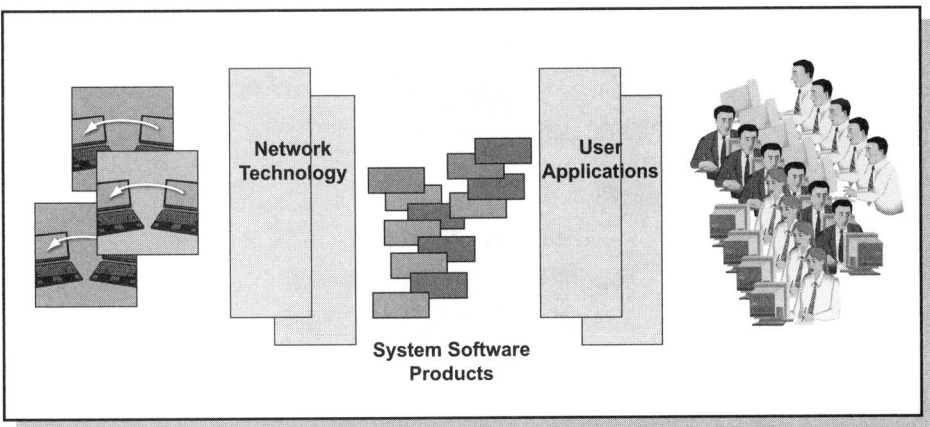

Figure 10.1   System Software Enables Rapid Development of New Applications

As evidence for this claim, consider the following: System software products typically provide both a development environment and a runtime, each of which requires a different type of training. The system administrator for the product uses the development platform to configure the product for a particular application or environment—for example, creating a base set of icons and window layouts for a graphical subsystem or defining the network topology of hosts that must communicate for a middleware product. Just as a database schema must be designed and defined to a DBMS before an application programmer can begin to work, the configuration of each system software product to be utilized must be completed before the programmer responsible for that portion of the application can begin work. Although this architecture has allowed organizations to build and maintain significantly more powerful and complex applications, the result has been that the knowledge of how the application is implemented now resides across multiple users with different types of knowledge, as depicted in Figure 10.2.

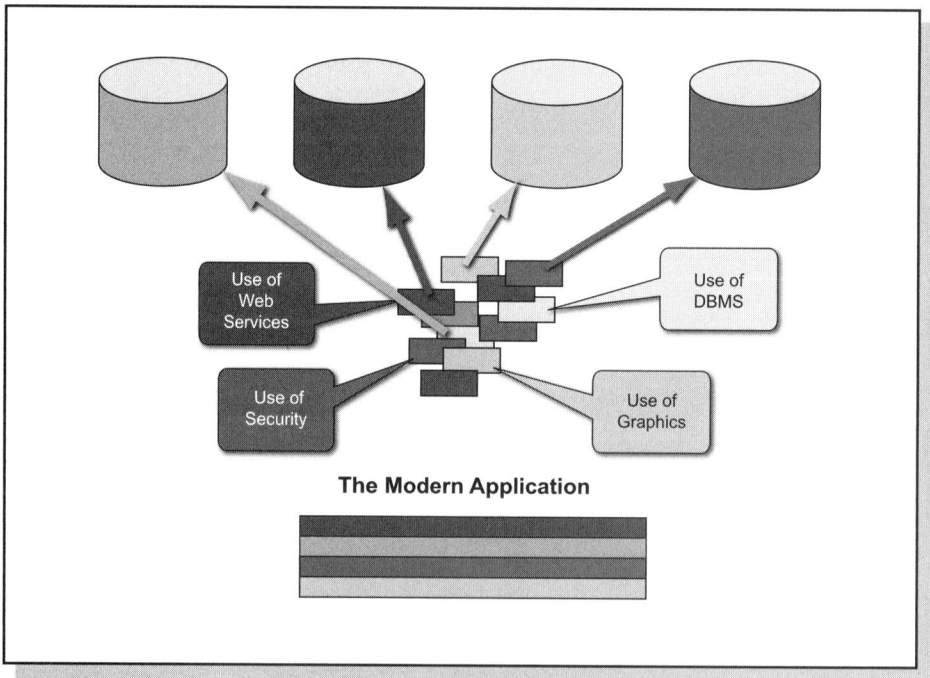

Figure 10.2 Specialized Skills Result in Fragmented Knowledge

This distribution of knowledge is reflected by various levels of metadata stored in each of the system software products used in building the application. Configuration information is analogous to a database schema (e.g., the icons and window layouts used by a product). The lower-level metadata represents the objects created by the user of the application during one or more application sessions and is analogous to the data values in a database. For example, consider the architectural drawings for a particular building created by manipulating the graphical objects in an application, where the graphical objects are defined by configuring a graphics package and session information is stored in that package, while the drawings themselves are stored in files.

Centralize Knowledge by Capturing Metadata

Reducing the cost of configuration requires some means of consolidating distributed knowledge in a persistent environment that can be queried by new users over time. One way of doing this would be consolidating the metadata across the various system software products used in building an application.

As illustrated in Figure 10.3, what one would like to see are development platforms that provide the same level of productivity to system administrators that system software provides to application programmers. In short, if we are to reduce the time spent on configuration and confirmation, we need a means of managing system

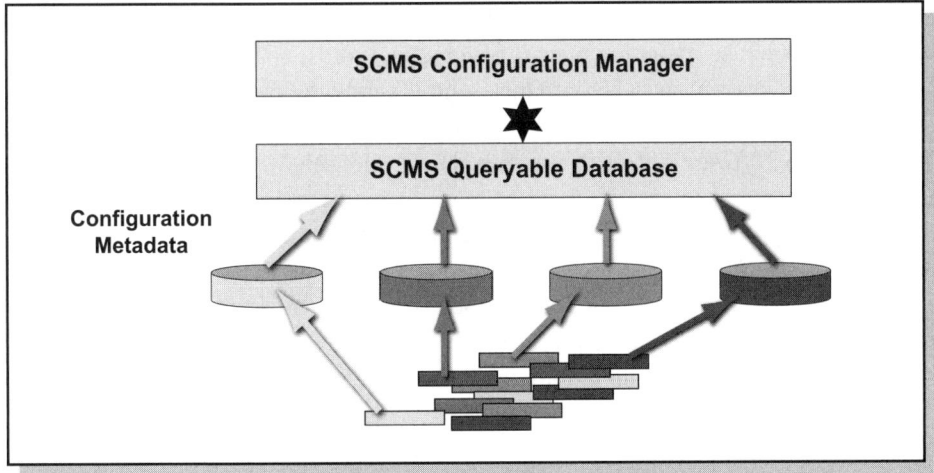

Figure 10.3   System Configuration Management System (SCMS)

software products at a higher level of abstraction so that we could have better information about how an organization utilizes its software assets—for example, which applications access a particular file, which users have accounts on multiple hosts, which hosts have the most free disk space, and so on. In fact, there are products that offer this capability for functional classes of system software (for example, those offered for UNIX system administration by IBM through Tivoli). Although this type of product is extremely valuable in a particular domain, what is needed is some kind of visibility into the full range of productivity products and applications in use by an enterprise.

Before dismissing this vision as unattainable, consider the following: The metadata required for efficient change management and auditability resides at the level of system software—the productivity software that allows programmers to ignore the details of operating systems and hardware. The development tools provided with these products allow programmers to configure the products to provide the desired behavior and usually provide persistent storage of this information to enable both efficient maintenance and reuse. Most can also export this information in file-based reports that can be parsed and interpreted like any data file. Similarly, the runtime of these products captures and/or logs the behavior of the software during execution. The primary motivation for these logs is often to assist developers in debugging problems and verifying (i.e., confirming) the behavior of the subsystem in the context of the overall design, but in conjunction with the configuration information, the information captured by these runtime logs could be extremely valuable in reducing the cost of confirmation (test).

A meta-system software product for managing the full range of system software products in use by an organization—in other words, a system software product for managing system software products—could provide the visibility required to reduce the costs associated with integration as well as confirmation and conversion. While system software products use metadata to describe the specific objects they manage, such as shapes on a screen or hosts in a network, a system configuration management system (SCMS) would acquire and manage the metadata used to configure those products and could be written in such a way as to be able to generate commands in the native APIs provided with these products (in much the same way that many integration and gateway products work today).

Such a product would require the following capabilities at a minimum:

- The definition of a data model for representing the range of capabilities afforded by these products. Note that this task is significantly less complicated than that of defining a common data model for an enterprise and/or an industry, because these products already work at the "meta-level" so their data models already contain a level of abstraction. As a result, a data model that was based on the union of the information captured by these products would be a good start.

- The ability to automatically retrieve the configuration information from these products to populate the data model.
- Making this information available in an environment that supported both graphical browsing and queries.

These capabilities would enable reuse and impact analysis. To the extent that the product could be built to generate the APIs for the underlying products, it could actually serve as a heterogeneous system management product.

This type of product could also help address one of the skills issues facing many large organizations. Most organizations have more than one instance of the same type of product. For example, most organizations have database products from at least two and often four different vendors. Currently, organizations must maintain staff with administration expertise for each of those products. One solution approach would be to consolidate onto one database technology, but that is rarely practical when COTS products are involved, because there may be no intersection between the databases supported by the various COTS products. Another solution approach is a centralized administration facility that allows the organization to train staff in the concepts of database administration and manage all vendors' products from a central "dashboard."

10.3   Conclusion

The principle of the conservation of complexity maintains that you can't make a complex problem simple. Too often when thinking that one technology is more efficient than some other, we have focused only on the code that will appear in an application and have forgotten to include the effort associated with configuration and any collaboration/communication required in the process of configuration. This approach generally leads to disappointing results and will continue to do so unless we begin to develop productivity platforms that address these neglected areas.

Building products that fully address the problem space is a difficult task. The past 50 years have produced impressive advances in software systems that support the creation of a wide range of different types of applications. But in some ways these systems are like power tools that enable the talented carpenter to build beautiful furniture. To take IT to the next level of productivity, we need productivity tools analogous to the assembly line. To build these types of productivity platforms we need tools and architectures that can automate integration, and these development platforms must provide an evolutionary path for integrating the applications and technology that are already in use. To design and build these platforms, one must understand the strengths and weakness of the software solutions that are already in place. Our hope is that this book has helped build a foundation for this type of understanding.

APPENDIX

A

On the Process of Writing

If you have majored in computer science or software engineering, it is quite likely that you haven't written a large number of papers in the process of completing your coursework. Yet writing will be an important part of your career if you want to advance to a senior position. Managers write business cases to justify expenditures or changes in strategic direction. Software architects not only have to document their designs, but also often have to justify them. Contractors and system integrators must respond to requests for proposals (RFPs). Most of the exercises in this book were designed to give you experience in this type of writing. The purpose of this appendix is to provide you with some techniques for helping you write these types of documents effectively.

A.1 Think First, Write Later

Some writing coaches, particularly those who focus on fiction, might encourage you to write first and worry about structure later. You may want to jot some notes down about points that you want to make, but with nonfiction you ought to think about each of the following topics before you start writing in earnest.

A.2 Understand Your Purpose in Writing

Most of the writing you will do in technology and business will have one of two goals (and often both):

- To *explain* something, for example, the design of a software product. The major challenge in this kind of writing is developing a strategy for breaking the topic down into meaningful sections that can be read and recalled. Unless you are writing a reference manual, the best strategy with a complex subject is usually top down, where you start with a high-level description of the major steps, stages, or components, followed by a more detailed description of each. In fact, depending upon the subject, you may need several levels of this type of "progressive disclosure."

- To *convince* the reader of something. In some cases, you may be in competition (e.g., to win funding for a project or a contract from a customer). But unlike other competitions, you win not by directly attacking the competitor, but by presenting an even-handed analysis that demonstrates that your approach is superior. More often, the competitor is unknown or very different (e.g., when you are making a case for some budget item). In either case, it's best to establish what you believe are the criteria for evaluation relatively early in the paper. In the case of an RFP, the customer may have provided the criteria, but even here it is beneficial to restate them, because often you can add a phrase or sentence to clarify your understanding in such a way as to create a problem for any responder that proposes a strategy other than yours.

Depending upon your career path, the following are the types of documents that you might be required to write:

- *Functional specifications and design documents*—A functional specification describes a software product or application from the user's (or users') point of view, whereas a design specification describes the software architecture, interfaces, and algorithms used to implement that product or application. In the past, writing these documents was tied to fulfilling milestones in the software development process. With the newer iterative development methodologies and improved development platforms, they are less important. On the other hand, with the rise in use of offshore and contract resources, the in-house staff frequently ends up doing more writing than coding. Regardless, this type of documentation remains important in commercial software environments because the functional spec is used in the development of marketing plans and training material, and the design spec is critical to developing comprehensive system tests.
- *White papers for presentation at conferences and articles for journals*—These can range from papers that explain the technical challenges of some application area or clarify the market positioning of a software product to highly technical papers that define algorithms.
- *Requests for proposals (RFPs), if you are a customer seeking to purchase a software product and/or services for your company*—Because of past abuses, the IT groups of large organizations usually have a formal process for deciding what to buy or whom to hire. These documents explain the organization's problem or project as well as any specific requirements for the bid. They also typically provide an outline for respondents to make it easier for reviewers to compare multiple responses.
- *Responses to RFPs*—These can sometimes run 100 pages in length or more and contain everything from explanations of the technical advantages of your company's approach to legal language regarding liability and damages. As a result, these documents are usually written by teams of individuals within the company, although there may be templates for different sections that can be reused across proposals.
- *Grant proposals*—You could be seeking funding for a project through an SBIR (Small Business Innovation Research) grant to develop some new technology for your business, or a stipend from some foundation

like the National Science Foundation. Each funding agency has its own set of guidelines about what it expects in a proposal.

- *Business plans to obtain funding*—This could be from either external investors, if you are an entrepreneur, or internal investors, if you are in charge of a business unit in an organization.

Obviously, there is no way to discuss techniques for addressing all these types of documents in this appendix, but in every case your writing should be clear and compelling. A poorly written document can "turn off" the readers so that they never get to your intended message. The following are some valuable techniques for helping you develop a strategy for a paper and can be applied across all types of nonfiction writing. Once we have discussed these general techniques, we briefly suggest how you might think about writing the different types of documents.

A.3 Steps in Developing a Writing Strategy

Characterize Your Reader

To write effectively, you should have in mind a model of your reader that includes:

- *Their position relative to you the writer*—Are they students, subordinates, or a prospective employer or customer? This information can influence the tone of your writing. For example, in writing training material, a humorous tone might be appropriate, whereas it would not be suitable in a document intended for a potential customer.
- *Their level of knowledge about the topic*—This information will help determine how much background information you need to provide and whether you should be careful about using specialized terminology.
- *How their beliefs differ from yours*—If you are presenting a new approach to some problem, it is important to be aware when you are making a statement that might cause the reader say to him- or herself "That's not right," because if you are not careful, he or she could simply dismiss the rest of the paper. Later in this section we will discuss a strategy for how to structure your paper to minimize this happening.

Organize Your Presentation

There are no "hard and fast" rules for organization that a skilled writer cannot violate and still succeed, but there are some basic strategies that are effective. The following are general guidelines that apply regardless of the type of document you are writing.

The Introduction Is Important

Use the introduction to tell the reader what you are going to write about and make them want to know what you have to say. As discussed in Chapter 6, there is strong evidence that perception and understanding are driven by expectations. The purpose of the introduction is to set those expectations. By the end of the introduction—which can take up to two or three paragraphs or be as short as one—the readers ought to know what the paper will be about, why you think the topic is important for them to know about it, and some idea about what they are going to read.

The introduction should not summarize every point you are going to make, but instead suggest what might be unique about your position. For example, after establishing the huge problem that back, leg, and neck pain pose to people and the adverse side effects of many surgical procedures and/or prolonged consumption of prescription drugs, an author might use a couple of statements like the following to close the introduction:

> Although most medical practitioners take a dim view of chiropractic therapy, the work being done by the practitioners of Network Spinal Analysis may bear a closer look. This paper examines the results of recent research in order to determine if HMOs should include this service as part of their healthcare offerings.

In these two sentences, the author suggests:

- A conflict, which typically engages a reader's interest
- Expectations about the type of material to be discussed:
  - More information about the risks of painkillers and surgery
  - A definition of Network Spinal Analysis and the research regarding its effectiveness
- A conclusion that will probably recommend that, at the very least, further research is needed to determine if HMOs should offer this type of treatment

Start with the Discussion that Establishes Your Credibility

Once you have interested the readers and set their expectations for the document, provide more background information about the topic, citing either references or your own qualifications to gain credibility. This material will ensure that you and your readers have a common understanding of terms and the like, as well as set up the problems that your later analysis will solve.

Note that it is important to be specific in establishing your (or your company's) credentials rather than making general claims. Statements like "Balboa Systems is the leading provider of solutions for Customer Relationship Management" sounds like only so much marketing unless it follows 1) an excellent analysis of the problem at hand and/or 2) a description of several verifiable successes in the area (e.g., As one of the three individuals responsible for patents in microbial applications of peyote, I have spent the past three years investigating . . .).

In an Argument, Start by Acknowledging Where You Agree

Once they have read the introduction, readers have one of three dispositions toward the document: 1) they hold no opinions about the topic but are interested because you have written such a compelling introduction; 2) they think they know something about the topic and think that they are likely to agree with you; or 3) they think they know something about the topic and think that you don't know what you're talking about because they know X, Y, and Z. Readers in the first two groups are ready to hear your argument, but before you present your case it is important to neutralize the readers in the third group. You do this by acknowledging first what skeptical readers are likely to agree with so that they cannot dismiss you as someone who doesn't know anything about the topic. In this process, you need to provide just enough detail to indicate that you have an understanding of the opposing view's evidence for their opinion without deflecting the primary focus of your paper.

Present Your Most Compelling Evidence First

Usually multiple arguments can be made in favor of one solution over another. If you have done a good job up until this point, all but the reader who is most adamant about some alternative is ready to believe you. If you lead with your weakest argument, then it might cause that reader to doubt that you have strong evidence. As a result, it is generally better to lead with your strongest evidence. In the case that there are different classes of evidence, you might want to introduce this section of your paper with an introductory sentence like, "There is evidence from at least three disciplines that suggests that computer systems will never be sufficiently robust to be trusted with making ethical judgments."

Conclude with a Forward-Looking Statement

Now that you have made your case, you should draw the paper to a close by reminding the readers what you have presented because this will help them recall your argument. In fact, there is an old saying that you should "tell them what you are going to tell them, tell them, and then tell them what you told them." Although this might sound repetitive, it is helpful because repetition is critical in transferring information from short-term memory to long-term memory.

Provide Sufficient (but Not Too Much) Detail

Now that you have the plan for your paper, it's time to write in earnest. That is not to say that you haven't been writing all these thoughts down. In fact, one of the greatest benefits of composing on computers is that it can be a great timesaver because you can cut and paste as you change your mind about which point you want to make first. But by the time you are ready to flesh out the sections, it is important to think again about your model of the readers you are targeting in order to decide how much they need to know. For example, if you are writing for a technical audience with a strong background in the topic, you are likely to need more specific detail than if you are writing for a more general audience. If you are writing for both types of readers, you might want to put the more detailed information in an appendix that you reference somewhere in the body of the paper so that you don't overwhelm the less technical reader with too much information.

Match the Tone and Language to Your Audience

You should choose your language and the tone you take so that they are appropriate to your intended reader. For example, in more formal writing it is usually better to avoid the use of the second person pronoun (that is, *you*) because that can strike the reader as too familiar. (Think of a Nobel laureate reviewing your grant proposal if she reads a sentence like "You may not realize it, but...".) On the other hand, if you are writing instructional material, it's fine to use informal language, particularly if you have some sense that the material could be forbidding to the reader—like a section on writing. In all cases, unless you are writing for a highly specialized set of readers, be very careful about jargon and acronyms. Use both sparingly and be sure to define them clearly when they are first introduced.

Use Correct Grammar and Punctuation and "Flag" Transitions

If you want your readers' respect, you must respect them. Misspelled words, incorrect punctuation, and/or bad grammar indicate to the reader that you are either lacking in education or sloppy in execution. We all make these mistakes from time to time, and part of what makes it difficult to catch them is that, as we discussed in Chapter 6, reading—like the perception of spoken language—is a predictive process. In short, we see or hear what we expect to see or hear. As a result, proofreading what you have recently written takes serious concentration. If you are worried about this, ask a friend to review what you have written.

Also, help your reader know when you are moving from one section of the paper to another by using headings, subordinate clauses (e.g., While this evidence might seem compelling . . .), or transitional phrases (e.g., In contrast, . . .), or some combination of these three techniques.

A.4 Suggestions for Specific Types of Documents

The general process described so far is beneficial in writing any of the types of documents we have been discussing. However, depending upon the type of document, the organization may differ. The following provides some additional notes about things to consider when writing a particular type of document.

Functional Specifications and Design Documents

These are usually detailed descriptions of relatively complex topics. If you simply document every capability or component in a sequential fashion, it can exceed the reader's capacity to recall what they have read. The following type of organization often helps:

1. Motivate the reader either by describing the importance of the problem or by using an analogy that suggests the importance of the problem.

2. Describe the capabilities that are required to solve the problem.

3. Provide a high-level overview of the architecture with a short description of the function of each major component, explaining how it relates to the capabilities described in #2. In a functional spec, this may be tied to the functionality provided to different types of users or for different types of activities. In a design spec these capabilities typically correspond to major components in the code.

4. Write a section for each component that describes it in detail, providing examples of when it would be used.

5. Make sure that your format/numbering allows users to quickly traverse from the overview in #3 to the appropriate detailed description.

White Papers and Articles

The general guidelines are sufficient for organizing these types of documents, although one must make sure to follow the published style sheet and formatting instructions provided by the conference coordinator or the editor of the publication.

Requests for Proposals (RFPs)

Although most companies have their own overall structure for these papers, the following is intended for the portion that describes the technical requirements. A poorly written technical specification provides a general statement of the organization's problem and—in the case of product evaluations—a long list of features and functions. This results in responses that are very hard to compare.

Your goal in crafting the technology section of an RFP is to present your company's challenge in sufficient detail to give vendors the opportunity to be specific enough in their responses that you can understand how the product and/or service they offer can meet your organization's specific needs. In addition, the relative importance of each requirement should be clear for both the vendor and the internal reviewers of the response. Otherwise, vendors responding to the RFP may misunderstand your requirements and answer the wrong questions.

Responses to RFPs

Most RFPs give precise instructions about the organization of the response, although within that structure, there are usually several sections where you are able to provide fairly extensive answers. At the appropriate point(s) in the response, you should take the opportunity to restate the problem(s) that the prospective customer is trying to solve—and expand upon the discussion to talk more specifically about the technical problems that must be solved. In this way, later in the response you can articulate how you would solve them (and hopefully reference successful past experiences with customers that could be references). This information provides the prospective customer with a sense that you have an understanding of their needs and also gives you an opportunity to (implicitly) introduce additional requirements that your competitors cannot meet.

Grant Proposals

Like responses to RFPs, the structure and content of grant proposals is determined by the guidelines published by the funding agency. Obviously, the general rules apply in terms of developing a model of the reader, setting expectations, and so on. The important thing to remember in this type of document is that foundations tend to fund research that would not normally be conducted by established businesses or individuals. As a result, in your proposal it is important to emphasize not only the important benefits of the proposed work, but also why it is unlikely that this work will be done in the normal course of events.

Business Plans

In many ways, this is one of the most important documents one can write because if you are a technical entrepreneur and you are successful in raising money, you are expected to execute the plan you described. As a result, the more thoughtful you are in the process of developing the plan, the more likely you are to succeed. Like RFPs and grant proposals, this type of document has a standard organization, and there are many books and courses about writing business plans. Instead, we focus here on characterizing the readers of business plans.

Just as there are different readers for a response to an RFP (e.g., technical staff, contracts, legal, etc.), there are two major types of readers of business plans for technology-based businesses: the financial reader and the technical reader. However, unlike the case of the response to an RFP, where each section can be evaluated relatively independently, the two types of readers must be convinced of the soundness of the plan in its entirety—both the potential for the product and its market strategy *and* the financial viability of the business model. The problem is that in many cases these two types of individuals have a limited understanding of each other's area of expertise. In fact, if you are the typical technical entrepreneur, you probably have a very limited understanding of how companies are evaluated financially.

The primary goal of the financial readers of a business plan is to determine whether they believe that they can at some later point sell the stock they purchased with their investment for significantly more money than they invested. The key to convincing the financial reader of the viability of your plan is to understand what he or she is looking for. There are three potential scenarios that allow investors to sell their interest in a private company: taking the company public so they can sell their shares on the open market, selling the company, or a management buy-out. In the first two cases, the company's historical financial performance must exhibit industry-specific characteristics for a successful exit (e.g., revenue, growth in revenue, profit, growth in profit, earnings per share, performance relative to competitors, market size, etc.). As you can see, most of these factors have to do with the *scalability* of the business model, because it is the potential for growth in both revenue and profit that makes a company valuable to a buyer or public investor.

Ideally, investors in technology-based companies have some technical background, because often the initial risk facing a technology start-up is the viability of the product. However, even if they do have a technical background, in evaluating the technical portions of the plan they rely on the judgment of some technical reader who typically has more recent and in-depth experience. The value of technical experience on the part of financial readers is that it allows them to abstractly characterize the type of product being proposed so they can compare it to the success of other companies offering products with similar characteristics. In fact, *comparables* are used by financial analysts in assessing the value of a company for sale or its potential value in recommending a stock. Note that this type of evaluation is not precise; rather, it is more of an art than a science, which is why it is not surprising that so many technology-based start-up companies fail.

As a technical entrepreneur, your biggest risk in developing a business plan is likely to be less the definition of the product or market need than the definition of a viable business model that will yield the type of growth that provides your investors—and you—with a successful exit. There is the old saying that "The best product doesn't necessarily win." In fact, some might even say that the best product usually doesn't win because management spent more time on product than market strategy.

If you want to minimize the chance of failing, you—or your co-founders—must put as much work into designing your business model as you put into product design by going through the same thought process as the financial investor. Read books like Geoffrey Moore's *Crossing the Chasm* (1991) to understand why other technology companies failed. Look for comparables. Think about scalability. For example, if your business model is direct sales and $1 million a year is the most that can be generated by any salesman, you may build a viable company, but it will not be one that provides the kind of growth that a venture investor would be interested in. In short, use the requirement for a business plan as just that—the opportunity to build a plan that you can use to develop the nontechnical aspects of a company. Like software development, the process of planning is iterative but just as necessary to business success as the breakthrough product.

A.5   In Conclusion

People tend to favor tasks that they are familiar with or for which they have a particular talent. If you haven't done much writing, the task of writing can seem formidable. However, the process of writing can be very stimulating if you think of it as a game of strategy; even more important, it can become a form of exercise that develops your mental prowess in ways that can benefit you both personally and professionally. You may never learn to love to write, but if you follow the process described in this appendix, you can become proficient at it.

REFERENCES

Agile Alliance. 2001. *The Agile Manifesto* (accessed *http://www.agilemanifesto.org*).

Dublin Core Metadata Initiative (accessed http://*www.dublincore.org*).

Fisher, David A. and Dennis Smith. 2004. "Emergent Issues in Interoperability," *Eye on Integration* (accessed http://www.sei.cmu.edu/news-at-sei/columns/eye-on-integration/2004/3/eye-on-integration-2004-3.html).

Fox News. May 22, 2006. "Social Security Numbers for Millions of Veterans Stolen from V.A. Official's Home" (accessed http://www.foxnews.com/story/0,2933,199465,00.html).

Gruber, T. R. 1993. "Toward Principles for the Design of Ontologies used in Knowledge Sharing," Technical Report KSL 93-04, Knowledge Systems Laboratory, Stanford University (accessed *http://66.102.1.104/scholar?hl=en&lr=&q=cache:bEGlN6p7UL4J:ra.crema. unimi.it/ontology/doc/ontology/gruber93toward.pdf+T.R.+Gruber*). An earlier version of this paper appeared in *International Journal of Human-Computer Studies* (43, pp. 907-928).

IDC. 2004. *Software Development Study 2004,* Framingham, MA: IDC.

Joint Task Force, Association for Computing Machinery (ACM), The Association for Information Systems (AIS), and The Computer Society (IEEE-CS). 2005. *Computing Curricula 2005: The Overview Report* (accessed *http://www.acm.org/education/curricula.html*).

Inmon, Bill. 1996. *Building the Data Warehouse.* New York, NY: John Wiley & Sons.

IT Governance Institute. 2004. *IT Control Objectives for Sarbanes-Oxley: The Importance of IT in the Design, Implementation and Sustainability of Internal Control over Disclosure and Financial Reporting,* Rolling Meadows, IL: IT Governance Institute.

Joy, Bill. 2000. "Why the Future Doesn't Need Us," *Wired* 8.4 (accessed http://www.wired.com/wired/archive/8.04/joy.html).

Kurzweil, Ray. 2005. *The Singularity is Near: When Humans Transcend Biology*, New York, NY: Penguin Books.

Leiner, Barry M. et al. 2003. *Brief History of the Internet* (accessed *www.isoc.org/internet-history/brief.html*).

Litan, Robert E. and Roger G. Noll. 2004. "The Uncertain Future of the Telecommunications Industry, Policy Brief #129" (accessed *http://www.brookings.edu/comm/policybriefs/pb129.htm*).

Marco, David. 2000. *Building and Maintaining the Metadata Repository*, New York, NY: John Wiley & Sons.

McGuinness, Deborah L. 2003. "Ontologies Come of Age" (accessed *http://www-ksl.stanford. edu/people/dlm/papers/ontologies-come-of-age-mit-press-(with-citation).htm*). Appears in

Fensel, Dieter et al., editors. 2003. *Spinning the Semantic Web: Bringing the World Wide Web to Its Full Potential,* Boston: MIT Press.

Miller, G.A. 1956. "The Magical Number Seven Plus or Minus Two, or, Some Limits On Our Capacity for Processing Information," *Psychological Review* (63, pp. 81-96).

Moore, Geoffrey. 1991. *Crossing the Chasm,* New York: NY: HarperCollins.

Morgan, Gareth and John Geralds. 2002. "Ford Ecommerce Unit Put on the Scrapheap," Accountancy Age (accessed *http://www.pcw.co.uk/accountancyage/news/2030595/ford-ecommerce-unit-put-scrapheap*).

Nadeau, Jean-Benoit and Julie Barlow. 2006. *The Story of French,* New York, NY: St Martin's Press.

Sapir, E. 1921. *An Introduction to the Study of Speech*, New York, NY: Harcourt Brace & Company.

Searle, John. 1969. *Speech Acts: An Essay in the Philosophy of Language*, Cambridge, UK: Cambridge University Press.

Siegel, Daniel J. 1999. *The Developing Mind—How Relationships and the Brain Interact to Shape Who We Are*, New York, NY: The Guilford Press.

Sowa, John F. 2006. *Semantic Networks* (accessed *http://www.jfsowa.com/pubs/semnet.htm*). An earlier version of this paper appeared in Shapiro, Stuart C., editor. 1992. *Encyclopedia of Artificial Intelligence*, 2nd ed., New York, NY: John Wiley & Sons.

Standish Group. 2003. *The CHAOS Chronicles Version 3.0*, West Yarmouth, MA: The Standish Group International, Inc.

Taylor, Kit. 1998. "The Brief Reign of the Knowledge Worker: Information Technology and Technological Unemployment," paper delivered at the International Conference on the Social Impact of Information Technologies (St. Louis, MO, October 12-14).

Toffler, Alvin. 1970. *Future Shock*, New York, NY: Random House.

Webster's New World College Dictionary. 1999. 4th ed. New York, NY: Webster's New World (J Wiley).

Whorf, B.L. 1956. *Language, Thought, and Reality: Selected Writings.* Boston: MIT Press.

Wikipedia. 2007. "Web Service" (accessed: http://en.wikipedia.org/wiki/Web_service).

World Wide Web Consortium (W3C). 2001. *Semantic Web Activity Statement* (accessed http://www.w3.org/2001/sw/Activity).

World Wide Web Consortium (W3C). 2001. *Web Services Description Language (WSDL) 1.1* (accessed http://www.w3.org/TR/wsdl).

INDEX